HOW TO BE A ROCK STAR

Have an Attitude

"I resent performing for fucking idiots who don't know anything."
(John Lennon)

Understand Your Art

"The idea is to keep it as simplistic, as innocent, as unassuming, and as stupid as possible."
(David Lee Roth, on Van Halen's music)

Have a Head for Business

"I live for meetings with men in suits. I love them because I know they had a really boring week and I walk in there with my orange velvet leggings and drop popcorn in my cleavage and then fish it out and eat it. I like that. I know I'm entertaining them, and I know that they know."
(Madonna)

Pick Your Political Allies Wisely

"Bill Clinton's gorgeous. I'd love to sleep with him."
(Boy George)

Cultivate a Nasty Reputation

"I can't think of anything I fear more, except possibly a nuclear holocaust."
(A Fort Worth hotel manager, on Led Zeppelin's imminent arrival)

. . . And Never Let Death Get in the Way of a Good Time

"Knowing me, I'll probably get busted at my own funeral."
(Jimi Hendrix)

Also by Coral Amende

Hollywood Confidential: An Inside Look at the Public Careers and Private Lives of Hollywood's Rich and Famous

Country Confidential: The Lowdown on the High Living, Heartbreaking, and Hell-Raising of Country Music's Biggest Stars

Random House Famous Name Finder

If You Don't Have Anything Nice to Say . . . Come Sit Next to Me

Supermodels . Heroin Overdoses . Banned Recordings . Excessive Spending . Kooky Religious Beliefs . Financial Impropriety . Devil Worship . Backstage Sex Marathons . Trashed Hotel Rooms . Blind Egoism . Shameless Comeback Attempts . Strange Appetites . Bizarre Accidents .

ROCK *Confidential*

Coral
Amende

A PLUME BOOK

PLUME
Published by the Penguin Group
Penguin Putnam Inc., 375 Hudson Street, New York, New York 10014, U.S.A.
Penguin Books Ltd, 27 Wrights Lane, London W8 5TZ, England
Penguin Books Australia Ltd, Ringwood, Victoria, Australia
Penguin Books Canada Ltd, 10 Alcorn Avenue, Toronto, Ontario, Canada M4V 3B2
Penguin Books (N.Z.) Ltd, 182–190 Wairau Road, Auckland 10, New Zealand

Penguin Books Ltd, Registered Offices: Harmondsworth, Middlesex, England

First published by Plume, a member of Penguin Putnam Inc.

First Printing, March, 2000
1 3 5 7 9 10 8 6 4 2

Ⓟ REGISTERED TRADEMARK—MARCA REGISTRADA

CIP data is available.
ISBN 0-452-28157-1

Printed in the United States of America
Set in Amerigo
Designed by Coral Amende

CONTENTS

Contents

YOUR FILTHY LITTLE MOUTH

Contents

Contents

STAIRWAY TO HEAVEN

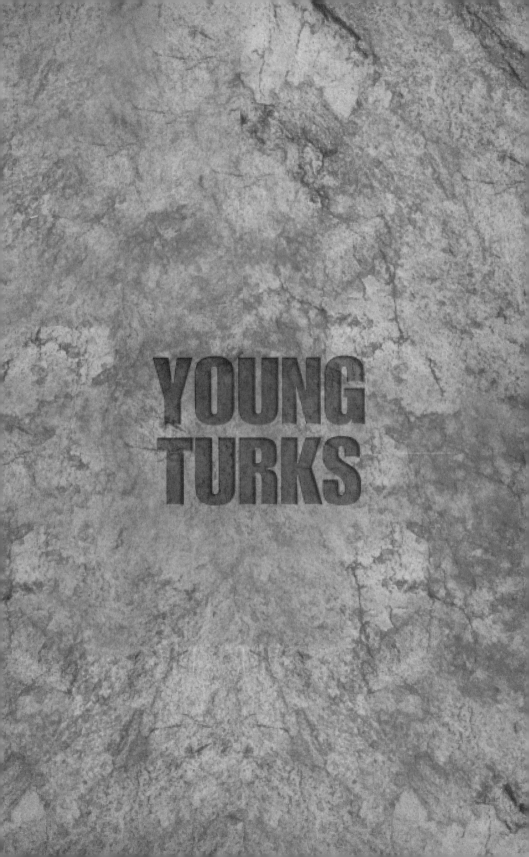

YOUNG
TURKS

"Rock is very, very important and very, very ridiculous."
(Pete Townshend)

life is just a fantasy

Rock 'n' roll has never ceased to daze and confuse, amaze and amuse—not only because of the music itself, which, beginning in the fifties, brought about a sea change in the popular musical landscape, but also because of the outrageous antics of its stars, which brought about a sea change in defining the limits of acceptable behavior. Whether it was **Chuck Berry** being thrown in the clink for a Mann Act violation in the fifties, **Jim Morrison** being hauled offstage by cops for whipping out his flesh flute in the sixties, **Led Zeppelin** cavorting with groupies in tubs of baked beans in the seventies, the **Go-Go's** being tossed out of **Ozzy Osbourne**'s backstage lair for being too unruly in the eighties (truly an astounding feat), or **Scott Weiland**'s continuing heroin-related legal antics in the nineties, we have continually been shocked, entertained, and—let's admit it—titillated by the way rock stars live their wild lives.

Living the life of a rock star means being able to indulge your every adolescent whim—exotic sports cars, sexy supermodels, designer drugs, your own table at your favorite strip club. Hangers-on hang on your every word, and handlers are employed to extricate you from (and sometimes take the rap for) almost any kind of trouble you get yourself into. Beautiful babes fall at your feet, even if you're a pencil-necked geek (and you are). You can stay up as late as you want and sleep until you damn well feel like getting up, surrounded by your choice of the most comely women (or men, if that's what floats your boat). You have groupies to ease the loneliness and drugs to lessen the stress, and life becomes a purple-hazy netherworld of sex, drugs, and decadence, with few of the consequences that mere mortals suffer.

But a glimpse through the portal of fame shows us there's a darker side to this rock 'n' roll fantasy. Drug use can turn into drug addiction (**Aerosmith, Mötley Crüe**); sexual indulgence can lead to serious legal problems (**Gary Glitter**); fast cars can have a deleterious effect on one's health (**Rick Allen, Razzle Dingley**). And as old appetites are sated, new ones develop, meaning it takes more to get the same jolt out of life—an escalating cycle that often leads to a downward spiral of substance abuse, arrests, mental illness, and early death.

Oasis's infamous **Gallagher** brothers are today's epitome of rocker-dude behavior, unrepentant throwbacks to a bygone era of licentiousness. They're constantly, publicly getting into brawls, stomping out of airports in petulant rages, marrying and splitting and reconciling with actresses, getting absolutely shitfaced, attacking members of the press—and, lest we forget, making some damn fine music in the process . . . a sharp contrast to the nineties trend of moaning, personality-free alt-rockers whining about how hard life is and what losers they are (on that point, at least, we are agreed), all the while raking in the rubles and enjoying the spoils of superstardom. Even determinedly shocking **Marilyn Manson**, who unabashedly cops to his love of sex, drugs, and decadence, couldn't quite pull off one of his profession's prototypical acts: the trashing of a hotel room. When called on the carpet for staining some bathroom fixtures with hair dye (*oh my gosh*), among other rather mild-mannered misdeeds, Manson immediately proffered a meek apology and a check in the full amount of the damages. Now, we know this is the right thing to do—but where's the trademark rock-star style? The brazen disregard for society's rules? The unabashed flouting of behavioral mores? The *fun* of it all?

> "There's an elevation to popular music that is the sound of a summer spilling out of someone's car and the moment you break up with somebody and the moment you first get sex . . ."
> *(Courtney Love)*

My advice to aspiring rockers: Do drugs—lots of drugs. Sign away your soul in an unholy pact with the devil. Callously use and discard as many groupies as you can get your mitts on. Overdose and refuse to go to rehab. Flip a car or two. Spend, spend, spend (when you're older and a has-been, you can always sell the rights to your back-catalog to revive your cash flow, as "legend" David Bowie did). And above all, be proud you're part of a long and noble tradition—the hedonistic, narcissistic, self-indulgent world of rock stardom.

Papa Was a Rolling Stone

*"I had a plastic Beatle wig when I was very small. That's what
started me buying records."*
(John Lydon, a.k.a. Johnny Rotten)
Yeah, you can really hear that Beatles influence in the Sex Pistols' music.

Life wasn't always a bed of roses for aspiring rock gods. In fact, for some it
was more like a bed of nails—many of today's hottest hunks used to be
sunken-chested nerds who couldn't make the baseball team, much less get
to first base with the popular chicks. No wonder, then, that they seem to
have a marked tendency to flaunt what they have now—showing the world
that they've got the most money, the loveliest lasses, the speediest sports
cars, the coolest clothes. But I digress.

*"Teachers always asked me, 'How come you hate everything?' That
was the catchphrase of my life."*
(Rob Zombie)

The seeds of greatness are sown in the fallow grounds of troubled child-
hoods. Big girl **Bette Midler** was an overweight youngster whose jumbo-size
personality reflects her childhood (and sometime adult) physique. (The Diva
Patrol also suggests that Midler's extra-large persona—despite being an obvious overcompensation for the traumas she endured as a tot—could use a
little toning down sometimes.)

"The first musical instrument I played was myself."
(Marty Balin, Jefferson Starship)

Ozzy Osbourne is a textbook case of a deprived childhood leading to depraved adulthood. The put-upon
youth was hardly a great student, and on top of that,
his classmates loathed him. Tony Iommi, who went
to school with Ozzy and was later his Black Sabbath
bandmate, says, "I used to hate the sight of him. I
couldn't stand him, and I used to beat him up whenever I
saw him. We just didn't get on at school. He was a little
punk." (Proving that some things *do* change—now Ozzy
is a big punk.)

In his teens, Ozzy fell headlong into a life of crime (unsuccessful crimes, to be sure . . . the kind you see on *The World's Dumbest Criminals*, to be exact). Court case in point: He wasted three months of his life in lockup after being nabbed for burglary. How was he fingered? He'd worn fingerless gloves while committing the crime, and left his prints scattered all over the house! Another stretch in the big house resulted from an incident where the hapless wannabe thief was making off with a stolen television set and had to scale a wall to make his getaway. Well, the obvious happened—he pulled a Humpty-Dumpty, and the weighty set tumbled down on top of him, knocking him silly. Back to the brig for the maladroit malefactor.

> **"Oh god, it's so hard for me and my father to understand each other. I mean, his favorite artist is Celine Dion."**
> *(Madonna)*

Barely there Beach Boy **Brian Wilson** suffered abuse throughout his boyhood (perhaps explaining his troubled later life) by his boozing bully of a father, Murray Wilson (who once made the boy defecate on a newspaper when he'd misbehaved). As an innocent infant, Brian was regularly backhanded by his bad dad (probably causing his partial deafness, which was evident by the time he was two—and which was exacerbated when Murray ripped the better part of one of his ears off). Murray's malignant behavior carried on even after Brian entered adulthood—he installed himself as manager of the blossoming **Beach Boys** and ruled the group with an iron fist (he lasted about a year—until band member **Mike Love** challenged him to a duel and knocked him senseless after a performance one night . . . better late than never).

> **"I studied the part of Snow White forever and had it down. And they gave me—without even auditioning me—the part of the evil witch. And that's when I was *eight*."**
> *(Courtney Love)*

Trouble magnet Axl Rose was a difficult child who was arrested four times by 1982, when he was ordered by a court to attend an alcohol-abuse program. "I was told my mental circuitry was all twisted," Axl admits. No kidding.

FAMILY AFFAIR

Jim Morrison, banned from an L.A. club after performing a song graphically detailing his Oedipal fantasies, wasn't the only one to express his, um . . . affection for dear old mum. J. J. Burnel, of the Stranglers, admits, "I just wanna fuck my mother, basically—always have done. Not so much now, because she's getting a bit older. She's losing her grip on her looks. She's a cute little French girl." (Eeeeeuuuuuw!)

Tiny tot Brian Warner (better known these days as the "Antichrist" himself, Marilyn Manson), had a pretty warped family, including a grandfather who, he claims in his hard-to-swallow autobiography, *The Long Hard Road Out of Hell*, was fond of playing around with XXX-large sex toys. The Warner clan fully support their sartorially strange son—especially dad, who confesses he spends "my time collecting memorabilia. Of Marilyn Manson. I have every article, every picture—in duplicate—that he has ever had his name associated with. I have in our family room every magazine cover that he's ever been on—framed. It's quite a museum, you might say." Okay, old-timer—you're elated that your odd offspring has accomplished so much with so little. So who's owed the lion's share of credit for sonny boy's stunning success? Dad bashfully basks in the glory: "I'm the true god of fuck," he proudly proclaims. " . . . I created the Antichrist." (Why aren't *you* the star, then, you old coot?)

"What if a little girl picked up a guitar and said, 'I wanna be a rock star'? Nine times out of ten, her parents would never allow her to do it."
(David Lee Roth)

Captain Beefheart was a precocious lad—he spent most of his childhood in his room sculpting, stopping only for short meal breaks (his understanding folks shoved his chow under the door). Strange Stranglers singer Hugh Cornwell was also the artsy type—he "used to go out into the garden and sing to the flowers," he says. And Siouxsie Sioux got her start in performance art well before her first official stage show. As a child, "I was very

SCHOOL'S OUT

"What I remember about junior high school is some of the questions the teachers would ask: 'True or false? The Russian people are bad.' "
(Short person Randy Newman)

"I had to fax them back and say, 'I regret that I shall not be taking up your offer, since unfortunately I have become an international rock star. ' "
(Ash singer Tim Wheeler, on why he decided not to accept admission to Glasgow University)

"I wish I was with my friends tonight, destroying my hometown. You know, I stole seventeen cars in high school. I derailed a train with a rock. Me and my friends blew up all the thermostats in school with plastic explosives. We stole bowling balls and threw them into buildings from our cars at ninety miles an hour. We got rancid whipped cream from garbage cans at the Reddi Wip factory and put it in fire extinguishers and sprayed it on people. It was the best time of my life."
(Mark Mendoza, The Dictators)

lonely, actually," she confesses. "When I was eight, I tried to commit suicide to get noticed by my parents. I used to do things like fall on the floor upstairs so they'd think I'd fallen downstairs. And I'd always have bottles of pills in my hand." Her earliest memory? "Pretending to be dead. My mum used to step over me while I was lying on the kitchen floor."

> **"I basically can't remember doing anything as a kid apart from watching TV, and every memory I have as a kid is somehow based around TV. That was my whole life, one hundred percent."**
> **(Rob Zombie)**
> *Hence his last name.*

Phony street-cred alert: Then there are the heartrending (yet oh-so-happily ending) tall tales of the hardscrabble youth of Robert Van Winkle, better known as Vanilla Ice (cool as his namesake for at least two seconds in the eighties, and currently struggling to make an alterno-style comeback with a refreshing new look: a manly-man goatee . . . gee, not a cliché or anything). He was, he claimed, "a kid that grew up in the ghetto," and also confessed that he'd been mixed up with rough, tough street gangs, during which time he'd been stabbed five times. He then turned his myriad talents to Motocross racing, and also began pursuing his unbelievable (and unbelievably short-lived) career in rap music. Incredible!—literally: Ice's dramatic stories of his misspent childhood are all products of his overactive imagination . . . in reality, he was raised in a nauseatingly normal middle-class home. (Once a doofus, always a doofus.)

> **"I never was a teenager."**
> **(Mick Jagger)**

Start Me Up

"Until we got our first advance from CBS, we all lived in an apartment together and I spent my money on Boone's Farm and blue crystal meth, which I kept in the refrigerator."
(Steven Tyler)

Getting started in the cutthroat world of music is never as simple as picking up a guitar, growing your hair, and getting together with a few other like-minded slobs (except maybe in the case of grunge bands). Nope, it takes determination, hard work, and most of all the desire to show all those people who didn't believe you'd ever amount to a hill of beans that *you are number one*. With a bullet. Unfortunately, that usually means a long spell of *paying your dues*—a euphemism for storing your few possessions in your car, dining out every night on ketchup from little plastic packets, and hanging out wherever you can find a place to lay your addled head. Guns N' Roses axman **Slash** (the one with the kinky bangs hanging two feet over his beady eyes) admits he used to "fuck girls just so I could stay at their place."

"We predicted ourselves into being rock stars, and we became them."
(Twiggy Ramirez, Marilyn Manson)

If you're lucky, paying your dues can also mean playing with successful musicians. **Boz Scaggs** was an employee of the **Steve Miller Band** prior to establishing a career of his own, and **Matt Sorum**, before joining **Guns N' Roses**, pounded skins for **Tori Amos's** first album. Poodle-permed **Sheryl Crow** warbled for **Michael Jackson**, from whom she "learned that it's very important to learn the names of those who work for you. He never learned my name. In eighteen months, he never once called me by my name, and in a situation the name is everything—it's your identity, and if someone can't be bothered to ask you your name, then there is no identity. You can't have people give their time and their energy and their lives to you and you don't even know their name. Forget it." (Hmmm . . . maybe if she hadn't been a *girl* . . . and a little *old* . . .)

> "On our first gig, we were so loud and horrifying that most of the teachers, students, and parents fled screaming from the room."
>
> (John Cale, Velvet Underground)

Limp Bizkit's (love that name, guys) career picked up steam after their record company, Flip/Interscope, paid muchos pesos to a Portland radio station to play the band's single, "Counterfeit." Payola? Why *no*, of course not—it was simply a well-thought-out marketing strategy . . . an "advertisement" for the group, pure and simple. Admits Bizkit belter Fred Durst, "It worked, but it's not that cool of a thing. Some stations won't play your shit even though kids want it, so we had to pay to get 'em to play it."

Gimme Some Lovin'

Why they got into rock 'n' roll

> "Money and girls were the two big motivations—that's what it was for everybody."
>
> (Don Henley)

> "I never set out to be a businessman. I just wanted to have fun, fuck chicks, and do drugs."
>
> (Ozzy Osbourne)

> "I didn't start up a band because I couldn't get laid. I started a band because I wasn't getting laid *enough.* So I decided to launch a proactive assault. 'Note to self: Start band.' "
>
> (Greg Dulli, Afghan Whigs)

> "I wanted to perform, I wanted to write songs, and I wanted to get lots of chicks."
>
> (James Taylor)

"The reason we first started strumming guitars is because we wanted women—and lots of them."
(Gene Simmons)

"You were at school and you were pimply and no one wanted to know you. You get into a group and you've got thousands of chicks there. And there you are with thousands of little girls screaming their heads off. Man, it's *power* . . . phew!"
(Eric Clapton)

"You could say that I got into music for the sex. I never harbored a burning desire to sing my heart out or be a star. So when I was fifteen, it was a big surprise to suddenly be asked to join a rock band. The invitation was extended by the lead singer, in a desperate move to seduce me. Until his request I considered him a complete arsehole. I loathed his New Romantic tucker boots, his lipstick, and his unmitigated rudeness. Then I heard him sing. I can still remember turning my head in shock and horror, thinking, 'He has the most beautiful voice.' I quickly fell in lust, and as he was very keen on me, I joined his band—and shortly thereafter his bed."
(Shirley Manson, Garbage)

Girls, girls, girls . . . what would rock stars do without 'em? "[Jane's Addiction's] first manager was a prostitute," says Perry Farrell. "That's where the song 'Whores' came from. She would get the money up for us to do shows." What an angel! (I don't wanna know how she was paid for her efforts.) An angel of a different ilk—in the form of devilish Kiss star Gene Simmons—fronted the fledgling, not-yet-famous bad boys of Van Halen enough dough to make their first few demos. So when the hard-rockin' hell-raisers hit paydirt, did they do the right thing? Hell no. "The guys still owe me a couple thousand bucks," fumes Simmons.

"It used to drive us mad to think that we were up there working so hard, playing our guts out while all these guys were sitting around and chattering. So we turned up the volume louder and louder until it was impossible for anyone to have a conversation."
(Black Sabbath drummer Bill Ward, remembering the band's early pub performances)

Dirty Work

"If I had to do something else, I'd like to be an osteopath. I'd like to cure arthritis and make people's bones work."
(Ray Davies)

It's all well and good to be cutting-edge and rebellious, but sometimes reality intrudes and you've just got to get a job (or you'll be *sleeping* at the Salvation Army instead of just *shopping* there). It's interesting to learn what rockers deemed acceptable, work-wise, while they awaited their big breaks. Some had low-end, low-paying jobs, barely earning enough to scrape together the rent money at the end of the month. Others, like Jon Bon Jovi, had positions that proved to be fertile training grounds for their future careers—and taught them about rock-star behavior, to boot. Learning by doing—always the best way.

Paula Abdul: waitress

Damon Albarn (Blur): recording studio gofer

Pat Benatar: bank teller; singing waitress

Chuck Berry: hairdresser

Jon Bon Jovi: Burger King employee; recording studio assistant

"I saw Aerosmith do more blow than I'd seen in my whole lifetime. I saw Gene Simmons of Kiss walk around all day with his hand in front of his face because he was afraid someone was looking at him, even though he didn't have any makeup on and they didn't wear it then anyway."
(Jon Bon Jovi)

"She chewed me out big-time when I walked in to deliver her a message and called her Diana. She said, 'Can't you read, you moron? It's "Miss Ross" to you. Now get the fuck out of my studio.'"
(Jon Bon Jovi)

David Bowie: commercial artist; model; art teacher

Jackson Browne: kaleidoscope assembler ("If one more person came up and said, 'Oooh, oooh, oooh, look at that!' I would have lost my mind. I lasted a week.")

Belinda Carlisle: gas station attendant

"As you know, I was once married to Barbra Streisand."
(Elliott Gould, when asked to name his worst job)

Chubby Checker: chicken plucker

Joe Cocker: plumber

Elvis Costello: computer programmer

Roger Daltrey: sheet-metal worker

Terence Trent D'Arby: army corporal

Jonathan Davis (Korn): live-in coroner's assistant

Bo Diddley: construction worker

Peter Gabriel: travel agent, milliner

Liam and Noel Gallagher: shoplifters

Bob Geldof: pea sheller; meat packer; journalist for England's *NME (New Musical Express)*

David Gilmour (Pink Floyd): model

Daryl Hall: apple picker

"To be honest, it was very boring. I found it very, very dull in the end. Standing there with the window open to keep your nipples firm was not very good."
(Geri Halliwell, on her former gig as a topless model)

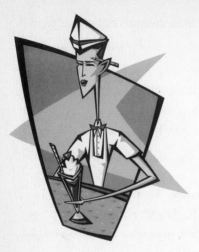

Deborah Harry: Playboy bunny; bartender at Max's Kansas City; secretary in the New York office of the BBC; beautician

Chrissie Hynde: waitress ("I was lousy because I had to serve meat to people, which pissed me off. I couldn't be courteous or polite when I wanted to go out and bury the meat like it should have been.")

Ice-T: jewel thief

Chris Isaak: tour guide in Japan

Mick Jagger: ice-cream vendor

Rickie Lee Jones: waitress

Cyndi Lauper: racehorse walker

Simon LeBon: lumberjack (he's so . . . outdoorsy and rugged)

Lemmy (Motörhead): roadie for Jimi Hendrix and Pink Floyd

AFTER THE GLITTER FADES

What are they doing now?

Peter Green's post-Fleetwood Mac occupation: grave-digging

M. C. Hammer, after completely decimating his more-than-thirty-million-dollar fortune, worked as a spokesmodel for Taco Bell, and has now begun a brand-new career as a televangelist (on the Trinity Broadcasting Network). God help us.

Teenybopper heartthrob Bobby Sherman now works as an emergency medical technician.

"It's like you've been an astronaut and you've been to the moon. What do you do with the rest of your life?"
(Paul McCartney)

Annie Lennox: fish filleter, waitress

Till Lindemann (Rammstein): Olympic swimmer

Courtney Love: stripper, groupie (and, according to her father, with whom she briefly lived in Ireland when she was sixteen, Love also worked as a hooker . . . so *that's* where she got her look)

Frankie Lymon: pimp

Madonna: lifeguard

George Michael: movie usher

Bette Midler: go-go dancer

Keith Moon: plaster salesman

Vince Neil: electrician

Stevie Nicks: Bob's Big Boy hostess

Elvis Presley: truck driver

Twiggy Ramirez (Marilyn Manson): pizza maker ("I was there by myself for hours and I was bored. So I tried fucking . . . the pizza dough before I cooked it. But then I threw it away. I was just bored. Something to do.")

Dee Dee Ramone: rent boy

"You'd be walking down the street and run into Dee Dee with some old guy and he'd get embarrassed and say, 'Hey you guys, have you met my uncle?' "
(Johnny Thunders)

PAINT IT, BLACK

Commercial-artist trainees

**David Bowie
Ian Hunter
Pete Townshend
Leo Sayer**

Lou Reed: accountant's assistant

Keith Richards: ball boy at a tennis court

Henry Rollins: ice-cream store manager

Tom Scholz (Boston): computer designer

Bon Scott (AC/DC): roadie, chauffeur, and business advisor to the band while waiting for their original lead singer to quit—it took a few months

Gene Simmons: schoolteacher

"I wanted to kill those little pricks."
(Gene Simmons, on why he chose to quit teaching)

Nikki Sixx: record-store clerk

Sting: schoolteacher

Neil Tennant (Pet Shop Boys): assistant editor of *Smash Hits* magazine

Tina Turner: maid

Dave Vanian (The Damned): grave digger

Tom Waits: vacuum-cleaner salesman

Wendy O. Williams: dominatrix in a live sex show

Bill Withers: installed toilets on 747s

Wyclef Jean (Fugees): fast-food worker

"I used to work at Burger King to save up enough money to get into the studio. I'd say to my boss, 'One day, you'll see—I'm going to be a big superstar.' And he'd say, 'Listen, give me nine Whoppers, six fries, and hold the dream.' "
(Wyclef Jean)

Frank Zappa: made custom porno flicks (specialized in providing "the fetish of your choice" for three hundred bucks a crack)

Rob Zombie: bike messenger; art director for sleazy porn rags like *Over 40* and *Tail End*

Stage Names

Inspiration comes in mysterious ways, as we learn by finding out how rock groups came up with their names—and what some of these monikers mean. (The term "rock 'n' roll"—derived from a term used by blues players, like rock music itself—is slang for sexual intercourse.) It's easy to cop a handle from an existing influence, like a movie or book (although frankly, most musicians aren't that well read), and many bands have done just that. Others have adopted or adapted the names of famous places or people, and a few try to be clever by mixing up the alphabet or dreaming up acronyms with "special" meanings. But the best names are those where a bit of inventiveness was employed (like **Led Zeppelin**, who got their name after **Keith Moon** chuckled  that the band would go down like a "lead balloon"), creating an instantly recognizable appellation that stands the test of time. **Nine Inch Nails? Marilyn Manson? Third Eye Blind? Smashing Pumpkins?** I don't think so.

The **B-52s** took their name from the retro-inspired foot-high hairstyles sported by members **Kate Pierson** and **Cindy Wilson.**

The rock press had **Blind Faith** that the supergroup led by **Eric Clapton** and featuring **Steve Winwood, Ginger Baker,** and **Rick Grech** would be stunningly successful (and they were right).

Eric Clapton, Ginger Baker, and **Jack Bruce** thought of themselves as being at the very top of the musical heap—the **Cream,** as it were.

Dire Straits named themselves after their typical financial state.

Eurythmics was a method used for teaching children music through movement. (And a method of teaching listeners boredom through bad songs.)

Fugees is a diminution of "refugees."

Foo Fighters were what World War II pilots called UFOs (or what they thought were UFOs).

The eof Four was a radical Communist faction in China.

Guns N' Roses was comprised of former members of Los Angeles bands L.A. Guns and Hollywood Rose.

Husker Du is an old board game (the name means "Do you remember?").

Iron Maiden: Steve Harris explains that "an Iron Maiden is a vicious torture device . . . you know, it's a metal case with these nails set inside of it, and if you fasten it over someone's head they get kind of spiked. Very unpleasant." (Like their music.)

The Joy Division was what the Nazis called Jewish women kept segregated in the camps to "entertain" the Germans.

The Lemonheads were named after the sour little candies.

Megadeth: Dave Mustaine says the name means "the act of dying, but, like, really mega!" Duuuude! Cooool!

The name Nine Inch Nails, according to Trent Reznor, has no meaning whatsoever (makes sense, considering the source), although some of the group's fans insist it's meant to refer to either the Statue of Liberty's fingernails or the nails used to put Jesus up on the cross. Get a life.

Alan Vega and his bandmates came up with the name Suicide because, Vega explains, "We looked around this room and they were all artists—great this and great that—and they're all just shooting up and trying, like, to off themselves. And we just said, 'Suicide,' and one look around and we said, 'Of course, of course,' and that was it."

The Tears for Fears and Primal Scream names were both taken from phrases used in psychiatrist Arthur Janov's "primal scream" therapy.

The UB40 is a government form needy Brits must fill out in order to receive public funds.

Life and Letters

ABBA was crafted from the initials of each of the group's members: Agnetha, Benny, Bjorn, and Anni-Frid (or Anni-Frid, Bjorn, Benny, and Agnetha). Must've taken them all afternoon to come up with that.

Blue Öyster Cult is an anagram of Cully Stout Beer—what the guys were swilling as they attempted to think up a name for their fledgling act.

EMF may stand for Every Mother Fucker (their record label denies this—surprise, surprise), or, alternatively, Epson Mad Funkers (a group of groupies of the band New Order).

KLF stands for "Kopyright Liberation Front" (lurn too spel).

L. L. Cool J stands for "Ladies Love Cool James" (the man obviously doesn't have an insecurity problem).

Axl Rose is an anagram of . . . an activity of which the singer is evidently quite fond.

W.A.S.P. stands for "We Are Sexual Perverts"
. . . or maybe "We Are Stupid People."

PLAYING DUMB, PART 1

The world's most idiotic album titles

Achtung Baby (U2)

Oy Vey Baby (David Bowie & Tin Machine)

Melon Collie & The Infinite Sadness (Smashing Pumpkins)

Outlandos d'Amour and Zenyatta Mondata (The Police)

The Dream of the Blue Turtles (Sting)

Cosi Fan Tutti Frutti (Squeeze)

Supposed Former Infatuation Junkie (Alanis Morissette)

If You Can't Lick 'Em, Lick 'Em (Ted Nugent)

For Those About to Rock, We Salute You (AC/DC)

The Spaghetti Incident? (Guns N' Roses)

Ringo's Rotogravure (Ringo Starr)

See Jungle! See Jungle! Go Join Your Gang! Yeah. City All Over! Go Ape Crazy (Bow Wow Wow)

Seven and the Ragged Tiger (Duran Duran)

Now and Zen (Robert Plant)

Dirk Wears White Sox (Adam & The Ants)

Koo Koo (Debbie Harry)

High Concept

Blue Cheer was a type of LSD.

One of the **Doobie Brothers** explains, "We were passing around a joint—a doobie—and someone said, 'We're all doobie brothers.' " (It sure beats their original name: "Pud.")

AU CONTRAIRE

Contrary to popular belief, the Beastie Boys name does not stand for "Boys Entering Anarchistic States Toward Inner Excellence," Kiss doesn't stand for "Knights in the Service of Satan" or "Kids in Satan's Service," and Bee Gees doesn't mean the "Brothers Gibb" (in fact, the treble-toned trio took their handle from the initials of a man who was instrumental in their career: racetrack promoter Bill Good).

The **Gin Blossoms** named themselves after the oh-so-attractive red "blooms" (groups of burst capillaries) one sees adorning the skin of chronic alcoholics.

In British slang, a **Motörhead** (without the metal-dude umlaut, of course) is a speed freak. Gee, wonder if **Lemmy** had anything to do with that moniker?

Pearl Jam was a psychedelic concoction with a special secret ingredient: peyote.

Heroes and Villains

Bob Dylan says he "didn't change my name in honor of Dylan Thomas. That's just a story. I've done more for Dylan Thomas than he's done for me. Look how many kids are probably reading his poetry now because they heard that story." *Yeah, and look how many kids won't ever turn on their radios again after hearing you.*

Buffalo Springfield is a manufacturer of steamrollers.

Jethro Tull was an eighteenth-century British farming expert who invented agricultural tools, including the seed drill, precursor to the modern plow.

The **Softnamed** themselves in honor of **Buddy Holly's Crickets**.

Most **Marilyn Manson** band members cobble two monikers together to form their unsavory appellations: the first name of a beauty icon, and the surname of a notorious murderer (the more brutal, the better). Thus we have Marilyn himself (Marilyn Monroe + Charles Manson), **Twiggy Ramirez** (the stick-thin sixties model + the "Night Stalker," Richard Ramirez), **Madonna Wayne Gacy** (the immaterial girl + John Wayne Gacy), and so on. Sooooo brilliant.

The name **Pink Floyd** is also a glued-together hybrid—of a pair of wacko **Syd Barrett**'s all-time-fave blues masters: Pink Anderson and Floyd Council.

Mansun were forced to change their name to the way it's currently spelled after some bizarro Charles Manson followers made threats against them.

In the spirit of *not* milking it to the last drop, a surprisingly levelheaded **Ozzy Osbourne** ix-nayed wife Sharon's idea of naming his act "Son of Sabbath" after he was booted out of the group.

The **Ramones** used a **Paul McCartney** pseudonym as the name of their band.

The **Yardbirds** were fans of jazzman **Charlie "Yardbird" Parker**.

A Word in Spanish

Black Uhuru: Uhuru means "freedom" in some stupid language.

Kraftwerk is German for "power station."

Before shortening their name, the **Pogues** were called "Pogue Mahone," which means "kiss my ass" in Gaelic.

Sepultura means "grave" in Portuguese. And "posing metal dudes" in American.

WHAT'S IN A NAME?

Alice Nutter of Chumbawamba once played drums with a band called Ow My Hair's On Fire.

Hitting the Books

Amboy Dukes: 1942 novel (about New York street gangs) by Irving Shulman

Boomtown Rats: The guys took the phrase, used to describe Oklahoma oil-field newcomers, from Woody Guthrie's autobiography, *Bound for Glory.*

Counting Crows: An olde English rhyme

Darling Buds: From Shakespeare's Sonnet 18 ("Shall I compare thee to a summer's day? Thou art more lovely and more temperate: Rough winds do shake the darling buds of May, And summer's lease hath all too short a date.")

Depeche Mode: Literally "fast fashion," a French couture magazine still in existence

The Doors: Aldous Huxley's *The Doors of Perception*

The Fall: Novel by Albert Camus

A Flock of Seagulls: *Jonathan Livingston Seagull* by Richard Bach

Heaven 17: A rock group in Anthony Burgess's *A Clockwork Orange*

Hole: A line in *Medea* ("There's a hole burning deep inside of me"). Courtney Love says she picked it because "I knew it would confuse people." (Dang, she's just so media-savvy.)

Marillion: A shortening of the book title *Silmarillion* (J. R. R. Tolkien)

Mott the Hoople: The novel by Willard Manus

Sad Café: Carson McCullers's *The Ballad of the Sad Café*

Soft Machine: The novel by William Burroughs

Steely Dan: A steam-powered dildo featured in William Burroughs's *Naked Lunch*

Steppenwolf: The Herman Hesse novel

Supertramp: *Autobiography of a Supertramp* (1908) by W. H. Davies

Velvet Underground: The title of a book (topic: sadomasochism) that one of the band members found on a New York City sidewalk. Right. They *found* it.

10,000 Maniacs: *2,000 Maniacs* (a cult horror flick)

Black Sabbath: 1935 Boris Karloff film

"I asked myself, 'Why is there a line of people with money in their hands, paying to get the shit scared out of them?' It's because people get a thrill out of being evil."
(Ozzy Osbourne, on the horror-flick theater across from Black Sabbath's rehearsal hall)

Cinderella: A porn movie

Duran Duran: *Barbarella*'s mad scientist, played by Milo O'Shea

Faster Pussycat: Russ Meyer's movie *Faster Pussycat! Kill! Kill!*

Fine Young Cannibals: *All the Fine Young Cannibals* (1960 flick starring Natalie Wood and Robert Wagner)

Mudhoney: Another Russ Meyer film

Terrorvision: Another cult horror flick

White Zombie: Yet another cult horror flick

Keepin' the Faith

Cosmic, dudes: **Air Supply** came to "spiritually in tune" member **Graham Russell** in a dream, as did **Soul Asylum** to **Dave Pirner**.

Alice Cooper: A Ouija board said that Vincent Furnier (Cooper's godawful given name) was the reincarnation of this seventeenth-century witch. A Ouija board session also gave guitarist **Rick Nielson** the **Cheap Trick** name, he claims.

Earth, Wind & Fire took their name from the three dominant elements in **Maurice White's** astrological chart. Deep, man.

Grateful Dead: **Jerry Garcia** found this name in an Egyptian prayer.

Fields of the Nephilim is a mythological hell, and **Styx** is a mythical river that's on the *way* to hell. I'll say.

Going Places

Bay City is a town in Utah, after which the **Bay City Rollers** decided to name themselves despite the fact that none of them are from there.

Bush is a shortening of the London suburb of Shepherd's Bush, where the band once lived.

Heavy metal's **Rammstein** took their name from a West German air base where disaster struck: During an air show, three jets collided, killing the pilots and more than forty members of the audience. To commemorate the event, Rammstein set fire to themselves each time they perform—to bring a sense of the shock and horror of the event (not to mention the concert itself) to the crowd.

The **Cabaret Voltaire**, in Berlin, was a dada café and "performance space." Whatever.

Chicago was originally known as The Big Three, then they expanded their lineup and changed their name to The Chicago Transit Authority, then CTA, then eventually just Chicago. (If you guessed that these folks are from the Windy City, you get a gold star.)

The members of the **Coasters** hailed from L.A. (a.k.a. "the Coast").

Oasis were named for a Manchester club where the **Beatles** once played.

PLAYING DUMB, PART 2

The world's most idiotic band and performer names

1910 Fruitgum Company
10,000 Maniacs
Ace of Base
Air Supply
Al B. Sure!
Animotion
Bad English
Bananarama
Ben Folds Five
Better Than Ezra
Bile
Blind Melon
Blue Öyster Cult
The Chocolate Watch Band
Chumbawamba
Color Me Badd
Cradle of Filth
Def Leppard
Dexys Midnight Runners
The Electric Prunes
A Flock of Seagulls
Foghat
Goo Goo Dolls
Haircut One Hundred
Hooters
Hootie & the Blowfish
Icicle Works
Jamiroqui
Johnny Hates Jazz
Kajagoogoo

Sex Appeal

Of the school principal who suspended a student for wearing a **Korn** T-shirt to school, guitarist **James "Munky" Shaffer** says, "She must have heard that Korn stands for 'kiddie porn.' You know how that goes. Kids make things up, and then people start to believe that the rumors are true." Munky and his equally stupidly named bandmate "Head" say it's actually the band's inside joke about a kinky sex incident (we don't wanna know).

The Lovin' Spoonful is slang for the male "emission." And 9CC is the average amount of semen in a normal ejaculation, so 10CC must be better, right?

Isn't it obvious? The **Buzzcocks** are named after something you probably wouldn't buy for your mother.

Tusk is Mick Fleetwood's slang for an erection, and the title of Fleetwood Mac's 1979 album. Mick lied to *People* magazine when they asked him about the record's title: "We just liked the sound of the word in the abstract," he told them. And they bought it.

Making a Name for Themselves

Luther Vandross has a strange middle name: Ronzoni (in honor of the only comestible his mom could keep down during her difficult pregnancy).

Why did **Prince** change his perfectly good (if a little grand) moniker to that stupid unpronounceable symbol? According to **TAFKAP** himself (who now goes by simply "**The Artist**," as if there were no others), "It was a way of cutting the chaos off, cutting off the outside voices. I heard 'Prince is crazy' so much that it had an effect on me. So one day I said, 'Let me just check out.' Here there is solitude, silence—I like to stay in this controlled environment. People say I'm out of touch, but I'll do twenty-five or thirty more albums—I'm gonna catch up with Sinatra—so you tell me who's out of touch. One thing I ain't gonna run out of is music." (Or ego. Or dumb clothes.)

Then there are the nicknames: **Keith Richards** and **Mick Jagger** are known as the "Glimmer Twins" (is it the stardust, I wonder?), Aerosmith's **Joe Perry** and **Steven Tyler** are known, for obvious reasons, as the "Toxic Twins," and Def Leppard's dynamic guitar duo, **Phil Collen** and **Steve Clark**, were known for the same reasons as "The Terror Twins." **John Bonham** was called "The Beast" because of his behavior when he'd knocked back a few (or a few dozen) drinks, and **Sid Vicious**'s girlfriend/murder victim, **Nancy Spungen**, was known by all and sundry as "Nauseating Nancy" because of her . . . er, *vivacious* personality.

PLAYING DUMB, PART 2 (CONTINUED)

Korn
Life of Agony
Limp Bizkit
Lipps, Inc.
Men Without Hats
Moby Grape
Mr. Mister
Nitty Gritty Dirt Band
Pet Shop Boys
Porno for Pyros
Quarterflash
REO Speedwagon
Right Said Fred
Scritti Politti
The Smashing Pumpkins
Sniff 'n' the Tears
Snot
Soft Cell
Squirrel Nut Zippers
Strawberry Alarm Clock
Swing Out Sister
Tears for Fears
'Til Tuesday
Timbuk 3
Toad the Wet Sprocket
Vanilla Fudge
Was (Not Was)
Wham!

After rock god **David Lee Roth**'s trademark long, fluffy mane started thinning, industry wags started calling him **David "Weave" Roth**.

"Diamond" Darrell renamed himself **"Dimebag" Darrell** to better reflect his band **Pantera**'s hard-edged sound. He tough.

Iggy Pop, born James Westerberg, says, "Iggy was a nickname hung on me—that I didn't particularly like—when I was in high school and was in a band called the Iguanas. Iggy is short for Iguana."

Motörhead's **Lemmy** picked up his name because of his habit of asking everyone to "Lemmy a fiver!" when he was a struggling musician.

"Cars" singer **Gary Numan**, born (the rather bland) Gary Webb, appropriated his moniker from a plumber he found in a telephone book.

Slash got his name from his "slash and burn" guitar-playing style.

 **Johnny Rotten** got his moniker because of his typically rotten English teeth. And personality.

Original Sins

Good thing they didn't stick with their original handles

The Beach Boys: Carl and the Passions

The Beatles: Johnny and the Moondogs

The Black Crowes: Greasy Little Toes; Mr. Crowe's Garden

Black Sabbath: Earth

Blue Öyster Cult: Soft White Underbelly; Oaxaca; The Stalk Forest Group

The Boomtown Rats: The Nightlife Thugs

David Bowie: David Jones and the Lower Third

Boy George: Lieutenant Lush (while working as a backing vocalist for **Bow Wow Wow** in 1980)

Bush: Future Primitive

The Butthole Surfers (used to change their name for every gig before settling on this winner): Nine Foot Worm Makes Own Food; Abe Lincoln's Bush; The Inalienable Right to Eat Fred Astaire's Asshole

The Cars: Cap'n Swing

Kurt Cobain: First band was named Fecal Matter

The Cranberries: The Cranberry-Saw-Us

The Cult: Southern Death Cult; Death Cult

Culture Club: Praise of Lemmings

The Cure: Goat Band

Def Leppard: Atomic Mass; Deaf Leopard

Earth, Wind & Fire: The Salty Peppers

The Eurythmics: The Tourists

Green Day: Sweet Children

The J. Geils Band: The Hallucinations

Joy Division: The Stiff Kittens

Kool and the Gang: The Jazziacs

Liz Phair: Girly Sound

Lynyrd Skynyrd: My Backyard

Mötley Crüe: London

Motörhead: Bastard

The New York Dolls: Actress

Pearl Jam: Mookie Blaylock; Reenk Roink

Tom Petty: Mudcrutch

Pink Floyd: The Screaming Abdabs

Queen: Smile

Pulp: Arabacus Pulp

The Ramones: The Tangerine Puppets

Simon and Garfunkel: Tom and Jerry

Simple Minds: Johnny and the Self-Abusers

The Talking Heads: The Artistics

U2: Feedback; The Hype

Van Halen: Rat Salade; Mammoth

The Who: The High Numbers

XTC: The Helium Kidz

Mirror Mirror

"When I first realized I was good-looking, I was naked, looking at myself in the mirror. Then, later, I got around to looking at my face."
(David Bowie)

When considering a career in rock, several things must be taken into consideration: Do you look good? Can you play (not critical)? Can you write the odd catchy tune here and there? Do you have the desire and drive to succeed at all costs? Oh, and by the way, do you look good? To be successful in the rock arena, it's not enough to be a great songwriter or a virtuoso on that Stratocaster—in fact, it's not necessary in the least. What's paramount is having a good look (or at least a good "rock" look—if you're not some combination of goateed, pierced, big-breasted, and tattooed, don't bother applying).

"I can't see what the fuss is all about. I mean, if I saw a five-foot-three spotty degenerate, I wouldn't flip out."
(Steve Marriott, Small Faces)

The Sex Pistols are a textbook case of this "image *uber alles*" philosophy—its members were recruited based on their ability to fit in with the look and attitude dreamt up by wacky, avaricious bondage-wear-merchant-cum-punk-impresario Malcolm McLaren. So when the bass player in the original lineup walked out, London street tough Sid Vicious was tapped to join the band. Now, Sid was not the brightest bulb on the string, and he didn't have a lick of musical talent or experience. No matter—he did have the most important

PISTOL WHIPPED

"I was just a haberdasher, selling the odd whip or chain."
(Malcolm McLaren)

"It was just like being in the Monkees."
(Glenn Matlock)

"The band is much more handsome since I joined."
(Sid Vicious)

"I only got involved with the Sex Pistols to sell more trousers."
(Malcolm McLaren)

thing going for him: he fit the Pistols' carefully crafted image so well—both in looks and in his jaded-before-my-time outlook—that he was a perfectly natural fit (and anyway, the rest of the band was similarly talent-free).

> **"I'm not, like, horribly unattractive."**
> **(Lemonheads sex symbol Evan Dando)**

The story was the same for the Clash's pretty **Paul Simonon** who, according to **Mick Jones**, "looked so great that we said, 'Just do something. Can you sing "Roadrunner"?' It didn't really work out, but he really wanted to be in a band, so we ended up painting the notes on the neck of his bass and teaching him the rudiments of bass guitar."

Similar Features

> **"It's written in rock 'n' roll that all you need is love. But you also need a great nose."**
> **(Bono)**

CARRY THAT WEIGHT

> **"I've got all this pressure to keep trim as Sporty Spice. I used to drink lager and blackcurrant, but I had to stop because I was getting a beer gut. I could have ended up being Fat Old Lazy Spice."**
> **(Mel C)**

> **"Singing is the love of my life, but I was ready to give it all up because I couldn't handle people talking about how fat I was."**
> **(Stevie Nicks)**

How do rockers feel about themselves?

"My teeth—I don't like the way they protrude. . . . Apart from that, I'm perfect." (Freddie Mercury)

"If a hundred belly buttons were lined up against a wall, I could definitely pick out mine." (Madonna)

Now, that's an achievement to be proud of.

"[I'll] always be stuck with the glasses thing and the bloody glittery image."

(Elton John)
Don't forget your trademark pudginess and the silly hair transplant.

"Express yourself. If you feel like you want to paint yourself pink, paint yourself pink, walk down the street and piss some people off 'cause it's really cool. You can't grow old thinking, 'Why didn't I? Why didn't I?' Just do it. Hair can be cut off, holes put in your face . . . they heal up. Just do it." (Keith Flint, Prodigy)

"I think I've always been glamorous; this is just a different version. For the next album, I'm thinking about removing my head altogether." (Marilyn Manson)

"It hasn't always been like this. They didn't use to write on my school reports, 'Jarvis could do better in this subject . . . and he's a sex god.'" (Jarvis Cocker, Pulp)

FLAPS DOWN

No collagen here, just lips that naturally look like the dime-store wax variety.

Steven Tyler

Mick Jagger

Natalie Imbruglia

Bob Geldof

David Johansen

Tim Curry

ROCK'S BLACK EYES

Enough with the eyeliner, already!

Ozzy Osbourne

Michael Stipe

Marilyn Manson

Keith Flint (Prodigy)

Scott Weiland

"I've always wanted to be a sex symbol, but I don't think I am. I think I'm really hideous and ugly and fluffy and wrinkly and disgusting, so I can't imagine anyone thinking that I was sexually attractive. And if they do, where the fuck are they?" (Sinéad O'Connor)

"I don't feel overly attached to my body, in that I don't think it is exactly who I am." (Alanis Morissette)

"I can't help it if I've never looked healthy." (Keith Richards)

"I manage to look so young because I'm mentally retarded." (Deborah Harry)

At First Blush

"People are really works of art, and if you have a nice face, you might as well play about with it." (Marc Bolan)

"Cosmetics is a boon to every woman, but a girl's best beauty aid is still a nearsighted man."
(Yoko Ono)
Certainly true in her case.

"Let's go watch Mick put on his makeup— that's always good for a laugh." (Ron Wood)

"I started wearing [lipstick] because it made me feel confident and more attractive. I'm completely featureless without it. But onstage, I always used to lean my mouth on the mic and shut my eyes so I wouldn't have to see the people. And at the end I'd come off with lipstick smeared all over my face, so I thought I might as well go on with it like that and make it look intentional." (Robert Smith, The Cure, on his horror-show maquillage)

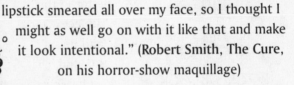

"When I put on my face, I feel that I am in a garden of paradise alone with beautiful ladies. They are the essence of my soul, a purity that cannot be tainted." (Tiny Tim)

IF I WERE A CARPENTER

"We're Pat Boone, only a little cleaner."
(Richard Carpenter)

"The image we have would be hard for Mickey Mouse to maintain."
(Karen Carpenter)

"Imagine taking off your makeup and
nobody knows who you are."
(Steven Tyler)
Imagine making an idiotic Gap commercial
that proves you can't sing.

Public Image

"The thing is, to the kids in the audience AC/DC pose no threat. I mean, they can take a look up and say, 'That could be me. In fact, I look smarter than him.'" (Brian Johnson, AC/DC front man)
And in fact they probably are.

"We like to look sixteen and bored shitless." (David Johansen, New York Dolls)

"I've always looked like a bank clerk who's freaked out." (Elton John)

"We try to keep a sharp image because the public wants it. Who would have wanted to see Clark Gable without his false teeth?" (Paul Stanley)

"It doesn't matter what we do. We are just perceived as being unhip. I think it will always be like that. That's just the way it is, for whatever reason." (Geddy Lee, Rush)

"Damn, I look good with guns." (Ted Nugent)
He'd look better at the other end of a gun.

"I've seen bands doing queer bits in their underwear to get attention." (Steve Miller)

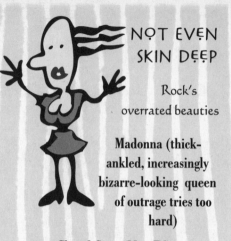

NOT EVEN SKIN DEEP

Rock's overrated beauties

Madonna (thick-ankled, increasingly bizarre-looking queen of outrage tries too hard)

Sheryl Crow (Mrs. Ed)

Sting (pomposity and blandness don't mix)

Tori Amos (too much curly hair)

Michael Hutchence (looked like a dissolute gigolo)

The new, improved, surgically enhanced Janet Jackson (intemperately tattooed, prodigally pierced)

Celine Dion (Hansel and Gretel would be terrified)

Mariah Carey (slutty-looking, overdone maquillage, too much hair . . . and can she even *sit down* in those skirts?)

Spice Girls (got some serious baby fat going on there . . . and it wouldn't hurt to lighten up on the makeup a little)

Oasis (dirty-looking, and that single eyebrow thing is revolting)

Jewel (squinty-eyed girl-next-door is really just kind of plain, and somehow got the idea she's *really* profound)

"Cock Rock"

"Basically, rock stardom comes down to the cut of your trousers."
(David Bowie)

Sexuality is a big part of the appeal of rock, and male rock stars tend to outfit themselves in such a way as to emphasize ye olde family jewels. Blues legend Ella James remembered one night when "that little package [Mick Jagger] wears in his pants" fell out of position during a concert, and said he was forced to hide behind some stage equipment while he reset *his* stage equipment.

"Maybe if the audience can see a cock through a pair of trousers, that must make you a sex symbol."
(Robert Plant)
You bet it does, baby. At least if it's big enough.

Rod Stewart, according to ex-wife Britt Ekland, "wore very shiny, very tight pants onstage, which were particularly tight around his bum. And because he wiggled it so much onstage, he wanted to keep it nice and smooth. But he couldn't have his instrument hanging all over the place, because it would dangle, and it was very uncomfortable. And he couldn't wear those . . . things that men wear, those horrible little packets . . . because they looked so ugly. So he used to take my knickers and pull them up real tight and stick the teeny-weeny part up his bum so that all that was covered were the parts he wanted covered. The panties were so thin and delicate that nothing showed."

HOW DEEP IS YOUR LOVE

"I'm a pop star! I have a big cock!"
(David Bowie)

"Some of my lady fans have accused me of putting bananas or socks down my pants to fill them up, so naturally I have to let 'em come up for a feel to show them they're wrong."
(Jim Dandy Mangrum, Black Oak Arkansas)

"My hose is my own. No Coke bottle, nothing stuffed down there."
(Freddie Mercury)

Hair Raising

"I looked at all the superstars. What is their different thing? Their hair. . . . I wanted to be a star. I said, 'I have to fix my hair.' "
(Rob Pilatus, Milli Vanilli)

Hair makes the man, as they say, and in music we've seen it all: from lionlike manes to razor-sharp Mohawks, kinky Afros to poodle perms. Today's major metal trend is the tough I-so-Rasta dreadlocks sported by the likes of the bad boys from Korn, Soulfly, and White Zombie. (Rob Zombie, now embarking on a successful solo career, looks *scarier* than he did in his White Zombie days, if possible, with that tangled mess hanging down his back plus a glamorous, ZZ Top–like facial fringe tinged with gray.) You know, come to think of it, I'll bet this came about because of the guys' dedication to their music—since they only have to wash their hair once every six or eight months, it gives them that much more time to hone their craft. Think how much more work would get done if we all just stopped taking showers.

"We had tremendous success in America. The bigger my hair got, the more records we sold."
(David Coverdale, Whitesnake)

CROSS HAIRS

A few fascinating follicular factoids

Ian Astbury and Billy Duffy of The Cult cut off their long hair in 1992 to prove a point: that "rock is dead." Point made. And so well.

Gary Numan ("Cars") has had a hair transplant, as has Sir Elton "Prince Valiant" John.

Jon Bon Jovi is the son of a hairdresser. Yeah, big surprise to me too.

. . . BUT NO ONE
PLACED A BID

When Michael Bolton chopped
off his long, distressingly ratty
hair, he saved the limp locks to
be auctioned off for charity.
No word on who the lucky
winner was.

In the eighties, **Poison** and **Mötley Crüe**
were the epitome of one of heavy-metal's
hallmarks: the goofily glammy L.A. "hair
band"—groups of skinny, guitar-wielding
shredders sporting down-to-your-ass,
bleached-to-a-pulp, pineapple-shaped
haystacks atop their pointy pates. Each
vied to have the highest follicular heap,
using enough Aqua Net (the sticky, holds-
like-cement staple of hair sculpture) in the
process to create a permanent hole in the
ozone directly above Sunset Strip.

"I don't like men with long hair. I think a man should be a man."
(Boy George)

On the sideburn side, awards for most impressive muttonchops go to the
Allman Brothers, **Lemmy** from **Motörhead**, and **Slade's Noddy Holder** (Britain's
Q magazine noted that his were so big they "hindered peripheral vision,
making him vulnerable to predators").

"I've changed my hairstyle so many times now [that] I don't know what I
look like." (**David Byrne**)

"I've tried changing it many times, but it refuses to lie down. I did have it
all whipped off once, but I looked such a twat, I grew it all back again. I'll
probably take it to the grave with me."
(**Rod Stewart**, on his roosterlike 'do)

"Every morning, I wake up with dreadlocks, so whatever product promises
me better hair, I buy. I'm a
complete junkie for that,
but I'm always disappointed
because nothing helps,
really." (**Nina Persson**, The
Cardigans)

"Fuzzy hair is radiant. My hair
is electric. It picks up *all* the
vibrations." (**Jimi Hendrix**)

LEADING WITH
HIS CHIN

**"There are plenty of
goatees around, just
not as gay and tidy as
mine."**
(George Michael)

Fashion Show

"Twenty years ago, they'd have said I was weird."
(Todd Rundgren)
Twenty years ago, they did.

Fashion is just as important a part of rock 'n' roll as looks and makeup. From the psychedelically hip hippie to the flamboyant seventies sex gods and masters of prog-rock pomposity (epitomized—and I mean that in the worst possible way—by codpiece-sporting Ted Nugent and fey Ian Anderson of Jethro Tull) to the wasted-junkie punk look of the eighties to the homeless-person-with-a-guitar look of the nineties, being a rock star has meant dressing in clothing others would never dare (or care) to don. But has anyone noticed that these convention-defying, rebellious young nonconformists all look *exactly the same*?

"[I am] a total slob. A pig. Everything is on the floor in my closet, but what does it matter when everything is black? It all matches."
(Gene Simmons, Kiss)

One of rock's more notable fashion fads was the punk look, which borrowed heavily from the fun bondage 'n' discipline crowd and featured lots of black rubber, leather, chains, heavy boots, and fright-mask Kabuki makeup. Adam Ant found it "really gray and sexless. I'd rather dress up as Liberace"—and he did. Ant was one of the pioneers of yet another (mercifully) short-lived music-as-an-excuse-for-fashion fad: the "new romantic" movement, which consisted in its entirety of silly, frilly duds, a few buckets of eyeliner and pancake, and completely meaningless musical maunderings.

LADY LOVE

One of the most radical makeovers in rock was that of Courtney Love, once grunge's grungiest fashion victim. When the hygiene-free and decidedly *non*-glam gal lucked into a Hollywood acting career, she suddenly and startlingly switched her whole loser look to a high-maintenance, Marilyn Monroe–ish one. Unfortunately, efforts at changing her prickly personality have been somewhat less successful.

Courtney Love,
looking every inch
the film star

"When I see some dirty old geek in a bloody plaid shirt and torn jeans, I get depressed. I don't want to look like a car mechanic."
(John Lydon/Johnny Rotten)

"Grunge was shooting so low. Do you wanna look like a rock star or do you wanna look like you work in a gas station? I'm an entertainer. I'm not here to pump gas."
(Marilyn Manson)

There's almost nothing left that will shock the jaded public—although girlfriend-of-Marilyn-Manson, talented cult actress/fashion fatality Rose McGowan, certainly made a valiant attempt: in 1998, she arrived at the MTV Video Music Awards show dressed in a little wisp of nothing fashioned from a few metallic ropes swingin' low across her ample bottom (Marilyn accompanied her to the event in a lovely, froufrou leopard-print glitter suit with a faux-fur collar—cocktail hour in lounge hell). It was evident that the poor girl had suffered from a temporary spell of amnesia, too, because she seemed to have left most of her underwear at home.

MTV dry-cleaned the entire venue after the pair departed.

"I don't know what I'm supposed to base myself on. When do I have to cut my hair and quit wearing jeans and my leather jacket and going on motorcycle rides? When do I have to start wearing a bun and stay home?"
(Cher)
Now would be good.

"People get used to a diet of beige, and they can't handle it when something shocking pink comes along"
(Rose McGowan)

"I'll wear anything as long as it hasn't been on George Michael's back."

(Boy George)

Another (mercifully short-lived) fad was the "is it a male or female" look worn by the gods of glam, who donned tourist-from-hell ensembles like purple satin pedal pushers with red-and-yellow-striped knee-highs and sky-blue, sky-high platform boots. What *were* they thinking? Maybe **Brian Eno** can explain it for us: "I was not gay, but I wanted to look great, and looking great meant dressing like a woman." Speaking of that sort of thing, it's not uncommon for rockers to borrow women's clothing to supplement their own wardrobes. **Casey Niccoli**, **Perry Farrell's** ex, confessed that "Perry and I kind of became one person. We shared each other's clothes. If I put on a dress and he liked it, then I had to take it off so he  could wear it for a gig. He stretched out all my lingerie." And I'll bet he looked awesome in it, too.

"I really just put any old thing on. Not like Mick, with his fabrics and colors. He's like fucking Greta Garbo."

(Charlie Watts)

Back in the days before body-piercing became de rigueur, **Mick Jagger** had a gem inset into one of his rather large choppers, and, obviously to enhance his ginger pulchritude, another Mick (Simply Red's stumpy **Hucknall**) has had a

ruby drilled into one of his yellowing incisors. There's not much such excessive rock-star flash today—the "look" seems to be no look, unless you count the little goatee-piercing-tattoo-dorky shorts-'n'-baseball-caps getups a "look." Ya-a-awn.

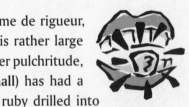

SUNGLASSES AT NIGHT

"The only reason we wore sunglasses onstage was because we couldn't stand the sight of the audience."

(John Cale)

Tattoo You

An excerpt from the Rock Star Rule Book: Get a tattoo. Get multiple tattoos. Cover your entire body in tattoos. Then start in on the piercing and (new!) subdermal body art. Don't worry what you'll look like when you're seventy—you probably won't live that long.

Permanent markers: some of rock's notable tats

"I have a tattoo on the inside of my upper left thigh of the Roadrunner saying, 'Beep beep.' My dad has the same one in the same place." (Sebastian Bach, Skid Row)

Cher: flower on butt, chain on arm—but maybe not for long . . . she's having all her tats removed because "It was just me and Janis Joplin who had them in the beginning. They were a symbol of rebellion. Now every model has them."

"I was always afraid to get my ear pierced, so I got a tattoo of an earring instead. It's kind of like killing two clichés in one stroke." (Alice Cooper)

"[I have a] reset button under my left arm. When you get all the way down and you hit that bottomless pit, you gotta reach under the arm and hit that reset button. I've only hit it two or three times so far, but that's what it's there for." (Dimebag Darrell)

"On my butt I have a tattoo of the planet Jendel, my birthplace." (Ace Frehley, Kiss)

Tommy Lee: too numerous to enumerate (one notable tat, however, is ex-wife Pamela's name—her full name—inked on one of his most private parts)

"I was gonna have a tattoo on my dick of my dick, but bigger. But I couldn't stand the pain." (Lemmy, Motörhead)

"I just had my back done. Tiger stripes. I'm striped all the way from the top of my neck down." (Vince Neil, Mötley Crüe)
Gee, that sounds sexy.

"I've got an *M* on each butt cheek that spells 'MOM'—unless I stand on my head; then it spells 'WOW.' " (Ricky Parent, Enuff Z'Nuff)

Ziggy and the Duke

Image Wizard David Bowie

David Jones was always a little "different," starting from an early age when a schoolyard punch-up almost cost him his left eye (he was in bed for eight months afterward) and left him with his strange multihued ocularity—his right eye is pale blue, and his left (injured) eye is pale gray, with a big ol' oversize pupil. Kinda cool, actually.

When Jones reached young adulthood, he decided to become a rock star. After performing for a while as "David Jones and the Lower Third," he hit upon a stroke of genius. With a name change (from Jones to Bowie), a dusting of glitter and a smattering of thrift-shop chic, he transformed himself into ultrafab "Ziggy Stardust," a fantastical (and, scandalously for the time, openly bisexual) space-being from Planet Glam. After his stunning transformation, Bowie saw his career rise to meteoric heights (and spawn a legion of pathetic imitators). Sadly, Bowie retired Ziggy—his most original and creative persona—at the finale of his 1973 tour.

His next too-cool persona was Aladdin Sane (get it?) from the not-quite-as-cool album of the same name. Then came the Thin White Duke, who debuted on the 1976 album *Station to Station,* after Bowie moved to decadent Berlin (with his good pal and partner in profligacy, Iggy Pop). During this period, Bowie made half-cocked comments like, "When you think about it, Adolf Hitler was the first pop star. It certainly wasn't his politics. He was a media pop star"; and "Hitler was a terrible military strategist, but his overall objective was very good. He was a tremendous morale-booster." Bowie called his Nazi costume–wearing, fascistic Duke creation "a very nasty  character," but later claimed he couldn't remember much about either the identity or making the album, having been too blitzed at the time. Fortunately, the Duke phase didn't last long, and after that Bowie was (and remains) . . . well, just Bowie.

"I'm sick of being Gulliver . . . I just want to go home to Beckenham and watch the telly."

"I feel like an actor when I'm onstage, not a rock artist."

"I already consider myself responsible for a whole new school of pretension."

"Didn't I retire in 1990? I can't remember."

"I wasn't at all surprised that Ziggy Stardust made my career. I packaged a totally credible plastic rock star—much better than any sort of Monkees fabrication. My plastic rocker was much more plastic than anybody's."

Holding Back the Years

Codger Rock

> "There are problems with being in an old, established band. It's disappointing to feel that you've become part of the establishment rather than staying at the sharp end. You felt that you were really radical, and suddenly everyone's going, 'Ugh—they're really boring, really old.' "
>
> *(Nick Mason, Pink Floyd)*

Rock 'n' roll is a young man's game (it is, after all, anti-authority, and we tend to *become* the "authority" as we get older). So how has the aging process affected the onetime rebels of the airwaves? Well, **Eric Clapton** still has an edge—but it's a decidedly fuzzy, simperingly sentimental one (want proof ? Listen to his dopey "Change the World" ditty). Dwarf-size singer **Steve Perry** has a hard time touring with **Journey** . . . because of his arthritis, he just can't kick up his elfin heels like he used to. And ax-shredder **Eddie Van Halen** had an artificial hip put in late 1999. Ah, how the mighty have fallen.

"No smoking around **Judas Priest**!" (K. K. Downing, Judas Priest)

 "You go into their dressing room before a show and there's a dead silence. They're all sitting around having a glass of milk and reading the *Evening News*." (Rod Stewart, on Deep Purple)

"A lot of people have asked us if we still think we're relevant." (Jim Kerr, Simple Minds)

I could answer that one for you right now.

"I don't want to be the world's oldest living folk singer." (Joan Baez)

"You know something? I really hate feeling too old to be doing what I'm doing." (Pete Townshend)

"People always said the Kinks would never last, but we survived the silly sixties, the sordid seventies, and the hateful eighties." (Ray Davies)

"Gram Parsons had it all sussed. He didn't stick around. He made his best work and then he died. That's the way I'm going to do it. I'm never going to stick around long enough to churn out a load of mediocre crap like those guys from the sixties." (Elvis Costello)
Too late, Elvis.

STONE AGE

"I'd rather be dead than singing 'Satisfaction' when I'm forty-five."
(Mick Jagger)

"You can't go on doing that thing for years. I mean, just imagine having to sing 'Satisfaction' when you're forty-five."
(Marianne Faithfull)
Yeah. Imagine.

"I'm twenty-eight now. Why thirty-three? I don't know—what the fuck. Look at Mick Jagger. You see this man in tight yellow pants, bouncing around as if he's in a step-aerobics class [and] . . . you think, 'This is not going to happen to me.' "
(Foo Fighters singer Dave Grohl, on his vow to cease performing at age thirty-three)

"Getting old is a fascinating thing. The older you get, the older you want to get."
(Keith Richards)

"People have this obsession: they want you to be like you were in 1969. They want you to, because otherwise their youth goes with you, you know."
(Mick Jagger)

BE MY BABY

"I can see the glamour thing, but not the sex thing. I've tried to stay away from that. I don't feel comfortable with any sort of overtly sexual image. I have to be a role model—I'm a mother now."
(Belinda Carlisle)

"I'd never even picked up a baby before I had one. I just thought they were like a load of Martians."
(Chrissie Hynde)

"I'm not interested in songs about seventeen-year-old angst and drugs. I'm thirty-eight. These days I'm interested in songs about how difficult it is to get baby-sitters."
(Bill Drummond, The KLF)

"I see my exit as something like being run over by a bus. But I'm deadly serious about this: I'm not going to be around to witness my artistic decline." (Elvis Costello, who recently made a record with Burt Bacharach)

"I have a terrible feeling that I'll wake up on my thirtieth birthday and my looks will have gone." (Marianne Faithfull)

"Close up, my face is starting to resemble an Ordnance Survey map." (George Michael)

"Age? That scares me. I'm gonna have a face-lift. I'm gonna hold on to my looks as long as Miss Dietrich. They'll be wheeling me out in a wheelchair when I'm eighty and I'll be singing, 'If you don't wanna fuck me, fuck off!'" (Wayne/Jayne County)

"It's better to get to sixty years old thinking, 'I've been in bed with a ton of women, dyed my hair every color I've wanted to, I've got tattoos that are all saggy and baggy and I don't look like anything, but I don't care because when I was twenty-six I was tooting around feeling great.'" (Keith Flint, Prodigy)

"All the people I've known who were fabulous have either died, flipped, or gone to India."
(Lou Reed)

PERFORMING RITES

The Song Remains the Same

"That line [in 'Go Your Own Way'] about 'shacking up'? I never shacked up with anybody when I was with him! People will hear the song and think that! I was the one who broke up with him. All he wanted to do was fall asleep with that guitar."

(Stevie Nicks)

Rock musicians tend to adhere to the old adage "Write what you know." Where this gets interesting is when a romance breaks up, particularly if the parties involved are in the same band—witness Fleetwood Mac's *Rumours*, an entire album's worth of breakup and makeup songs like "Go Your Own Way," Lindsey Buckingham's scathing diatribe against Stevie Nicks. So if you think you're hearing something autobiographical in your favorite tune, chances are you're absolutely correct.

AC/DC

"Whole Lotta Rosie": a groupie who bedded singer Bon Scott (he was her twenty-ninth lover—that month!)

The Beatles

"If I Fell" and "We Can Work It Out": Paul McCartney's pre-Linda love, Jane Asher
"Hey Jude": Julian Lennon (written by Paul after he learned that John Lennon was divorcing Cynthia, Julian's mother, in order to marry Yoko Ono)
"Golden Slumbers": a sixteenth-century poem by Thomas Dekker

Chuck Berry

"Maybellene": "The only 'Maybellene' I ever knew was the name of a cow," confesses Chuck. That is gross.

RADIO, RADIO

"Sometimes I listen to radio in the States and I think 'This is crap' . . . and then they play my single."
(Joe Jackson)

"The other day, I was in a gym in Kansas, and the worst songs were playing on the radio. And then *my* song came on. I was like, 'I'm one of them! I'm a terrible love song!' It kind of scares me."
(Jewel)

THE WRITE STUFF

Songwriters on songwriting

"If you can't say it in a three-minute song, you can't say it at all."
(Noddy Holder, Slade)

"My friends won't come over. It's a hovel. My landlord is about ninety—he's always coming over and asking me if I live here. And my neighbor up front is a throwback to the fifties, an old harlot. . . . I wake up to that. But I need a place that's cluttered so I can see the chaos. It's like a visual thesaurus."
(Tom Waits)

"I don't expect 'Short People' to be a big commercial success in Japan."
(Randy Newman)

"The band called it 'the stupid ballad.' "
(Kevin Cronin, REO Speedwagon, on his song "Can't Fight This Feeling")

"I have trouble with words."
(Paul Simonon, The Clash)

"Don't interpret me. My songs don't have any meaning. They're just words."
(Bob Dylan)
Amen, brother.

Boomtown Rats

"I Don't Like Mondays": Troubled teen Brenda Spencer, who one day whipped out a gun and shot up her high school in San Diego. When asked why she had done it, she replied: "I don't like Mondays."

David Bowie

"I'm Always Crashing the Same Car": Bowie, in the throes of a bad breakup (and a severe drug problem), raced his car round and round a parking garage, hoping to hit a concrete column and end it all. Instead, he wrote this wonderful song.

Buffalo Springfield

"For What It's Worth": Not, as is popularly assumed, an anthem against the Vietnam War, but rather an anthem against the 1967 Sunset Strip riots (a cops-kids dustup)

Eric Clapton

"Layla": George Harrison's wife, Patti Boyd, with whom Clapton was in love. The title of the song, Clapton's pet name for Boyd, came from a book of Persian poetry. "Layla was about a woman I felt really deeply about and who turned me down," said Eric, "and I had to pour it out in some way. I mean, her husband is a great musician. It's one of those wife-of-my-best-friend scenes, and her husband has been writing great songs for years about her and she still left him."

"Tears in Heaven": Four-year-old son Conor, who died in a fall from his fifty-third-floor apartment window in New York (a housekeeper had opened the window to air the place out; the boy fell forty-eight stories, onto a five-story brownstone below)

David Crosby

"Triad" (The Byrds): An odious ode to ménages à trois

THE WRITE STUFF (CONTINUED)

"A friend of mine and I were goofing around my house one night. We were kinda drunk, and we were writing graffiti all over the walls of my house. And she wrote, 'Kurt smells like Teen Spirit.' Earlier on, we'd been having this discussion about teen revolution and stuff like that. And I took it as a compliment. I thought she was saying that I was a person who could inspire. I just thought it was a nice little title. And it turns out she just meant that I smelled like that deodorant [named Teen Spirit]. I didn't even know that deodorant existed until after the song was written."
(Kurt Cobain)

"I'm all for these sociological lyrics—I just can't be bothered to write them."
(Suggs, Madness)

"Now and then, ideas for songs seem to come from heaven and from other places I don't know where the heck they were. Melodies and stuff would come from heaven."
(Brian Wilson)

"A lot of tunes in the guise of romanticism have mainly fucking behind them."
(Randy Newman)

THE WRITE STUFF
(CONTINUED)

"The only two things that motivate me and that matter to me are revenge and guilt. These are the only emotions I know about. Love? I don't know what it means. It doesn't exist in my songs."
(Elvis Costello)

"There are certain things I feel need to be done in terms of music and performance, and what these things amount to is that the world doesn't need another posturing clown yammering away about his 'baby.' "
(David Byrne)

"After the *Comes Alive* album, the pressure was so great. There was so much thought that went into writing, as opposed to letting it happen. That can be dangerous. Then you manufacture a song as opposed to letting it come out from the heart."
(Peter Frampton)

"The problem with all those people relating to 'Satisfaction' is that they want to drag you back. Or they want you to drag them back, which is worse."
(Keith Richards)

"It's only rock 'n' roll—disposable crap."
(Tom Petty)

Deep Purple

"Smoke on the Water": Singer Ian Gillan wrote this song in 1971 after watching the Montreux Casino (in Switzerland) burn down.

John Denver

"Rocky Mountain High": Driving around on his motorcycle and stoned out of his mind on acid, Denver later remembered "what a far-out experience that was."

Dion

"Abraham, Martin, and John": Abraham Lincoln, Martin Luther King, John F. Kennedy, and Robert F. Kennedy

Bob Dylan

"I know who the 'Sad-Eyed Lady of the Lowland' really is, no matter who he says it's about."
(Joan Baez)

The Eagles

"Life in the Fast Lane": Don Henley says, "It's been mistaken as a song glorifying that type of lifestyle, when in fact it's not! I'm just trying to give others the benefit of my experience." *(And he's had a lot of experience.)*

Roberta Flack

"Killing Me Softly with His Song": Folk-rocker Don McLean

Jimi Hendrix

"Dolly Dagger": Supergroupie **Devon Wilson** (jumped or was shoved—no one really knows—out of a window in New York's Chelsea Hotel in 1972)

Rick James

"Mary Jane": Not about a girl, but about "the herb"

Billy Joel

"Just the Way You Are": A birthday present for his first wife, Elizabeth
"Uptown Girl": Christie Brinkley

Elton John

"Someone Saved My Life Tonight": Says Elton, "Some people think that's about me with my head in the gas oven, but it's actually about [another musician] . . . and, ahem, my troublesome sexuality. I was living with Bernie [Taupin] in a flat in Islington and I had a girlfriend, as you do, who I was gonna get married to and have kids and the whole thing. It had gone as far as me choosing the soft furnishings, the drapes and all that stuff. I went up to the Bag o' Nails club with Bernie one night and there was [the other musician]. I'd spent a long time in his backing band so I knew him pretty well, but I swear I had no idea he was gay. . . . So he comes rolling up to me and we catch up on things, with me telling him I'm going to get married. He turns to me and says, 'If you marry this woman, you'll destroy two lives—hers and yours.' He knew I was gay, and told me I had to get used to it or else it would destroy my life."

56

SONGS OF LIFE

Classic rock anthems

"Stairway to Heaven" (Led Zeppelin)

"Free Bird" (Lynyrd Skynyrd)

"Whipping Post" (The Allman Brothers)

"Bohemian Rhapsody" (Queen)

"Layla" (Derek and the Dominoes)

"Won't Get Fooled Again" (The Who)

"Smoke on the Water" (Deep Purple)

"(Don't Fear) the Reaper" (Blue Öyster Cult)

"Dream On" (Aerosmith)

"Roundabout" (Yes)

"Hotel California" (The Eagles)

"Hold Your Head Up" (Argent)

"Do You Feel Like We Do" (Peter Frampton)

"Frankenstein" (The Edgar Winter Band)

"Funeral for a Friend/Love Lies Bleeding" (Elton John)

"Magic Man" (Heart)

"Nights in White Satin" (The Moody Blues)

"Foreplay/Long Time" (Boston)

Korn

"Kill You": Singer **Jonathan Davis** wrote this about his overly strict stepmother.
"Pretty": Davis penned this sad song about a very young incest victim he saw while working as a coroner's assistant.

Led Zeppelin

"The Wanton Song": An early-seventies groupie

John Lennon

"Sexy Sadie": Maharishi Mahesh Yogi (Lennon wrote this after learning about the supposedly saintly guru's attempts to put the moves on actress **Mia Farrow**)
"How Do You Sleep": Paul McCartney

Don McLean

"American Pie": **Buddy Holly**

George Michael

"Miracle" (from *Ladies & Gentlemen: The Best of George Michael*): George says it's a "love song to the policeman who arrested me" in 1998 in Beverly Hills.

Joni Mitchell

"I hang my laundry on the line when I write."

"A Free Man in Paris": David Geffen
"Willy": Graham Nash
"I Had a King": First husband Chuck Mitchell
"The Last Time I Saw Richard": James Taylor

The Motels

"Suddenly Last Summer": Based on the Tennessee Williams play of the same name

Mötley Crüe

"Kickstart My Heart": About Nikki Sixx's near-fatal drugs/booze OD in 1987. Sixx was turning blue when paramedics arrived and "kickstarted his heart." (See story, page 274.)

Graham Nash

"Our House": Joni Mitchell

Roy Orbison

"Oh, Pretty Woman" and "Too Soon to Know": Wife Claudette (tragically killed in a motorcycle crash)

Pink Floyd

"Shine On, You Crazy Diamond": Former member/drug casualty Syd Barrett

George Michael: Coppin' to it

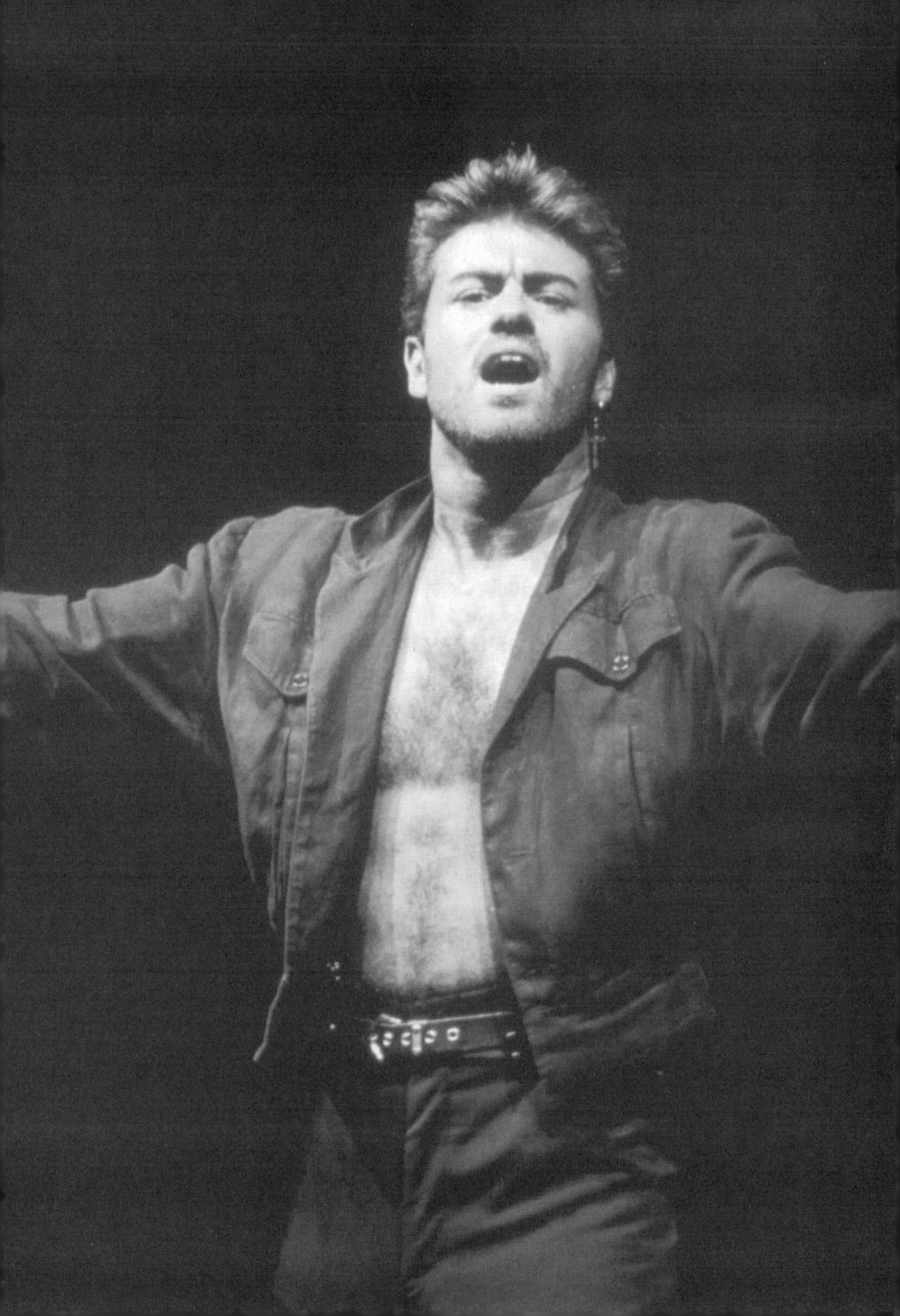

Placebo

"My Sweet Prince": The song is "about heroin and attempted suicide," according to singer/guitarist Brian Molko. "An ex-girlfriend of mine, when I broke up with her, tried to kill herself; she wrote in makeup on the wall, 'My sweet prince, you are the one.'" Creepy!

BE A PEPPER

Faces on the cover of the Beatles' *Sgt. Pepper* album

Fred Astaire
Aubrey Beardsley
The Beatles
Larry Bell
Wallace Berman
Issy Bonn
Marlon Brando
Bobby Breen
Lenny Bruce
William Burroughs
Lewis Carroll
Stephen Crane
Aleister Crowley
Tony Curtis
Marlene Dietrich
Dion
Diana Dors
Bob Dylan
Albert Einstein
W. C. Fields
Huntz Hall
Tommy Handley
Oliver Hardy
Aldous Huxley

C. G. Jung
Stan Laurel
T. E. Lawrence
Richard Lindner
Sonny Liston
Dr. Livingstone
Karl Marx
Merkin
Max Miller
Tom Mix
Marilyn Monroe
Sir Robert Peel
Edgar Allan Poe
Tyrone Power
Simon Rodia
George Bernard Shaw
Terry Southern
Karlheinz Stockhausen
Albert Stubbins
Stuart Sutcliffe
Shirley Temple
Dylan Thomas
Johnny Weismuller
H. G. Wells
Mae West
Oscar Wilde

The Pretenders

"Back on the Chain Gang": James Honeyman-Scott
"Don't Get Me Wrong": Tennis star (and pal o' Chrissie) John McEnroe

Red Hot Chili Peppers

"Under the Bridge": Heroin

The Rolling Stones

"19th Nervous Breakdown": Probably about **Mick Jagger**'s first supermodel love interest, **Chrissie Shrimpton**, who had a nervous breakdown because of Jagger's sudden fame, inflated ego, and alleged "relationship" with manager **Andrew Loog Oldham**

"Angie": Possibly **Angie Bowie**

"Brown Sugar": Singer **Claudia Linnear**, who was having an affair with Mick while he was married to **Bianca**

"Star Star": With a chorus comprised mostly of the word *starfucker*, you might imagine the song is about groupies—and you're right.

Leon Russell

"Delta Lady": **Rita Coolidge**

Neil Sedaka

"Oh Carol": **Carole King**

Carly Simon

"You're So Vain": Probably **Warren Beatty**, but possibly **Kris Kristofferson** or **Mick Jagger**

"You Know What to Do": Ex-*Dynasty* star **Al Corley**, also Carly's ex-boyfriend

"Anticipation": **Cat Stevens**

"Three Days": **Kris Kristofferson**

"James" and "Fairweather Father": Soft-rockin' ex-husband **James Taylor**

ONE GOOD REASON

Why the Rolling Stones called an album *Some Girls*:

"Because we couldn't remember their fucking names."
(Keith Richards)

Bruce Springsteen

"Nebraska": Twisted spree killer Charles Starkweather and his girlfriend/
accomplice, Carol Fugate

"Born in the U.S.A.": Inspired by Ron Kovic's book (later turned into the
sappy film starring **Tom Cruise**) *Born on the 4th of July*

"Darkness on the Edge of Town": Tom Joad's final speech in Steinbeck's *The
Grapes of Wrath*

Rod Stewart

"Maggie May": "She was
one of the first—if not
the first—woman I
ever loved. I forget
what her name was."
Touching.

Stephen Stills

**"A songwriter can do three
things with women: love them, suffer over them, or turn them into
hit records."**

"Suite: Judy Blue Eyes": Judy Collins

Styx

"The Grand Illusion": "This profession can really play tricks on your
head by the fact that you're out
there on the stage being what
everybody wants you to be, but
behind that facade you're still
trying to be the same person
you've always been." *(Tommy Shaw)*

U₂

"Pride (In the Name of Love)":
Martin Luther King Jr.

Rock Banned

Revolutionary, ahead of its time, dangerous: good ways of describing rock music. Afraid of change, concerned about the erosion of "family values," protective of the social order: good ways of describing the powers that be. Never the twain shall meet. Why is it that no one ever gives a thought to banning albums for the right reason: bad music?

Cover Me

Rock 'n' roll album covers that were ix-nayed

Yesterday and Today (The Beatles): Brutal Art

Showed "butcher" Beatles sitting around in white smocks with a bunch of bloody doll parts

Two Virgins (John Lennon and Yoko Ono): Nauseating Nudity

Featured the unconventional twosome entirely naked—front and back, on front and back covers. (Morals aside, this was a bad choice for aesthetic reasons alone.) The initial shipment to America (30,000 copies) was seized by authorities at Newark Airport in New Jersey, and one Chicago record store was actually shut down for displaying the cover in its window. The standoff was broken when the duo's label, Tetragrammaton, promised to wrap the offending discs in brown paper for the prudish Yanks.

Black and Blue (The Rolling Stones): Graphic Misogeny

Showed a well-used woman, bound and sitting spread-eagled on a cube with photos of the Stones' homely mugs on it

Sticky Fingers (The Rolling Stones): Overt Sexual Imagery

Cover was a crotch shot (no identification offered) showing a large-ish lump in a pair of tight jeans

Blind Faith (Blind Faith): Pedophilia

A nude pubescent girl holding a large phallus-shaped metal airplane model— pointing downward. Yecch.

Mom's Apple Pie (Grand Funk Railroad): Depiction of a Forbidden Zone

A hot and juicy "pie," which was actually a cleverly painted representation of a certain portion of the female anatomy (the band were ultimately forced to modify the art to "brick up" the offending opening)

The Man Who Sold the World (David Bowie): Nonstandard Sexual Imagery

Showed the sexually ambiguous singer wearing a dress. Too much for its provincial time.

Diamond Dogs (David Bowie): Ditto

A very strange painting of Bowie as a dog, with genitals (later airbrushed out) on full display. And the point would be . . . ?

A Nod's as Good as a Wink . . . to a Blind Horse (The Faces): Over-the-Top High Jinks

An insert included with the album was an on-the-road Polaroid scrapbook showing the band in all sorts of compromising, debauched positions with their good friends the groupies.

Appetite for Destruction (Guns N' Roses): Lurid Rape Scene

A tasteless painting of a robot ravaging a woman (only a few initial copies went out with the original painting; subsequent copies featured the GN'R cross logo)

"Sanctuary" single (Iron Maiden): Staged Murder of a Public Figure

Featured the band's horrific mascot, Eddie, knifing Margaret Thatcher

Ritual de lo Habitual (Jane's Addiction): Societal Taboos

The bizarre sculpture featured on this cover, crafted by idiot-savant band leader **Perry Farrell**, was a self-portrait of himself and two women—naked on a bed and encircled by occult paraphernalia. When American chain stores refused to carry it, Farrell replaced the cover "art"—with the First Amendment in bold type on a white background. Nyah!

Born in the U.S.A (Bruce Springsteen): Dissing an American Icon

Cover featured a photograph of Springsteen with his back to the camera, facing an American flag. Because of the somewhat less than patriotic emotions expressed in the songs on the album, some came to the conclusion that because he had his back to the camera, he was wee-weeing on the flag. Not so, protests Bruce: "It just turned out that the picture of my *butt* looked better than the picture of my *face*." I'll buy that.

Sinful Songs

Rock ditties that were outlawed

The Byrds, "Eight Miles High," 1966: Lyrics about Drugs?

Roger McGuinn: "Forty-two- or forty-three-thousand feet, or about eight miles high, is the altitude for military aircraft—[but people still believed] it was about drugs and not airplanes."

David Crosby: "Of course it was a drug song. We were stoned when we wrote it."

Frankie Goes to Hollywood, "Relax," 1984: "Overtly Obscene" Lyrics ("Relax, don't do it . . . when you wanna come")

BBC Radio One refused to play the song after a DJ took a hard listen to its lyrics (curiously, they had already played the song more than seventy times by that point).

The Kingsmen, "Louie, Louie," 1964: "Pornographic" Lyrics?

The song was banned by Indiana governor Matthew Welsh, who called it "pornographic" (despite the fact that to this day no one can understand the lyrics), explaining that his "ears tingled" when he heard it. He called for a ban of the song by the Indiana Broadcasters Association—causing the incensed publisher of the tune to offer a thousand bucks to anyone who could find anything "suggestive" in its lyrics (it must have been hard enough just finding *English* words in its lyrics). No takers.

Paul McCartney, "Give Ireland Back to the Irish," 1972: Unlawful Public Proselytizing

Banned by the BBC. The reason? A law that makes it illegal for public figures to make statements about events that are under investigation by the Crown. (How 'bout making a law against writing lame-o songs?)

The Rolling Stones, "Street Fighting Man," 1968: Fear of Bad Behavior

In some American cities, authorities were afraid the song might "incite riots and other forms of public disorder."

The Rolling Stones, "Star Star," 1973: Bad Words

Banned by the BBC because the chorus contains the word *starfucker*, repeated repeatedly

Frank Zappa, *200 Motels* soundtrack, 1971: "Obscene" Lyrics

Zappa was banned from performing at the Royal Albert Hall in London after authorities pronounced the lyrics on this album "obscene." Please.

Peccant Performers

Jim Dandy, Black Oak Arkansas:
"Sinful" and "Lewd"

Southern preachers got their backs up after hearing about Dandy's hypermasculine stage presence. Dandy responded in kind: "I don't mind no religion. But we don't nail our dicks to the cross, either. As for my pants—well, hey, that Nureyev feller wears them same kind of britches. I like to dance, too."

Screamin' Jay Hawkins:
Outrageous

"I'd go do my act and there'd be all these goddamn mothers walking the streets with picket signs. I mean, [they think] I'm some kind of bogeyman—I come out of coffins, skulls, snakes, crawling hands, fire . . . all that mess."

John Lennon: Blasphemous

In a 1966 interview with London's *Evening Standard*, the angry young rock star said, "Christianity will go. It will shrink and vanish. We're more popular than Jesus now." Despite the fact that he was merely making a point, rather than delivering a wholesale indictment of religion, disgruntled former fans began publicly burning Beatles albums, American radio stations refused to play the band's records, and during their live shows, the Fab Four were pelted with refuse. Lennon hastily issued an apology at a press conference.

Madonna: Sex and Religion Don't Mix

In April of 1989, Madonna lost her Pepsi endorsement deal (though she kept the five-million-smacker fee) after releasing her overtly, overly sexual "Like a Prayer" video, which featured scenes of the pop diva making love to a mysterious black man—in a church.

The Nice: Flag Burning

Banned from playing London's Royal Albert Hall after burning an American flag onstage during a performance in July of 1968. (Had the show been in France, the band probably would have been given an award.)

P. J. Proby (James Marcus Smith): Exhibitionism

P. J. was prohibited from appearing in several British venues and on the TV program *Shindig* after producers heard about the way he deliberately split his trousers during stage shows.

The Rolling Stones: Tardiness

Banned from recording for the BBC in 1964 because they were never on time. Come on—they're *rock* stars.

The Sex Pistols: Public Enemies

The band was prevented from entering the United States when they arrived for a tour on December 15, 1977, for various reasons, detailed per member by thoughtful government officials:

*Johnny Rotten, because of an indictment for drug possession (one amphetamine);

*Paul Cook and Sid Vicious, for "moral turpitude" (probably pretty accurate); and

*Steve Jones, because they didn't have enough hard info about his criminal past (of course, America lets terrorists in, but *rock 'n' rollers*? No way!)

Performance Art

> **"Just point me at the piano and give me my money, and in fifteen minutes I'll have 'em shaking, shouting, shivering, and shacking."**
> **(Jerry Lee Lewis)**
> *Only Jerry Lee could make you "shack."*

Performing is a major part of the rock 'n' roll art, and it can be a truly transcendant experience for star and fan alike. It also feeds a rocker's insatiable craving for attention, as evidenced by a somewhat apocryphal tale concerning **Jerry Lee Lewis** and **Chuck Berry**. As the story is told, Lewis was more than a bit miffed when promoters decided Berry should close the show, not Lewis. Jerry Lee, in true trouper style, did indeed go on first, and played his damndest—but, at the finale ("Great Balls of Fire"), booted his stool into the crowd, doused his piano with petrol, and lit it up—all the while continuing to play! As he passed Berry on his way off the stage, Lewis allegedly spat, "Follow that, nigger."

> **"Just because I cut the heads off dolls, they say I must hate babies. But it's not true—I just hate dolls."**
> **(Alice Cooper)**

ALICE IN WONDERLAND

> **"Offstage, I'm Ozzie Nelson."**
> **(Alice Cooper)**

Another of rock's more notable showmen is Alice Cooper, who brought camp horror-flick theatrics to the stage long before **Marilyn Manson** lifted his first lipstick. "I never really did anything that outrageous on stage," protests Alice. "The hanging had been done ten million times in every western. The guillotine had been done since 1925 in vaudeville shows. It's just the fact that it had rock 'n' roll behind it that made it sound so damn notorious." Cooper used a plethora of props in his show, including the aforementioned dolls and a large live snake, which performed for years with his metal master. Rock chick **Bebe Buell**, then-girlfriend of **Todd Rundgren**, who knew Cooper, remembered feeling

sorry for "that poor snake, but Todd would always say, 'Don't worry about it. The snake has been on the road for a long time; the snake drinks; the snake smokes; the snake has girl-friends—the snake gets laid more than any of us.' " (Sadly, the slithery one died of injuries from a rodent bite—inflicted by a rat he was eating for lunch!)

During their David Lee Roth days, Van Halen's stage set featured large statues of the devil that would "pee" bourbon (breakfast of champions) fifteen feet out into the audience. Self-destructive Iggy Pop cut his chest open onstage and broke his teeth by ramming a mic through them. (You couldn't say *his* audience didn't get their money's worth.) Jethro Tull's medieval Ian Anderson used to adopt an odd one-legged stance during his flute solos (yeah, we need more *flute solos* in rock 'n' roll).

NO SHOWS

Rockers who suffer from stage fright

Babs Streisand (mercifully—at least it meant we weren't treated to any of her performances for quite a few years)

Carly Simon (froze in fear once during her act, which resulted in her many-year retirement from performing)

Stage fright: not a pretty sight

The vomiters: Chaka Khan, Johnny Rotten, Cher, John Lennon

The back-turners: Lou Reed, Jim Morrison, and Rod Stewart (touring with the Jeff Beck Group in 1968, Rod cowered behind the band's towering speaker cabinets during the show)

The cupboard-hider: David Allen from Gang of Four (secreted himself in a cupboard to avoid performing on the tour's first gig, and he didn't get any better later—his stage fright was so bad that the remainder of the scheduled tour was canceled)

Joni Mitchell remembers, "I used to run offstage quite frequently. You get that shot of adrenaline and it's fight-or-flight."

NO SHOWS
(CONTINUED)

XTC's Andy Partridge, who had severe stage fright, would sob uncontrollably and freeze in fear; once, he even wet himself onstage, albeit behind a guitar. He eventually stopped performing altogether because it freaked him out so much. "The crunch came in Paris," he recalls. "I remember playing the opening of 'Respectable Street' and thinking, 'I don't feel well.' I could feel the others wondering why the hell I wasn't singing. I was dizzy. I thought I was dying. My stomach hurt, my legs were giving way, my head was throbbing, the audience was going to kill me with affection. It was like the dam had burst. I pulled off the guitar and just ran." (Partridge then turned into an agoraphobic, and said, "It got to the point where if I touched the front door knob, I wanted to throw up.") This may be one reason why the band never reached the top—although Partridge begs to differ. The problem, he explains, "is that none of us have a streak of showbiz in us."

"I was the best wiggler in the world."
(Marc Bolan)

Gloomy grunge-sters Nirvana would try just about anything to be "outrageous" during their concerts: Kurt Cobain wore dresses, the group members kissed each other, and the band destroyed their equipment even before they'd finished their show. Gee, how original.

"I smash guitars because I like them. I usually smash a guitar when it's at its best."
(Pete Townshend)

The Who's Pete Townshend is renowned for his ax-annihilating antics, but he wasn't so sure about the gimmick when he first started. Reveals Townshend about an early incident: "This was only going to be like the second guitar I'd ever broken, seriously. I went to my manager, Kit Lambert, and I said, 'Can we afford it? Can we afford it? It's for the publicity.' He said, 'Yes, we can afford it—if we can get the *Daily Mail*.' I did it, and of course the *Daily Mail* didn't buy the photograph and didn't want to know about the story."

> "We ain't never played no fruit rock, no punk rock. We never wore dresses onstage, put no paint on our faces, blew up no bombs onstage. We didn't suck off snakes onstage; we didn't wear tight pants and big rings. We didn't puke onstage or throw TVs out the windows."
>
> *(Levon Helm, The Band)*

One surefire way to generate some ink is to insert blatantly sexual elements into one's otherwise run-of-the-mill stage show. In the shot seen 'round the world in 1971 (and in fact to this day), glam ham David Bowie simulated oral sex on Mick Ronson's guitar during a performance. Adam and the Ants, in their early days, titillated the audience with a series of onstage sadomasochist vignettes (between Jordan, their manager, and Adam himself) during their live shows, and some strange girl fellated Marilyn Manson (for real) onstage during one of his oh-so-exciting sets (if your music doesn't have any substance, I guess you have to encourage that sort of thing). And the Stranglers once invited some strippers to share the stage with them during a performance of their song "Nice 'n' Sleazy." The girls, clad in nothing but the briefest of undergarments, shook their moneymakers (and were quickly joined by a few bold, completely nude dudes).

> "You should have seen [our] Atlanta show. There was full-on muff-munching and belt-beating. It was a genuine live sex show—and performed in front of an underage crowd, no less! We got chased out of town, and there's still a criminal complaint pending."
>
> *(Dave Wyndorf, Monster Magnet)*

> **"I resent performing for fucking idiots who don't know anything."**
> *(John Lennon)*

Punk bands were routinely "gobbed" (spat on)—all just harmless fun and an expected part of the show (except in the case of Billy Idol's Generation X, who were truly hated by the punks—and, frankly, just about everyone else). Fearless Stranglers front man **Hugh Cornwell** had a novel way of dealing with the practice: he'd haul the offenders onstage and administer spankings—ultimately so popular a ritual that he had to stop. But he took it past the limit during one concert in France, when a spitting fan was treated to another of Cornwell's peculiar punishments: a banana shoved up his bum. The revolted crowd picked up and left en masse. Ecch! Ptui!

One for the Road

> **"It keeps you fit—the alcohol, nasty women, sweating onstage, and bad food."**
> *(Bon Scott, AC/DC)*

Rockers, on "the road"

"We used to play clubs all the time and it was fun. It was good because you got to play and you got to get quite good on the instrument. But then we got famous and it spoiled all that. We'd just go round and round the world singing the same ten dopey tunes. Then you'd have a few weeks off and you didn't want to know about the guitar."
(George Harrison)

LOW "RIDER"

On Limp Bizkit's rider (the list that tells those in charge at the concert venue what's required by the visiting stars backstage): one case of Budweiser, one case of Corona, one six-pack of V8, and one pair of silk panties, size 5–6

"I did **Zeppelin's** last indoor shows at Earls Court in 1977. That was the biggest entourage I've seen. They had two bodyguards and a limo each, plus a whole team of bodyguards for the children. That was the closest I ever came to royalty." (**Robbie Wilson,** tour manager)

"It always helps to have a few rows of girls up front—that just makes it more rock 'n' roll." (**Tom Petty**)

"I like them [the audience] to go away feeling the way you do at the end of a good chick—satisfied and exhausted." (**Robert Plant**)

"If I don't get sexually aroused onstage, then there's something wrong." (**Michael Hutchence, INXS**)

"If you leave our gigs without your sexual glands being stirred, then you need therapy." (**Bobby Dall,** bassist, **Poison**)

"I don't think having a naked woman strapped to a rack is sexist at all. And I don't think the fact that we pretend to slit her throat is violent." (**Blackie Lawless, W.A.S.P.**)

"When you go on the road, there's nothing to do but do drugs and fuck." (**Steven Tyler, Aerosmith**)

"I'll tell you what's fun: finding the right stewardess and turning her upside-down in the back of the plane. Ever done it? You come so fast." (**Steven Tyler, Aerosmith**)

"It was 1968 and we were playing in Paris. Some girls had lost their clothes and were being carried over the top of the audience to the stage. It wasn't sexist like it would be today—they were enjoying it. It was part of the fun of being alive." (Arthur Brown, The Crazy World of Arthur Brown)

"The road can be full of surprises. Here are a few of the more memorable: Standing in a shower in Japan with a drink in my hand, getting a blow job from one young girl while two others folded my clothes and packed them in my case. In the same room, having sex with a girl and her music-biz boyfriend. (Although my performance was somewhat hindered by overindulgence in Peruvian marching powder, I did manage the odd slurp in the general direction of the girl.) Several instances of drunken sex in front of roommates, one of whom masturbated furiously during the whole sad event. And the predictable hummers [blow jobs] in the back of the tour bus." (Andy Cairns, Therapy?)

"[Depeche Mode's] Dave Gahan was in a right state . . . with ropey American rock chicks hanging around him—all ripped fishnets and stilettos, incapable even of putting their lipstick on straight." (Andy Perry, rock journalist)

"They had a roadie who would go out every night and pick out the fifteen or twenty most beautiful girls in the crowd and take them backstage, evidently for the Mode's pleasure." (Andy Perry, on Depeche Mode)

"[Primal] Scream always took along boxes of records and had a couple of decks in the dressing room, so there were people dancing, and Dave Gahan sitting in the middle of the room, apparently shoveling coke up his nose. Suddenly, he seemed to realize I was a journalist, and he pointed at me and one of his big flunkies came and got me. I had to kneel down beside the armchair to make it possible [for him] to talk to me. He started burbling on about how people didn't understand him, but then his mood changed and he said, 'I'm gonna curse you!' The next thing I know, he's bitten me on the neck." (Andy Perry)

BREAKING UP IS HARD TO DO

Aerosmith

When: 1979. Why: A spat between two of the band members' wives, which ended with Joe Perry's better half dumping a glass of milk over bassist Tom Hamilton's spouse. This was evidently so upsetting that it caused the band to break up. "It's true," laughs Steven Tyler. "We actually broke up over spilled milk." (Apparently the Toxic Twins' ongoing series of serious drug problems had nothing to do with it.)

"We had the same fights we had when we were poor, except 'That's my tomato you're eating' became 'That's my limousine—get your ass out.'"
(Alice Cooper)

Dire Straits

David Knopfler broke up the band after control-freak brother Mark said David "didn't practice enough."

BREAKING UP IS HARD TO DO (CONTINUED)

Fleetwood Mac

After their stormy, soap-operatic love lives splintered the group in the seventies, the members reconvened in the late eighties to discuss getting their act back together—but the meeting ended in hostility. Though they did ultimately decide to re-form, temperamental Lindsey Buckingham quit again after another meeting with Stevie Nicks, his former flame, turned into a violent brawl. Then Stevie quit the band in a huff after the 1990 release of Mick Fleetwood's sensational tell-all autobiography about the Mac's wild years.

Red Hot Chili Peppers

In July of 1996, drummer Chad Smith announced to the world that the band was splitting up. "It's not just an ugly rumor," he said. "The Chili Peppers are a great band and I'm very lucky to have been a part of it, but I think we should go out on a high note and not flog a dead horse. It's kind of a relief that the years of hell are finally over and I can get on with real life, instead of being a spoilt kid living in a bubble in a sea of retarded sexuality." But that's what rock 'n' roll's all *about*, dude.

"Marc [Bolan] paid for us to come on his tour, which was unheard-of then. . . . The only time he was wary was when we'd bring girls back to the hotel. He thought they were talking to us to get to him, and he was often right. We'd be in the hotel doing all sorts of dubious acts, and they'd be asking, 'What's Marc really like?' We'd tell 'em, 'I'll tell you later.' Disgraceful!" (Captain Sensible, bassist for The Damned)

"When I'm alone in my disheveled house, all the memories of tour-bus blow jobs, backstage fucks, and hotel debauchery are transformed from the glorious male bragging and pseudo-wank fantasies that they seem to be into the reality of the frequent speed-, coke-, and alcohol-fueled impotence and forty-second overexcited rush that they usually are." (Andy Cairns, Therapy?)

"The funny thing about touring is that you rehearse all the wrong things: the music, the stage show. That stuff isn't the problem, it's the other twenty-two hours of the day. That's the weird part." (Michael Hutchence)

"When I got off tour, I remember dialing room service on my home phone."
(Steven Tyler)

Ballroom Blitz

"I don't enjoy playing unless I see blood or get hurt."
(Henry Rollins)
We don't enjoy your playing even then.

Onstage violence

AC/DC

The show must go on: During a 1991 concert, three members of an AC/DC audience were trampled to death—but the hard rockers kept right on playing! Said a cop, "They had to lift the bodies up over the crowd. . . . If you're in the band, I don't think you could help but notice that."

Aerosmith

In October of 1978, Steven Tyler and Joe Perry suffered minor injuries when some hyped-up idiot chucked a cherry bomb onto the stage. Bloody but unbowed, the Toxic Twins performed behind a Cyclone fence for the duration of the tour.

BREAKING UP IS HARD TO DO (CONTINUED)

The Rolling Stones

Why longtime bassist Bill Wyman quit the superannuated supergroup: "Their music really annoyed me." I can relate.

The Sex Pistols

At a concert in January of 1978, Johnny Rotten ended the gig (and the band) with the immortal line, "Ever get the feeling you've been cheated?"

The Beatles

"As far as I'm concerned, there won't be a Beatles reunion as long as John Lennon remains dead."
(George Harrison)

Why: They were just sick of it all— particularly John Lennon. (Interestingly, Lennon, having decided he wanted to be a full-time house-husband, turned Paul McCartney away in 1975 when he showed up at Lennon's New York City apartment with guitar in hand.)

The Everly Brothers

Broke up after a July 1973 concert during which Phil smashed his guitar and stormed offstage (he'd been depressed over his drug habit, an impending divorce, and the duo's decline in popularity). Don continued the show, confessing to the audience that "the Everly Brothers have already been dead for ten years."

David Bowie

"I know that one day a big artist is going to be killed onstage, and I keep thinking it's going to be me."

At an Anaheim, California, concert in 1987, Bowie invited a female fan up to the stage. The woman happily obliged—then sunk her sharp choppers into his neck. They both tumbled to the ground, where they struggled until limpet-girl was forcibly disengaged.

Ted Nugent

The Motor City Madman was threatened by crazed fan David Gelfer, who pointed a .44 Magnum at his "hero" during a 1975 concert in Spokane. Gelfer was thrown to the floor by audience members and beefy security guards, and later charged with "intimidating with a weapon." (Nugent wasn't charged for "assaulting with terrible music.")

Jimmy Page, Led Zeppelin

"I was once informed that someone was set on killing me while I was in the States. Actually, it was a lot more serious than I thought. The guy was a real crazy, and had all these photographs on the wall with circles 'round them. . . . It was actually a lot worse than everyone at first believed, and eventually this guy was tracked down and got carted away to a hospital."

Lou Reed

A wild-man-fan at a 1973 **Lou Reed** concert jumped onto the stage and bit a chunk out of Reed's flabby posterior while screaming "Leather!" at the top of his lungs. After the show, Reed coolly observed that America "seems to breed real animals."

The Rolling Stones

At the Altamont Speedway in Livermore, California, during a free **Stones** concert on December 6, 1969, a fan was killed by the Stones' resident security force, a phalanx of mucho macho Hell's Angels. The victim, eighteen-year-old Meredith Hunter, was beaten to death with pool cues by one "Angel," who claimed he'd spotted a gun in Hunter's hand—pointed straight at **Mick**. (Later, the murderous Angel sued the Stones—see page 265.) "People were just asking for it. All those nude, fat people. They had victims' faces," remarked sensitive soul **Keith Richards**.

Van Halen

At the Castle Donington rock festival in August 1984, **David Lee Roth** saw a fan tossing a bottle up to the stage. Yelled Diamond Dave, "Don't throw no shit at me, man, because after the show you know I'm gonna fuck your girlfriend."

"We don't mind you throwing shit up at the stage—just don't hit our beers. They're our fuel, man!"
(James Hetfield, Metallica)

Fan Belt

Rockers and their fans

"We have fun, the kids have fun, the cops have fun. It's kind of a weird triangle."
(Jim Morrison)

"Our audience doesn't come to see theatrics. . . . They realize we're not performers, and that we're a group that's earnestly trying to accomplish something and we don't quite know what it is."
(Jerry Garcia)

"You know, I pride myself in sticking my head in the lion's mouth. I will set a ramp up that goes right up into the crowd and walk up into it, as long as my jewelry's tucked away, you know."
(Steven Tyler)

"When you fuck a lot, you learn how a woman moves. When you play a lot, you learn how the audience moves."
(Ted Nugent)

"A lot of girls scream and go, 'Oh my god!' . . . I don't really like it."
(Reluctant sex symbol Evan Dando)

"If they scream at me, it's probably in horror."
(Elton John)

"Beefheart freaks: I know the kind too well. 'I just love Captain Beefheart—I wouldn't want him over at the house, though.' "
(Captain Beefheart)

"Just because you like my stuff doesn't mean I owe you anything."
(Bob Dylan)

At a party in Stockholm, according to INXS crooner **Michael Hutchence**, "This girl said to me, 'Come here, I wanna show you something.' She leads me into the bathroom, and I'm like, 'Yeah, I think I've seen one of these before,' and she goes into the cubicle and says 'Listen.' And I hear this 'Tss, tss, tss, tssss, tssss, tssss, tssss, tssss, tss, tss' and I'm thinking, 'What's that?' And she starts getting very upset, and says, 'Don't you recognize it? It's [INXS hit single] 'Need You Tonight'—I'm peeing it for you."

During a gig on **Night Ranger**'s 1998 reunion tour, an unknown thief stole into the band's dressing room during their performance and made off with a vest belonging to **Jeff Watson**. No big deal, right? Well, it *was* a big deal after the AWOL garment started writing to him—that's right, postcards began to arrive, addressed to Jeff and signed by . . . the vest. The missives were of the "wish you were here variety," and came from various landmarks and touristy spots: London, Seattle's Space Needle, and a taping of Conan O'Brien's show in New York City! The mysterious kidnapper has yet to be apprehended.

> **"Bernie [Taupin] and I do seem to attract weirdos. I don't know why, because we're not really weird ourselves. People give me pineapples."**
> *(Elton John)*

> **"[People] want showbiz. They want to see you rush off in your limousine."**
> *(Freddie Mercury)*

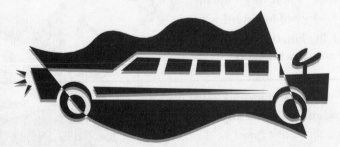

"Those of you in the cheaper seats, clap your hands. Those of you in the more expensive ones, rattle your jewelry."
(John Lennon)

"People say the fans love you, and you've got to be loyal to them. But in a year they're going to love someone else. Where will that leave me? Nowhere. No money, no fans, no nothing."
(Gary Numan)

"People who have memorized your songs—how can you not love them?"
(Todd Rundgren)

"If all we've achieved is someone wanting my autograph, then we've gone wrong."
(Joe Strummer)

"I signed a pussy lip once."
(Jerry Cantrell, Alice in Chains)

"Audiences are very much like the kids in Tommy's Holiday Camp—they want something without working for it."
(Pete Townshend)

"I'm still that surfer gas station guy that plays music. So I write fans back a normal letter and find myself becoming part of their lives."
(Eddie Vedder)

"Our fans in England are crazy. You can't stop them. They bite and claw their way onstage. We have to encourage the rest of the audience to beat them senseless."
(Sid Vicious)

High-Performance

"We're the Cecil B. De Mille of rock 'n' roll—
always wanting to do things bigger and better."
(Freddie Mercury)

"For the past ten years, all I've had to do is stand
in the background, sometimes put on a bit of
makeup, and look happy to be there."
(Bill Wyman, Rolling Stones)

"It would be fucking monotonous if every show
was good."
(Johnny Rotten)

"I hate it when Grace [Slick] does that sexy shit
onstage. Man, it really makes me want to puke.
She reminds me of my mother—she's *not* sexy."
(Marty Balin)

"I've always done me little theatricality bit of
throwing me arms about with the music."
*(Joe Cocker, whose trademark grimaces and arm-flinging were so
well parodied by John Belushi on Saturday Night Live)*

"Sometimes I thought it was detrimental to the
song if you're singing about attempted suicide
while jumping on the piano with high-heeled boots
on and feathers sticking out of your head."
*(Bernie Taupin, on writing partner Elton John's wild stage
show)*

"Music always is a commentary on society, and
certainly the atrocities onstage are quite mild
compared to those conducted in our behalf by our
government. You can't write a chord ugly enough
to say what you want to say sometimes, so you
have to rely on a giraffe filled with whipped
cream."
*(Frank Zappa, referring to the stuffed animal he brought onstage
to squirt whipped cream into the audience)*

Spinal Tap Moments

"There is definitely a thrill when the band is all together and it all is working. You can't beat being in a group. But the effort to put a band together, rehearse all the tunes, then you have to go out on tour for months to justify the expense—I don't know if I want to do that. I'm not going on a Spinal Tap tour."
(George Harrison)

The movie *This Is Spinal Tap* chronicled the adventures of a misbegotten band of crusty old rock 'n' rollers hitting the road for a "reunion" tour. The hilarious mockumentary has that unmistakable ring of truth: in fact, many of the incidents depicted are based on actual on-the-road accidents. The filmmakers seemed especially intent on skewering pompous prog-rockers—who, admittedly, needed their bombastic balloons punctured more than anyone else—but Spinal Tap–like incidents can happen to anyone . . . and do.

"I don't know how they managed it, but that film made us look like . . . buffoons. He filmed nights when we had no problem finding the stage, but did he use them . . . ?"
(Nigel Tufnel, Spinal Tap)

Black Sabbath

"I thought they'd had a spy with us."
(Terry "Geezer" Butler, on the movie This Is Spinal Tap*)*

The band, with Ian Gillan on lead vocals, used a quasi-atmospheric, quasi-mystical Stonehenge set during their 1983 U.S. tour. Unfortunately, Gillan wasn't very well rehearsed (he couldn't remember the words to the songs), and was unable to see his cue cards due to the thick-as-pea-soup dry-ice fog blanketing the stage. This resulted in musically heavy but lyrically sparse performances consisting of the Sabs' classic raunch 'n' roll riffs overlaid with Gillan's screaming one word—"Yeah!"—repeatedly. (During *his* performing debut with the band, dwarflike screamer Ronnie James Dio got lost onstage in the same miasma. Presumably they've learned their lesson.)

Alice Cooper

Welcome to my nightmares: Cooper fell off a Vancouver stage and broke six ribs during his 1975 tour; and during a run-through of his show in 1988, his safety tether broke while he was rehearsing his onstage hanging—which nearly turned into the real thing (luckily, a quick-thinking roadie came to his rescue).

Genesis

The band members were almost history one night when their roadies used a

brand of flash powder (low-grade gunpowder used in creating spectacular onstage explosions) they'd never tried before. When the explosion was set off, it literally ripped the venue apart. "Half the stage blew up," remembers Mike Rutherford. "Speaker cabinets went flying. We were nearly killed. Bits of wood were later found impaled in all sorts of things."

The Kinks

Why road managers should always remember to equip their band members with curb feelers: The Kinks were forced to cancel the remainder of their 1965 U.K. tour after guitarist Dave Davies (Ray's brother) was knocked unconscious when he crashed into a cymbal during a London concert.

Manic Street Preachers

During a gig in August of 1993, rowdy fans threw bottles and cans onstage, one of which hit bassist **Nicky Wire** in the head and caused a concussion (as well as the involuntary termination of the Preachers' performance). Groused singer **Richey James Edwards**, "Most bands look forward to their homecoming gig. I don't expect roses and petals at my feet, but the amount of grief we get here is nonstop."

Molly Hatchet

"I'd focused the light so directly on him that his hair caught alight. Now I know to focus *around* the guys." (Hatchet roadie X-Ray, on a gig where the keyboardist's hair caught fire because the lights were too hot)

Alanis Morissette

During a 1998 gig at Chicago's Metro Bar, a rock-rag photographer stumbled over some cabling and caused all kinds of technical glitches, forcing a brief intermission in the show. What did Morissette do? Improvised, of course—albeit badly: "Breathe with me," she exhorted the audience. "When was the last time any of you breathed properly?"

Mötley Crüe

"On one tour I had a drum kit that was supposed to fly into the audience over everybody's heads," **Tommy Lee** recalls. "As I was flying back toward the stage, I'd bungee-jump off the side of the drum riser. One night we got it wrong and I dropped seventy feet and landed head first onto the concrete stage." (Hmm, dropped on his head . . . could explain his recent behavioral problems.)

Nirvana

While performing at the 1992 MTV Video Awards show, **Chris Novoselic** threw his bass up into the air—and it fell right back down on top of him, knocking him silly.

Pearl Jam

At a September 1998 concert at Madison Square Garden, **Eddie Vedder** tried one of rock's trademark cool moves: swinging his microphone like a lariat. Unfortunately, the mic got caught in some lighting equipment, and he couldn't get it back—so he ended up just sort of standing there, looking like the goofball he is.

Primal Scream

"I was photographing the Primals when suddenly [guitarist] **Throb** just wasn't there anymore. He was so drunk he'd taken a tumble backward off the stage."
(Lucas Carr, photographer)

Ratt

During a 1997 gig, singer **Stephen Pearcy** fell fifteen feet from a concert stage to the floor after being temporarily blinded by stage lights. The tour was postponed to allow the wheezy old geezer to recover.

Patti Smith

In January of 1977, Patti spun around so wildly onstage that she lost her balance and fell off, breaking her neck and requiring twenty-two stitches. "I look like an asshole," she admitted.

The Tubes

During a concert in England in 1978, **Fee Waybill** fell off the stage and broke his leg.

U2

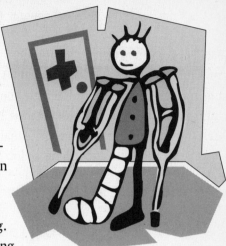

The band's 1997 Pop Mart tour featured a giant lemon-shaped pod, in which the band would play their encore. "It's great in there," gushed **Bono**. "There's drinks and everything. It's a great feeling. What we are saying with the lemon is, 'Here we are in the lemon. Fuck off.' " *What a rebel.* Unfortunately, in Norway the pod jammed shut, trapping the guys inside for an embarrassingly long time. Did they learn their lesson? Nooooo. During a Las Vegas gig later in the tour, **The Edge** couldn't even find his guitar through all the fog spurting from the uncooperative device. "I got engulfed in the smoke and got lost," he recalled. "I couldn't see a thing and didn't know where I was. It was the funniest thing that has ever happened to me onstage. I completely lost it and caught Bono's eye, and I was laughing hysterically, and soon he was, too. It was my **Derek Smalls** [a member of Spinal Tap] moment."

The Who

Roger Daltrey, rehearsing with porky alleged child-porno fan **Gary Glitter** for the Prince's Trust concert in 1996, was whacked in the kisser by a microphone swung by ol' fatty. Daltrey fell to the ground clutching his various injuries (fractured eye socket, cut mouth, minor concussion), but later made a full recovery.

Firing Squad

Just because you're not part of corporate America, don't think you can't be "downsized." The reasons musicians are axed are a little more dramatic, of course (I don't think anyone has ever been ousted from a rock band for stealing paper clips), but there's no such thing as job security.

What color are their parachutes?

Big Country

The band (remember them?) were dropped—after just a couple of days—from a tour with **Alice Cooper**. Why? Well, they were allegedly "too strange." (For Alice? Come on!)

Marc Ford, The Black Crowes

The Black Crowes fired lead guitarist **Marc Ford** because of chronic substance abuse problems (his, not theirs). Explains lead singer **Chris Robinson**, "I think that if Marc had stayed in this band, he would be dead. We were out there on tour, doing our thing, and I just told him, 'Look, brother, I can't deal with a corpse. Corpses are icky.' " (Earth to Chris: *Looking* like a corpse is icky too.)

Ronnie James Dio, Black Sabbath

Ronnie James Dio was fired from (or quit, depending on who you talk to) **Black Sabbath** when his fellow band members accused him of tampering with the mix of their album *Live Evil* (ooh, a palindrome) to raise the level of his vocals (volume-wise, not quality-wise)—at the expense of the other musicians in the band. Can anyone say "lead-singer-itis"?

Ozzy Osbourne, Black Sabbath

After Ozzy was fired from **Black Sabbath**, his life went down the toilet. "I ended up in the Park Hotel in Los Angeles," he recalls, "and I didn't open the drapes for three months. My dealer dropped off coke every other day, and I sent out for booze and pizza. The maid wouldn't come near the place." Sounds kind of fun, actually.

David Crosby, The Byrds

The Byrds axed **David Crosby** in the late sixties for a few good reasons: his passionate political diatribes (onstage—yaaaawn), endless tuning-up, shitty lyrics, and heavy LSD use. (After he left, the group, on their soon-to-be-released album *The Notorious Byrd Brothers*, replaced his photo with one of a horse.)

Mick Jones and Topper Headon, The Clash

In September of 1983, the **Clash** fired lead guitarist **Mick Jones** because they felt he'd "drifted apart from the original idea of the Clash" (whatever that was). The year before, they'd done the same to **Topper Headon**. The official reason was that they felt they had "a difference of political direction" with him, but the real cause was allegedly Headon's substance-abuse travails (severe enough that he landed in jail on drug charges in 1987).

Ian Gillan, Deep Purple

Watch your mouth, son: Hard-rock screamer **Ian Gillan** was axed from **Deep Purple** in 1987 for bad-mouthing their album *The House of Blue Light*.

ALL BY MYSELF

A few of the musicians who left the bands that made them famous to find success as solo artists (with varying degrees of success)

Phil Collins, Genesis

Fish, vocalist for Marillion

Peter Gabriel, Genesis

Steve Hackett, Genesis

Debbie Harry, Blondie

Billy Idol, Generation X

Janis Joplin, Big Brother and the Holding Company

Nick Lowe, Brinsley Schwarz

Morrissey, The Smiths

Smokey Robinson, The Miracles

Rick Wakeman, Yes (quit in June of 1974, then, when his solo career tanked, rejoined the band at the end of 1976)

Steve Winwood, Traffic

Bob Weston, Fleetwood Mac

Keep your hands to yourself: Fleetwood Mac guitarist **Bob Weston** was fired in the early seventies for having an affair with **Mick Fleetwood**'s wife, Jenny.

Syd Barrett, Pink Floyd

In 1968, **Pink Floyd** fired original member **Syd Barrett**, who was having trouble functioning (not just as a musician, but also as a human being) after years of overindulgence in psychedelics.

Pete Farndon, The Pretenders

In June of 1982, bassist **Pete Farndon** was fired from the **Pretenders** because of his "incompatibility" with the other members (in reality, a severe substance abuse problem). Ironically, Farndon was canned just two days before **Pretenders** member **James Honeyman-Scott**'s death from an overdose.

Jimmy Chamberlin, Smashing Pumpkins

In 1996, the band dismissed their drummer, **Jimmy Chamberlin**, because of his being in the room during the overdose death of their keyboard player, **Jonathan Melvoin**. (Melvoin and Chamberlin allegedly shot heroin together on the night of Chamberlin's death.) The **Pumpkins** issued a statement to mark the event: "Today we are very sorry to tell our friends and fans that we have decided to sever our relationship with our friend and drummer, Jimmy Chamberlin. We are seeking an immediate replacement for him so we can continue touring. For nine years we have battled with Jimmy's struggles with the insidious disease of drug and alcohol addiction. It has nearly destroyed everything we are and stand for."

DRINK AND DIVE

Musicians whose substance abuse problems led to their ouster

Pete Willis, Def Leppard (ironically, he was replaced by **Phil Collen**, who had an even worse problem)

Steve Adler, Guns N'Roses (must've been some problem to cause him to be kicked out of *that* band)

Dave Mustaine, Metallica

Shane McGowan, The Pogues

Runnin' with the Devil

Or, Gee, Van Halen is rough on singers

> "I run into you, you better wear a cup. I'm going to kick you in your nuts."
>
> *(Eddie Van Halen, to David Lee Roth)*

> "I was told to kick Roth in the balls if I ever saw him."
>
> *(Sammy Hagar)*

Eddie Van Halen has made many snide comments about "lead singer disease" (big talent, big ego, big mouth) in the past, and it was his hatred of this "illness" in original Van Halen singer David Lee Roth (together with Dave's determination to launch a solo career) that led to his decision to axe the legendarily egocentric frontman in the mid-eighties (Diamond Dave blamed the breakup on drug problems—theirs, of course). The divorce was *not* an amicable one—the name-calling (by both band and fans) went on for many years, despite both Van Halen's and Roth's separate successes.

MONKEE BUSINESS

> "You can't get the Monkees back together as a rock 'n' roll group. That would be like Raymond Burr opening up a law practice."
>
> *(Michael Nesmith)*

> "There are a stack of people who think the Monkees were a conspiracy. These tend to be people who live in the desert in a house made out of hubcaps."
>
> *(Michael Nesmith)*

> "I started seeing things. I was like, 'Hey, Sam, you've got to be a team player if you wanna do another record.' The way he treated [producer] Glen Ballard was an embarrassment. He basically spit in Glen's face."
>
> *(Eddie Van Halen, on Sammy Hagar)*

In what was seen as a match made in heaven, the band then hired veteran hard-rock screamer Sammy Hagar ("I Can't Drive 55"), and all was well . . . for a while. Due to increasing "personality conflicts," Hagar was fired in 1996, and Ed began making what seemed to be hatchet-burying moves

toward Diamond Dave. "I sensed a different guy than I used to work with," Eddie remembered. "Not necessarily humbled, but just normal. Like the LSD—that's what I call Lead Singer Disease—was gone. We apologized to each other about the childish mudslinging over the years, and then we sat around and bullshitted. Nothing to do with music—just life, telling jokes, having fun." Fans of the original lineup rejoiced, but the reunion turned out to be short-lived. . . . What happened?

"I asked [Roth] to do a song for the *Van Halen Best Of* because I wanted it to have something new. Then MTV and everybody else—including him—thought it was a reunion. I told him every fucking day, 'Dave, cut the crap. You're not in the fucking band.' Then we presented at the MTV Awards—a total embarrassment; what happened backstage between Roth and I, I won't get into, but the first thing that went out the window was the friendship. . . . I had no idea he was going to react like that. I was embarrassed, especially when I watched it on tape. The old Dave reared its ugly head backstage. On a personal level, I found out he hadn't changed."

(Eddie Van Halen)

(Note: The band's next vocalist, who presumably got on swimmingly with alpha-male Eddie, was nerdy, personality-free Gary Cherone, formerly of the nerdy, personality-free band Extreme, responsible for the simpering "More Than Words," who hasn't exactly set the world afire—Van Halen's first album featuring Cherone didn't even break the half-million mark in sales!)

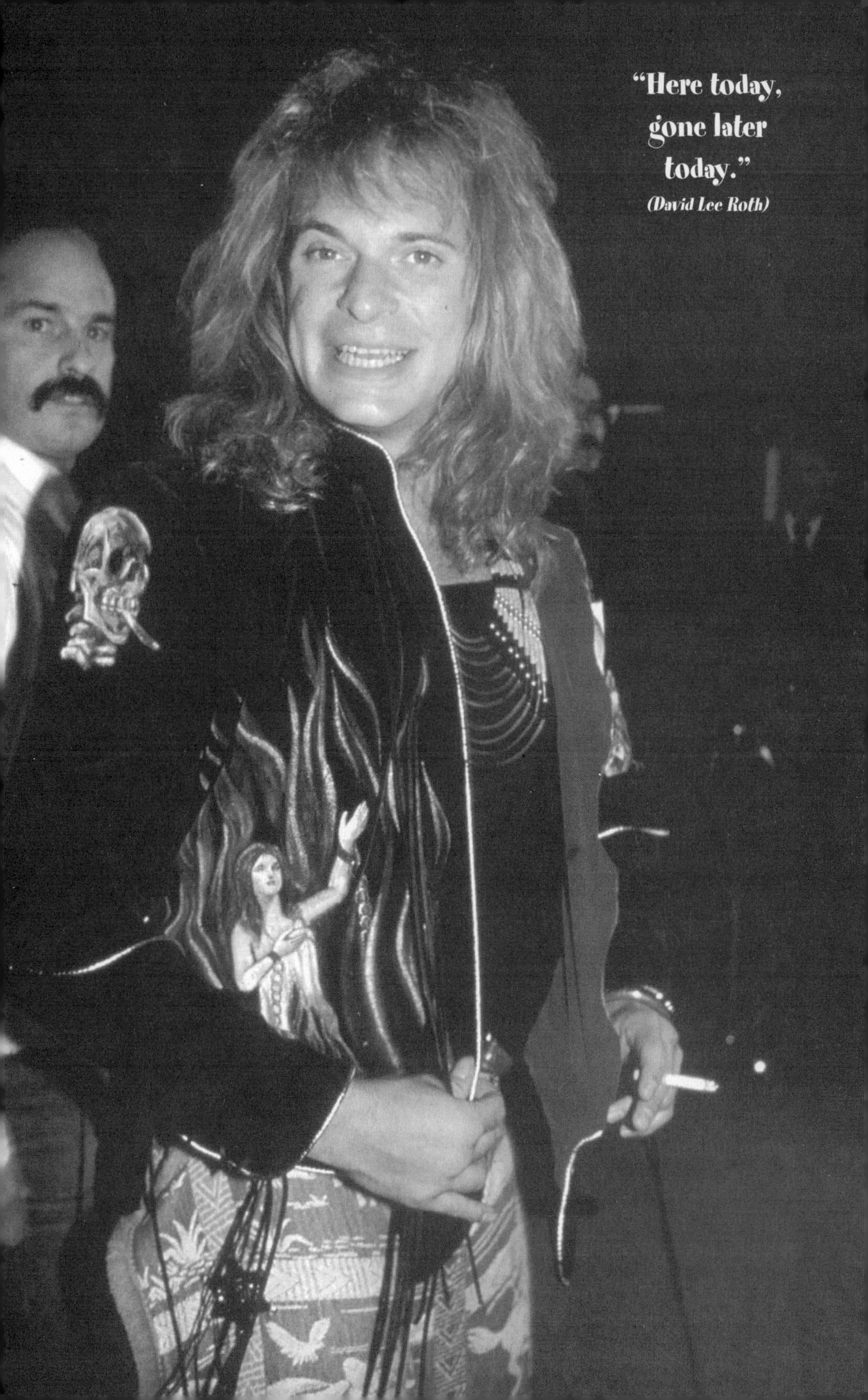

"Here today, gone later today."

(David Lee Roth)

Record Club

One of the perks of being a successful artist is being handed your own vanity label. Some are more successful than others—**Madonna**'s label, Maverick, for example, signed up angst-ridden best-seller **Alanis Morissette**, and saw sales skyrocket. But what has **Mariah Carey**'s record company done lately?

The Beatles: Apple Records
Luther Campbell: Luke Skywalker (in 1990 was ordered to ante up $300,000 to LucasFilms, owner of the *Star Wars* copyrights and trademarks, for unauthorized use of the name of Mark Hamill's character)
Mariah Carey: Crave
Jello Biafra: Alternative Tentacles
Def Leppard: Bludgeon Riffola (the label, named after a phrase used by a particularly brutal reviewer, was taken over in 1979 by Phonogram/ Vertigo)
Jefferson Airplane: Grunt Records
Elton John: Rocket Records

Korn: Elementree
Led Zeppelin: Swan Song Records
Madonna: Maverick
Metallica's Lars Ulrich: The Record Company
Gary Numan: Numa (shut down in February, 1987)
Joan Osborne: Womanly Hips
Ozzy Osbourne: Ozz Records
Prince: Paisley Park
Pulp: Gift
Andrew Loog Oldham, Rolling Stones manager: Immediate Records
The Rolling Stones: Rolling Stones Records (how original)
Frank Sinatra: Reprise
Sisters of Mercy: Merciful Release
Phil Spector: Philles
Dave Stewart (Eurythmics): Anxious Records

Therapy?: Multifuckingnational
U2: Mother Records
Paul Weller: Respond
Frank Zappa: Straight
Rob Zombie: Zombie A Go-Go

Acting Out

> "Whenever I see the news, it's about the same depressing things—wars, hostages, and people's arms hanging off with all the tendons hanging out, you know. So I tend not to watch it much. I prefer to go and see a movie or something where it's all done much more poetically. People getting their heads blown off in slow motion, very beautifully."
>
> *(Kate Bush)*

Rock stars' forays into acting can be stunning (Dwight Yoakam in *Sling Blade*, Cher in *Moonstruck*), pretty darn decent (Jon Bon Jovi in *The Leading Man*, Courtney Love in *The People Vs. Larry Flynt*), or com-

pletely and utterly embarrassing (Paul McCartney in *Give My Regards to Broad Street*, Madonna in almost anything). Those who have enoyed on-screen success include David Bowie, Harry Connick Jr., Brandy, and Sting (although someone should tell him to pick his projects a bit more carefully). But unfortunately, every time some idiot rocker hits it big, some studio is guaranteed to make some pseudo-rock-based star vehicle for their charismatic cash cow—witness Whitney Houston in *The Bodyguard*, Bette Midler in *The Rose*, and Babs Streisand in *A Star Is Born*, produced by her boyfriend at the time, celeb hairdresser-turned-big-time-Hollywood-honcho Jon Peters. (Frankly, it was a little difficult fathoming the Kris Kristofferson character's major attraction to this abrasive, lame-wisecracking pop tart.) Any day now, we're going to be treated to bony-breast-beating, expansive-gesture-making, grotesquely grimacing Celine Dion as one of these tragic femme fatales—can't wait.

DIRECT RESPONSE

Dude-for-all-seasons Rob Zombie was asked to write and direct *The Crow 3* (hopefully the last in the trash-goth series). But he had no experience! "Listen—I don't see directing a movie as any different from anything else," says Rob. "The thing that gives me the confidence to do stuff is when you meet the other people that are doing it. You think, 'Jesus Christ, if that retard can do it. . . .'"

"Film people are so fucking arrogant. I hate them."

(Elton John)

Somewhat of a pot and kettle situation here. . . .

Some of rock's more memorable moments on the silver screen

Performance (1971) starred **Mick Jagger** as a decadent rock star (what a stretch). We already knew he was a rock star, and they really didn't put any good scenes of decadence in the flick. You're better off trying to find a copy of the unreleased **Stones'** documentary *Cocksucker Blues*. Wild. Raunchy. Rock 'n' roll at its best.

Purple Rain (1984): A pretty good **Prince** vanity project, unlike his pair of stink bombs, *Under the Cherry Moon* and *Graffiti Bridge* (the latter, according to its omnipotent creator, was "not a failure. Maybe it will take people thirty years to get it. They trashed *The Wizard of Oz* at first, too").

Truth or Dare (1991), **Madonna**'s tour de force about her, er . . . tour de force.

Includes the immortal scene where **Kevin Costner** triggers Madonna's gag reflex by telling her he thought her show was "neat."

The Song Remains the Same (1976): **Led Zep**'s excruciatingly hokey live-concert/band-member-fantasy flick, which the band's mountainous manager, **Peter Grant**, called "The most expensive home movie ever made."

Remember **Vanilla Ice**'s feature-film debut, *Cool As Ice*? (Memorable if only for the sheer mountain of bad reviews it generated.) Confessed costar **Naomi Campbell**, "I did it as a favor to someone. Not many people liked it, so I guess it wasn't a good move. Please don't hate me." (Or at least don't hate her because of that—not when there are so many other, better reasons.)

Rock Stars Do Acting

"I'm not a very good actor, man. I went on a *Party of Five* audition and ran out of there grabbing my boobs, I was so scared. . . . I was mumbling through the lines and pretty much passed out and started crying. It was so embarrassing. It seems like there are much better ways to make yourself feel like a loser."
(Mark McGrath, Sugar Ray)

Ad-Rock (Adam Horowitz, of the Beastie Boys): Had a cameo in *The Equalizer*

Adam Ant: *Slamdance* (1987); *Cold Steel* (1988)

Jon Bon Jovi: *The Leading Man* (1998); *Homegrown* (1998); *Moonlight and Valentino* (1995)

David Bowie: *The Man Who Fell to Earth* (1976); *Just a Gigolo* (1979); *The Hunger* (1983); *Labyrinth* (1986); *Absolute Beginners* (1986)

Brandy: *I Still Know What You Did Last Summer* (1998)

Brandy and Diana Ross: Made-for-TV movie *Double Platinum* (1999)

SINGING OUT

Actors do rock: not a good idea. Does anyone remember the beautiful music created by these beautiful people?

Gillian Anderson

Kevin Bacon

Kim Basinger

Tia Carrere

David Hasselhoff (but the Germans love his vanilla pop musik)

Jennifer Love Hewitt

Don Johnson

Milla Jovovich

Joey Lawrence

Traci Lords

Eddie Murphy

Leonard Nimoy (did a classic version of "Proud Mary")

Keanu Reeves (At the "T in the Park" rock festival, held in July 1996, TV director Billy Sloan remembers, "We spent three months negotiating to film Keanu Reeves in his band, Dogstar, but when all the little girls mobbed him, he went back to his caravan and sulked. Then he agreed to play only if there were no cameras present. After two numbers, the crowd lost interest and drifted away.")

SINGING OUT
(CONTINUED)

Steven Seagal

William Shatner (did a classic version of "Lucy in the Sky with Diamonds" in the sixties, and was recently asked by Ben Folds (for his other band, Fear of Pop) to warble a track written specifically with Shatner in mind: "In Love." Said Shatner, "Movies are made with the support of music, but the music doesn't actually throb to the beat of the word. Here, it's intricately woven.")

John Travolta

Jack Wagner (Jon Bon Jovi confesses, "Years ago I'd see a Jack Wagner try to make a record and I'd certainly look down my nose at it, like, 'I don't know about this.' ")

Bruce Willis

Mare Winningham

Phil Collins: *Buster* (1988); *Hook* (1991); *Miami Vice* (who was the casting agent who looked at Collins and thought, "matinee idol"?)

Roger Daltrey: *Lisztomania* (1975); *McVicar* (1980)

Evan Dando: *Reality Bites* (1994)

Gloria Estefan: Starred with Meryl Streep in Wes Craven's dreadful *50 Violins* (1999)

Flea: *Back to the Future, Part III* (1990); *My Own Private Idaho* (1991)

Art Garfunkel: *Catch-22* (1970); *Carnal Knowledge* (1971)

Deborah Harry: *Videodrome* (1983); *Hairspray* (1988)

Levon Helm: *Coal Miner's Daughter* (1980); *The Right Stuff* (1983)

Whitney Houston and **Brandy:** Made-for-TV movie *Cinderella* (1998)

Chris Isaak: *Married to the Mob* (1988); *The Silence of the Lambs* (1991)

Jewel: *Ride with the Devil* (1999)

David Johansen: *Scrooged* (1988); *Freejack* (1992)

Gary Kemp: *The Krays* (with his brother, **Martin**; 1990); *The Bodyguard* (1992)

Meat Loaf: *The Rocky Horror Picture Show* (1975); *Roadie* (1980)

Bret Michaels (Poison) wrote, directed, and acted in *A Letter from Death Row* (1999), featuring pals **Charlie** and **Martin Sheen**. Who will, of course, appear in anything.

Alanis Morissette: *Dogma* (1999), with **Matt Damon** and **Ben Affleck**. She plays God. No, I mean in the movie.

Vince Neil: *The Adventures of Ford Fairlane* (1990)

Joe Perry: *Homicide: Life on the Street* TV show (Perry says, "It's a great part—not a walk-on, not a cameo.")

"I can't believe they gave me a badge and a gun—even as a joke."
(*Joe Perry, on his* Homicide *role*)

Iggy Pop: Appropriately enough, appeared as an alien in *Star Trek: Deep Space Nine* in 1998

Diana Ross: *Lady Sings the Blues* (1972); *Mahogany* (1975); *The Wiz* (1978)

After **David Lee Roth** left Van Halen, CBS gave him a budget of ten million bucks to make a movie based on his 1985 solo hit album, *Crazy from the Heat*. Diamond Dave produced an embarrassingly ego-driven audition tape featuring himself and a cast of hundreds. Method actors? No: bosomy babes. Roth's fledgling film career was summarily scrapped.

Ringo Starr: *Lisztomania* (1975); *Sextette* (1978); *Caveman* (1981); *Give My Regards to Broad Street* (1984)

Sting: *Quadrophenia* (1979); *Dune* (1984); *The Bride* (1985); *Julia & Julia* (1987)

Bernie Taupin (Elton John's lyricist): Appeared on ABC's *The Hardy Boys and Nancy Drew Meet Dracula* in 1977

Lee Ving: *Flashdance* (1983); *Streets of Fire* (1984)

Tom Waits: *The Outsiders* (1983); *The Cotton Club* (1984); *Ironweed* (1987); *At Play in the Fields of the Lord* (1991); *The Fisher King* (1991); *Bram Stoker's Dracula* (1992); *Short Cuts* (1993)

TRACK MEAT

Meat Loaf modestly summarizes his stunning success

"I got good *New York Times* reviews in Shakespeare even when Clive Barnes hated the production."

"One of my ambitions is to play the part of Henry VIII. I love the idea of behaving like a real slob and throwing bits of chicken over my shoulders."

> "The music and entertainment business [sic] are highly fueled on drugs and flavor-of-the-month and stuff like that. Who's popular at the moment. And how many people want to be around you because it makes them feel good about themselves 'cause you're famous or important or whatever. It's amazing how many people in the movie want to hang out with rock stars or be rock stars."
>
> *(Twiggy Ramirez, Marilyn Manson)*

And, in the spirit of saving the best for last: Can we even begin to describe the incredible beauty, talent, and drive of Renaissance woman **Babs Streisand**? Not only has she had a brilliant career as our generation's preeminent singer and actress, but now she's a true gal for all seasons—she's directing the movies in which she's starring! But the world still isn't giving a fair shake to women: Babs was shut out—nay, rudely *snubbed*—by the Academy for her fascinatingly multifaceted cinematic masterpiece *The Prince of Tides*. Speaking of that fine flick, Babs ran into a little problem during filming—the **star actress** of the picture (Babs) evidently felt a little embarrassed doing love scenes with Nick Nolte, so the **director** of the picture (that would be Babs) had to step in and cut the scene. Explains Babs herself (note: to facilitate understanding, individuals are identified in brackets), "A shy actress [Babs] got in the way of the director [Babs]. She [the actress, Babs] screwed the director [Babs] by yelling, 'Cut!' I know I [the actress, Babs] probably should have gone on, but you could say that the director [Babs] was really there and thought she got enough. I [the actress, Babs] did get very shy. I [the actress, Babs] thought, 'My god, how could I [the actress, Babs] be making love to  him [my costar . . . what's his name?] in the corridor here with my [the director, Babs] crew watching?' The director [Babs] was sensitive to the actress [Babs] by knowing she [the actress, Babs] was getting slightly embarrassed, and she [the director, Babs] cut for her [the actress, Babs]."

> "Barbra Streisand could play me in the film of my life. She played a man in *Yentl*, she comes from Brooklyn, and we've both got the same nose."
>
> *(Barry Manilow)*
>
> *Yeah, but you're waaaaaaaay better lookin'.*

I Love Rock 'n' Roll

Rock stars on music

"I like sound-effect records. Sometimes late at night I get a mint julep and just sit there and listen to sound effects. I'm surprised more of them aren't on the charts." (Bob Dylan)

"I think music is the main interest of the younger people. It doesn't really matter about the older people now, because they're finished anyway." (George Harrison)

"I think music should make people sit back and want to touch each other." (Jim Croce)

"Me and Nureyev have flaming rows about whether it takes more talent and discipline to be a ballet dancer or a pop singer." (Mick Jagger)

"I don't know anything about music. In my line, you don't have to." (Elvis Presley)

"Rock 'n' roll is instant coffee." (Bob Geldof)

"Pop music is just hard work, long hours, and a lot of drugs." (Mama Cass)

FOR THE RECORD

"I'm not going to tailor my music to what people are going to like next. I don't think in terms of radio and MTV."
(Trent Reznor)

"The goal was to create a record that, ultimately, you'll like—but probably not the first time you hear it."
(Trent Reznor)
Yeah, really wanna rush right out and buy that inaccessible music.

"My new double album, Incantations, is a load of rubbish, really. There are a couple of parts in which I'm expressing myself completely, not using irrelevant stupid things like emotions. The rest, though, is rubbish."
(Mike Oldfield)

"As a medium, it should not be questioned, analyzed, or taken so seriously. I think it should be tarted up, made into a prostitute, a parody of itself." (David Bowie) *Mission accomplished.*

"I once asked Lennon what he thought of what I do. He said, 'It's great, but it's just rock 'n' roll with lipstick on.' " (David Bowie)

FOR THE RECORD
(CONTINUED)

"I had no thought about the sixties when I made *Let Love Rule*. I just wanted to make real music with real instruments. It was also the beginning of my consciousness about the planet and how we're fucking it up."
(Lenny Kravitz)

"After I made my most recent album, *Buddha and the Chocolate Box*, I couldn't figure out what I was talking about."
(Cat Stevens)

"All my records are comedy records."
(Bob Dylan)
Hey, not true—only the ones where you sing.

"Rock has always been the devil's music." (David Bowie)

"One chord is fine. Two chords are pushing it. Three chords and you're into jazz." (Lou Reed)

"Rock 'n' roll is like a drug. I don't take very much, but when I do rock 'n' roll, I fuckin' do it. But I don't want to do it all the time, 'cause it'll kill me." (Neil Young)

"Rock 'n' roll is phony and false, and sung, written, and played, for the most part, by cretinous goons." (Frank Sinatra)

"It's boring chord movement and bad acting." (Joni Mitchell)

"I'll play it first and tell you what it is later."
(Miles Davis)

LOUD AND PROUD

"We're only in it for the volume."
(Geezer Butler, Black Sabbath)

"It's the old philosophy: if I'm too loud for you, you're too old for me."
(Stiv Bators, Dead Boys)

Acid House

"It was fuckin' great, acid house. Well, the music's bollocks in a way—but no, some of it's good. No, really! You've got to be on Ecstasy or acid to listen to it, of course. But that's no fuckin' different from punk and all the speed you had to take to listen to that, right." (Shane McGowan)

Alternative/Grunge

"I would rather listen to the **Spice Girls** any day of the week than to some Seattle band dressed like lumberjacks trying to convince me that they're suicidal and depressed when they're young, healthy, rich, famous, and getting all the pussy they want. I'm sorry, I don't buy that. For me, the Spice Girls have got much more credibility than any band trying to pretend they believe the world is all doomy and glum. Bullshit." **(Gene Simmons)**

"I don't know how much more of these waifish alternative singers I can take. Honey, just get out of that dirty bathtub and give me an old-fashioned, sweaty, big-titty bitch of rock 'n' roll." **(Sandra Bernhard)**

Disco

"Death to disco, mon." **(Peter Tosh)**

"I hate disco music." **(Barry Gibb)**

"They ruined a perfectly good theater by filling it with faggots in boxing shorts waving champagne bottles in front of your face." **(Keith Richards, on Studio 54)**

"It's musical soma." **(David Bowie)**

OUT OF HIS TREE

Captain Beefheart, whose voice was so powerful that it once destroyed a studio microphone, consulted with a tree surgeon during the recording of his 1969 *Trout Mask Replica* album because he didn't want the recording process to injure any innocent foliage that unwittingly happened to be standing nearby.

"We're a perfect example of the average uneducated 'twentysomething' in America in the nineties."
(Kurt Cobain)
Amen, brother. Nice outfit, by the way..

Folk

"I think it's all folk music, whether it's fast or slow. You've got three chords, an attitude, a story. I've always thought punk rock was folk music." (Dave Pirner, Soul Asylum)

"Folk singing is just a bunch of fat people." (Bob Dylan)

Glam/Glitter

"I have nothing against glitter bands or groups that wear makeup. But that doesn't mean I'll go drinking with them." (Ronnie Van Zant, Lynyrd Skynyrd)

Metal

"Our music is very angry, you see, and we can't really go onstage and sing about daffodils with 40,000 watts of power." (Rob Halford)

"The idea is to keep it as simplistic, as innocent, as unassuming, and as stupid as possible." (David Lee Roth, on Van Halen's music)

"I find it really funny to see a lot of those groups like Poison—not even Poison, but Warrant and Skid Row, bands like that—desperately clinging to their old identities, but now trying to have an alternative angle in their music. It gives me a small thrill to know that I've helped in a small way to get rid of those people." (Kurt Cobain)

Hippies, Flower Power

"If you can remember anything about the sixties, you weren't really there." (Paul Kantner)

"That love, peace, and granola shit went over real well." (David Crosby)

"The whole hippie scene is wishful thinking. They wish they could love, but they're full of shit." (Frank Zappa)

"A hippie is another word for a goat tick. If a guy's got flies buzzing around his head and a joint in his mouth, I think he's a sap." (Ted Nugent)

PIERCED EARS

Rockers with ravaged eardrums

Roger Daltrey, The Who

John Entwistle, The Who

Jerry Garcia, The Grateful Dead

James Hetfield, Metallica

Ted Nugent

Sting

Pete Townshend, The Who

Frankie Valli

Brian Wilson, The Beach Boys

"At the time, we were angry young kids and there were all these Haight-Ashbury bands happening. I hated the smell of incense. And when I heard the fucking words 'If you go to San Francisco, be sure to wear a flower in your hair,' I wanted to kill the fucking lyricist. I thought, 'This is fucking shit, man.' " (Ozzy Osbourne)

Punk

"If any of them punk rockers goes anywhere near my kit I shall kick them square in the knackers. I got fifteen years in this bloody business, and what do these bastards know?" (Keith Moon)

"I'm tired of the theory of the noble savage. I'd like to hear punks who could put together a coherent sentence."
(Lou Reed)

MUSIC TO MY EARS

Musicians on musicianship

"To me, a thing like tuning is so beside the point that it's totally irrelevant."
(Lenny Kaye, Patti Smith Band)

"Man, I took speed every night for three years and practiced."
(Duane Allman, on how he got to be so good)

"My solo guitar work is based around delay, repetition, and hazard, an approach introduced to me by Eno, directly and without explanation in September 1972."
(Master axman Robert Fripp)

"The big difference between us and punk groups is that we like KC and the Sunshine Band. You ask Johnny Rotten if he likes KC and the Sunshine Band and he'll blow snot in your face." (Chris Frantz, Talking Heads)

"We're the only honest band that's hit this planet in about two thousand million years." (Johnny Rotten)

"All the hype the Sex Pistols had was totally deserved. Johnny Rotten was the one I identified with; he was the sensitive one." (Kurt Cobain)

"It was like a case of premature ejaculation. Over in a flash and deeply unsatisfying." (Glenn Matlock, on his stint in the Sex Pistols)

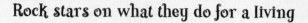

Sound Judgment

Rock stars on what they do for a living

"We're lucky in the fact that we're more of an art project than an actual musical band." (Twiggy Ramirez, Marilyn Manson)
And we're lucky you're not on the radio more.

"We're just a little band working as hard as we can to entertain the fans." (Modest Dave Mustaine, Megadeth)

"There's a lot to like about this band, because there's a lot of different things going on . . . from messages to tight pants." (Tommy Shaw, Styx)
. . . to lame pomp-rock.

"You don't always get a chance to fuck when you're horny or punch somebody in the face when you feel like it. . . . When people become disenchanted with the world, they turn to fantasy—and here we are." (Gene Simmons, who must be *someone's* fantasy)

"If it wasn't for Michael Jackson, I probably wouldn't make music now. *Thriller* changed my life. It changed the whole world." (Sean Lennon)
He wishes he had a tenth of Michael Jackson's talent. Or even his mother's.

"Our main criticism of Malcolm [McLaren, the manager who put Bow Wow Wow together] is that he's too intellectual. We do have intellectual elements in what we do, but the music is basically about shagging." (Leigh Gorman, Bow Wow Wow)
At last! A true rock 'n' roller!

"What occurred to me was how severely and despotically the God from the Old Testament acts. How He almost curses those people. And it seemed that I adopted that cursing voice in my singing." (Nick Cave)
Sounds more like a cursed voice.

Business Affairs

The business side of rock 'n' roll

"What most people don't realize is that the whole thing is about getting as much money as possible in as short a time as possible with as much style as possible."
(Malcolm McLaren)

STEALING THE SHOW

"All the flourishes, like big double octaves on the piano—we stole them like crazy."
(Elvis Costello, on Abba)

"What we do is derivative, very derivative."
(Mick Jagger)

" 'Twenty-five years old' is from Gilbert O'Sullivan's 'Alone Again (Naturally),' except 'sixty-five' is now 'twenty-five.' 'All around the world, statues crumble for me' is a Killing Joke thing. 'Who knows how long I've loved you?' is from 'I Will' by the Beatles. It's all [imitative]. But at least Sugar Ray can come out and admit it."
(McG [Joseph McGinty Nichols], video director/producer for Sugar Ray)

" 'My Generation' was our biggest seller, and we never hope or want to produce anything like it again."
(Pete Townshend)

"The only way to be a star again is to spend my life promoting myself in a way that I find cheapening."
(George Michael)
And you should know how that *feels by now.*

"Sometimes I have to remember that this isn't a record retail store I'm running. It's supposed to be some kind of art." (Paul McCartney)

"The days of the fucked-up, half-pissed, half-stoned pop star with black leather kecks, winkle-picker boots, and long black hair, staggering down the corridor clutching a bottle of Jack Daniel's and thinking he's Keith Richards, are over. It's not that I sit in an office with a fax machine, but I keep an eye on what's going on."
(Noel Gallagher, Oasis)

"I live for meetings with men in suits. I love them because I know they had a really boring week and I walk in there with my orange velvet leggings and drop popcorn in my cleavage and then fish it out and eat it. I like that. I know I'm entertaining them, and I know that they know." (Madonna)

"I've always seen **David** as a building. I visualize him as a building. Something rather like the Pan Am Building on Park Avenue." (Tony DeFries, Bowie's manager)

"Can I just say that **Richard Branson's** got ridiculously enormous teeth? One day all these cretins with big teeth and long hair and cheesecloth shirts started turning up at our gigs. These people were from Virgin Records." (**Andy Partridge, XTC**)

"Sure I lie, but it's more like . . . tinting. It's all just negotiating theatrics." (Irving Azoff, Eagles manager)

"In an industry riddled with drug addicts, homosexuals, and hangers-on, I am one of the few real men left." (**Don Arden**, manager of huge rock acts like Black Sabbath)

"I have no use for bodyguards, but I have a very specific use for two highly trained certified public accountants." (Elvis Presley)

THE RULING CRASS

"They have the odd idea that democracy is the best way to run a band. It is the worst way."
(Marty Balin, on Jefferson Starship)

"Everybody argues, then we do what I say."
(Bono)

"It's crucial that I should be marketed in the right way." (Deborah Harry)

"Look, if they're going to buy lunch boxes, they may as well buy David Cassidy lunch boxes." (David Cassidy)

"You go and meet him and he's this pleasant, corporate cocksucker. They're making a doll of him." (Liam Howe, Sneaker Pimps, on Marilyn Manson)

Another Day in Paradise

"I only remember a city by its chicks."
(Jimi Hendrix)

A rock 'n' roll travelogue

America (general)

"There are many things about America I like—things that Americans take for granted, like a good telephone system. And they don't force you to go to bed at 10:30 P.M. by switching off all the TV programs and stopping the trains." (Jimmy Page)

Nebraska

"I've never been hated by so many people I've never met as in Nebraska in the mid sixties. Everyone looked at you with a look that could kill. You could tell they just wanted to beat the shit out of you." (Keith Richards)

Chicago

"You look for certain things in certain towns. Chicago, for instance, is notorious for sort of two things at once. Balling two chicks, or three, in combination acts." (Jimmy Page)

Las Vegas

"A thorough survey may prove that it is impossible to buy a plain white or decently tasteful shirt in the whole of Las Vegas." (Jann Wenner, editor, *Rolling Stone* magazine)

Los Angeles

"The chicks are stunning, the climate's better, and everything's half-price." (Lemmy)

"L.A. . . . yuck! This place is one big parking lot. It's like walking through an endless supermarket. The pizzas taste like wafers covered in garlic." (Deborah Harry)

"[The groupies in Los Angeles are] real thick. If you're married to somebody in rock 'n' roll, there are definitely places where you don't let your husband go without you—unless you want him to completely have nights of decadence, because it's just like the way it goes in L.A. These women are very loose out there. Women coming up to you, 'Do you want a blow job?' I mean, give me a break—what guy doesn't? They're crafty. They'll come up to you and go, 'Want us to take you shopping? We know all the great places to go.' If you come into L.A. for the first time and you don't know your way around, two of them take you shopping and two of them go after the guy. This is where you're talking hard-core groupie here—the girls that really have the science down." (Bebe Buell)

"I would meet these horrible little girls there who were fifteen and were fearing becoming nineteen. And that's not healthy, that's sick." (Iggy Pop)

"L.A.'s okay, I guess, if you want to be the bronzed goddess driving around in your Cherokee Jeep in your satin shorts with your asshole jerk-off rock 'n' roll star boyfriend with his shorts full of cocaine." (Chrissie Hynde)

"That fucking place should be wiped off the face of the earth." (David Bowie)

New York

"Living in New York is like coming all the time."
(Gene Simmons)

"A bowl of underpants." (Captain Beefheart)

"It's like living on top of a rotting corpse—vampire
life." (John Hiatt)

South America

"Argentina, the World Cup 1978. When I got there, they said, 'You have to be careful of the bandits. Let us give you a couple of security guards. We'll take you to the best restaurant in Buenos Aires.' Sure enough, I was sitting there when these guys held up the restaurant, told everyone to get on the floor, and started taking everyone's watches off. Then the police turned up and started firing into the restaurant. They shot two bandits inside and the other one was shot trying to escape. One of the waiters was shot in the back. The police lay the bodies outside in the gutter. That was it. We had a bottle of brandy, then the owner of the restaurant gave us the bill. Cheeky cunt!"
(Rod Stewart)

"Great" Britain

"England's terrible. It has the worst air, the worst water, the worst food, the worst anything you want to name. It's the pits. Every single person smokes cigarettes and they all have brown teeth and rotted-out gums. Everything is black from coal—the buildings are black, the streets are black." (**Fee Waybill, The Tubes**)

"There's a certain lack of big tits in England." (**Nigel Mogg, The Quireboys**)

"I have absolutely no respect for the English people. They make me sick." (**Kurt Cobain**)

"I think you have a cute little country." (**Randy Newman**, to an English journalist)

"Parisians love the **Sex Pistols** because the French really hate England." (**Malcolm McLaren**)

"Everybody is either heterosexual or homosexual in London, but no one ever gets laid." (**David Johansen**)

"London is the only city in the world that is run entirely on bullshit." (**Boy George**)

"London's a kind of massive souvenir shop—a facade of how London used to be. It just isn't English anymore. It seems very Americanized, which is something to dwell upon with horror." (**Morrissey**)

France

"The French are just useless. They can't organize a piss-up in a brewery." (**Elton John**)

The Fame Game

"If people ask me what I do, I always say I'm a chartered accountant, unless there's a lot of time to explain things."
(Brian Eno)

What life is like when you're rich and famous

"Being a rock star is like having a sex change. People stare at you, follow you down the street shouting comments, they hustle you and touch you up." (Bono)

"Everyone's scared of you; you can't really make any friends; they want to have a big Hollywood meeting with you just so they can stare at you for ten minutes." (Courtney Love)

"Of course you can do things like going into a pub. The thing to do is just go in and have a drink. But if you walk in wearing a double-breasted mink jacket, obviously people treat you as something different." (Cliff Richard)

"It's bizarre—everybody just automatically assumes you're being an asshole or a dick because you're being yourself. . . . When people automatically think you're a dick, you have to be extra nice to everyone just to be an all-right guy." (Twiggy Ramirez, Marilyn Manson)

HIT PARADE

"I feel a bit silly. If somebody's looking at me with rapture all over their face, I want to throw a bucket of water over them."
(Ian Dury)

The Cult's Ian Astbury once strolled into a hotel in England, only to encounter a horde of tourists. What did the sightseers do? Surrounded the pop star and just stared. What did Astbury do? Broke a wine bottle over his own head.

"I was standing at the bar the other day and a guy came up to me and said, 'Ray, I like your songs. I think you're a very underrated songwriter—a poet, really.' So I hit him over the head with a bottle."
(Ray Davies)

Love to love you,
baby

"A lot of musicians that get real famous have this feeling that everyone that's dealing with them wants something from them." (Flea, Red Hot Chili Peppers)

"It's strange how people appear to be well meaning and they're not. They're after something that you've got. You always think that they want your friendship, but they don't. They want what comes with your friendship—the money, the fun, the parties, the free ride. When you're not selling records and your wife's left and they're all gone, then you suddenly realize that maybe you don't have any friends." (Mick Ralphs, Bad Company)

"The very weird religion of celebrity scares me. It's like people are creating fake heroes because they don't have any real ones. The politicians have failed us, religion has failed us, so who do people turn to? Celebrities. It's wrong." (Michael Stipe)

"I very rarely talk to an audience. If you talk to them, you can become human. And they don't want you to be human. They would rather have you on a level where you're not human." (Alice Cooper)

"You've been there, done that: bought the T-shirt, got the poster, *been* the poster." (Cher)

"We played in my hometown of Sheffield. All of the relatives who for ten years had been saying, 'When are you going to get a proper job?' were saying, 'Isabel got a **Pulp** bag and a T-shirt. Why haven't I got any souvenirs?'" (Jarvis Cocker, Pulp)

"It's much easier to make it than it is to stay there." (Peter Frampton)

"Fame is like the ocean: it looks pretty from a distance, but if you're gonna jump in, you'd better learn to swim." (**Michael Hutchence**, waxing philosophical)

"I love being famous. . . . It makes me feel wanted and loved and noticed." (**Michael Hutchence**)

"I love being a star more than life itself." (**Janis Joplin**)

"The best thing is that I never have to wait for a table at a restaurant. The worst thing is that I can't put my trash out in front of my house because people always go through it. That's the spectrum." (**Madonna**)

"Suddenly girls were queuing up to sit on my face, which I thought was really pleasant—if they'd washed beforehand." (**J. J. Burnel**, The **Stranglers**)

"They say, 'Well, fucking Rod's gone off to Hollywood with a movie star.' The cunts! I come from the same background they do. In England, all rock 'n' roll comes from the working class. That's your only way of getting out of the rabble. I come from nothing. Then all of a sudden I'm faced with a lot of glamorous women. What the fuck am I going to do?" (**Rod Stewart**)

"It really dawned on me how secure the situation was, the fact that we could go on for the next ten years making records, getting hit records, getting bigger and bigger and all the rest of it. That frightened me because I realized we were going to end up the same like the rest of them." (**The Jam's Paul Weller**, explaining that he broke his band up so they wouldn't end up making dinosaur rock like The **Who** and The **Stones**)

Hard Pressed

We hate the press! We loathe the press! We can't do without the press!

"To all those who criticized, condemned, berated, lambasted, denounced, defamed, defiled, or otherwise desecrated the Monkees—go fuck yourselves." (Mickey Dolenz)

"If I read anything cruel, I have to have a couple of days to get over it. If it came at me all the time, I'd go around throwing acid into people's faces." (Deborah Harry)

"You better get your fat hips out of here!" (Michael Hutchence, to a photographer)

"As long as my picture is on the front page, I don't care what they say about me on page ninety-six."(Mick Jagger)

"It's amazing to me that people want to know about my soap opera." (Mick Jagger)

"It's really difficult to get out of gossip columns once you're in them." (Mick Jagger)

"There's no such thing as bad publicity. Not for the Stones, anyway." (Keith Richards)

"I think freedom of the press ought to be about uncovering abuses and exposing tyrants, not about whether or not I'm walking down the beach in a junky sweater."

(Babs Streisand)

"If you want to take my picture, it'll cost you a fiver. If not, I'll smash your camera."
(Sid Vicious)

"In Texas one time, a guy reviewed the show and said we just sucked. Then he started mentioning names of songs that we didn't even play. So I called this guy up at the paper and said, 'Now you gotta tell me—were you at the concert?' And he said, 'No, ha, ha, ha.' I felt like going there and killing the guy." (Steve Walsh, Kansas)

"Rock critics like Elvis Costello because rock critics look like Elvis Costello." (David Lee Roth)

"I'm tired of being victimized by people who are dedicated to a snappy phrase." (Linda Ronstadt)

"[*Rolling Stone*] made this elaborate diagram charting all these hearts I broke. I mean, I can't date? Am I a sinner for dating? That was kind of shocking. And it was the men on the list who called me up and said they were gonna make a complaint. After that, I was told that the magazine had a policy not to ever say anything nice about me." (Joni Mitchell)

"[Rock writing is] so jivey. I found myself looking things up in the dictionary a lot just to see what the guy is saying." (Tom Petty)

"Rock 'n' roll is not meant to be criticized. If you can find someone who's willing to pay you to be a critic, then you've found a sucker." (Paul Stanley, Kiss)

"Rock journalism is people who can't write interviewing people who can't talk for people who can't read." (Frank Zappa)

Everybody Wants to Rule the World

Proof (as if any were needed) that living the rock 'n' roll lifestyle is not always conducive to keeping oneself grounded in reality

"There's nobody in the world [that] can make better records than I do." (Phil Spector)

"I am blessed with a terrific voice. It's a God-given thing." (Roy Orbison)

"When I hear the birds singing, I think, 'Is that me?' " (Brian Wilson)

"I am a brilliant guitarist." (Ritchie Blackmore)

"I don't need people to tell me how good I am. I've worked it out for myself." (Eric Clapton)

"I'm still a metal god to many people, and I'm proud to carry that with me." (Rob Halford, Judas Priest)

"I know we're the best group in the world." (Ian McCulloch, Echo & the Bunnymen)

"They were taking themselves so seriously about being musicians, they were forgetting that they were actors and comedians. I mean, Belushi was saying, 'Did you hear Aykroyd on the harp? Better than Paul Butterfield!' And I said, 'Whoa . . . time to remember who you are.' That's when my job gets a little dangerous. Belushi didn't talk to me for six months." (Legendary photographer Annie Liebovitz, on the Blues Brothers—John Belushi and Dan Aykroyd)

"If I was going to listen to anybody, I'd listen to me. I love the stuff I do. I mean, it's the greatest, so what the hell?" (Ted Nugent)

"I don't mean to sound bigheaded, but I honestly don't think we've put a foot wrong in twenty years." (Mike Rutherford, Genesis)

"We weren't too ambitious when we started out. We just wanted to be the biggest thing that ever walked the planet." (Steven Tyler)

"I'm the greatest fucking rock star that ever walked this planet." (Noel Gallagher, Oasis)

"You know, sometimes I look back on my life and wonder just how one man could achieve all I've done." (James Brown)

"We have changed the history of pop music. We know that. It's fantastic. But it has its downside. We are tired." (Liam Howlett, Prodigy)

"If I had a dream of how others would see me, in all humility it would be for people to see me as a pioneer, a woman's woman, a maverick . . . in fact, *maverick* is a word I like, and I think it's great that **Madonna** named her label after me. . . ." (Rock chick **Bebe Buell**, whose biggest claim to fame is that she dated a lot of rock stars)

"I epitomize America." (John Denver)

"Real estate is the only thing that doesn't depreciate—other than me." (Jerry Lee Lewis)

"One thing's for sure—now when I look at *Funny Girl*, I think I was gorgeous. I was too beautiful to play Fanny Brice." (Babs Streisand)

"I think I'm a genius. Point fucking blank." (Terence Trent D'Arby)

"I'm just an advertisement for a version of myself." (David Byrne)

"I'm just the same as ever—loud, electrifying, and full of personal magnetism." (Little Richard)

"I have a lot of respect for my own opinion." (Paul Stanley, Kiss)

"Pretend I'm stupid? If that's the alternative, I'd rather be a pretentious wanker." (Sting)
He's certainly made good on his word.

"John's just jealous because I'm the brains of the group. . . . They were so useless they had to come to me because they couldn't think of anything by themselves." (Sid Vicious)

"The most important thing in the world is to dig yourself, and if you can't do that, why in hell parade yourself around in front of an audience?" (David Johansen)

"I don't think people mind if I'm conceited. Every rock 'n' roll star in the world is conceited." (Mick Jagger)

"I think Townshend's always wanted to be me." (Roger Daltrey)

"[Bob] Dylan once said to Keith, 'I could have written "Satisfaction," but you couldn't have written "Tambourine Man." ' " (Mick Jagger)

"I am the Nureyev of rock 'n' roll." (Meat Loaf)

"I feel I'm as good as Beethoven or any of the greats." (Marvin Gaye)

"I'm very misunderstood, you know. It's the price I have to pay. Beethoven and Michelangelo were misunderstood in their time too. I'm not concerned about now, but when I leave this earth I'll be appreciated." (Marvin Gaye)

"There's shit on this record Mozart wishes he could have thought of." (Ted Nugent)

"I really believe that I have more talent in my little finger than Tony Bennett or anybody like that can possibly ever hope to achieve in a lifetime." (Elton John)

"I'm a lot like [John] Lennon in a way. He was very controversial with what he had to say." (Marilyn Manson)

"I love talking about the various ways in which I am unappreciated." (Leonard Cohen)

"I feel like I could be president of the United States. People laugh, but if I set my mind to it, within the next fifteen years I would be president." (Will Smith)

"God had to create disco music so that I could be born and be successful." (Donna Summer)

"I can do anything. One of these days I'll be so complete I won't be a human. I'll be a god." (John Denver)

"I won't be happy until I'm as famous as God." (Madonna)

"I guess I've always wanted to be God. What that really means really is that I was to be It. Mr. Cool. Mr. Top. And there's nothing higher than God. I don't know if I want the responsibility of knowing that all the atoms in the universe are going all right. But it would be great to have your name repeated all the time—'Thou art great, Thou art this, Thou art that.' Yeah, I sure am." (Gene Simmons)

"Yes. I am God. I am God the almighty." (Noel Gallagher's response to a journalist who asked if he believed in a higher power)

You're No Good

"The whole music business works on the principle 'You scratch my back and I'll claw yours.' We keep our nails pretty well sharpened."
(Bob Geldof)

Meow!

The Beatles

"The Beatles never had anything to say. It was always nice, happy stuff. What *did* they ever say?" (Lou Reed)

"The Beatles misused that responsibility and turned a whole generation on to drugs. We're going to be very careful about how we use our new fame." (Daryl Dragon, The Captain & Tennille)

Jeff Beck

"Jeff Beck is pathetic." (Pete Townshend)

Ben Folds Five

"All we want to do is bring heavy back into rock 'n' roll. Because goddamned Ben Folds Five sucks." (Jonathan Davis, Korn)

Chuck Berry

"I think for the life span he's lasted, Chuck Berry's productivity has been nil, more or less." (Elton John)

Jon Bon Jovi

"He's a wimp." (Nikki Sixx)

"I think Jon Bon Jovi should decide what he wants to be. Is he in the Mafia? Is he a cowboy? Is he an Indian?" (Sebastian Bach, Skid Row, wondering about Jon's constantly changing image)

Bono, U2

"Bono would love to be six-foot-tall and thin and good-looking. But he's not—he reminds me of a soddin' mountain goat." **(Ian McCulloch, Echo & the Bunnymen)**

David Bowie

"David Bowie is the most insane-looking human creature I've ever had the misfortune of laying my eyes on." **(Frank Sinatra Jr.)**

"David Bowie's like a sponge, soaking up everything he can get. I wouldn't let him near me with a ten-foot pole." **(Johnny Thunders, New York Dolls)**

"He has a great potential for true idleness." **(Angela Bowie)**

"He's a little too fairyish-looking for me." **(Patti Smith)**

"I think Bowie was so innovative because he was a bit mad. He started the character Ziggy Stardust and then he said he actually started believing he was this character that was like a god." **(Suggs, Madness)**

Boy George

"I'd like to pistol-whip him for about an hour. Though he originally came out against drugs, how many people did he suck?" **(Ted Nugent)**

David Byrne, Talking Heads

"He should be the first guy indicted for crimes of such extreme pretension that he's actually physically jailed." **(Bob Guccione Jr.)**

Chumbawamba

"I hope they disappear very quickly, and I'm sure they will. I just hate everything they stand for—I don't find any soul or genuine concern for people in their music." **(Steve Mackey, Pulp)**

Elvis Costello

"Elvis Costello is terrible—all fat and sweaty. Can't dance, either." (Ian McCulloch, Echo & the Bunnymen)

"I believe in glamour. **Tom Waits**? Why would I want to listen to him? He's ugly and grubby. They call **Elvis Costello** 'four eyes' for a reason. How can you look at him and get off?" (Lou Reed)

The Cranberries

"I saw The Cranberries' first gig in London, and **Dolores [O'Riordan]** was frumpy, in a bad Kensington Market Indian smock, with bad sandals and a gorgeous voice—and really shy and charming. Then she just turned into this mountain-goat-stomping, faux-political southerner from Cork, freak-singing about the troubles in Northern Ireland." (Courtney Love)

John Denver

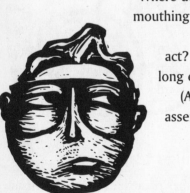

"Where does that pompous creep come off bad-mouthing me like that when he never even met me and probably hasn't even seen my act? . . . Just for that, I'm gonna stick around long enough to piss on John Denver's flowers!" (Alice Cooper, upon hearing of Denver's assertion that he'd be around when Alice was long forgotten)

Devo

"It's nice to see an act whose audience can't relate to them." (Leonard Cohen)

Bo Diddley

"I still like Bo Diddley. If he ever gets out of the chord of E, he might get dangerous." (Jerry Lee Lewis)

Celine Dion and Babs Streisand

"Have you ever seen that 'duel' between Celine Dion and Barbra Streisand? I watch that and say, 'God, this can't be happening.' When I see them high-five each other after hitting some soaring high note, I'm like, 'What's going on here? Is this music or is this *Top Gun*? It's all so forced and contrived. . . .'" (Holly Cole)

Duran Duran

"Duran Duran are completely disgusting and crass and offensive." (**Mick Hucknall**)

Bob Dylan

"Dylan gets on my nerves. If you were at a party with him, I think you'd tell him to shut up." (**Lou Reed**)

"He never initiates conversation, but he'll answer a question if you ask him." (**Jimmy Carter**)

"I don't like Bob Dylan. I don't like his attitude or his records. . . . All that protest thing was a load of rubbish. I don't hate listening to his records, but I can't stand it when people say he's a genius." (**Tom Jones**)

"I never liked Dylan's music before I played with him. I always used to think he sounded like Yogi Bear." (**Mick Ronson**)

"I've already forgotten who Bob Dylan was." (**Elvis Costello**)

"What will Bob Dylan be doing in twenty years? To be truthful, who cares?" (**Andy Partridge, XTC**)

Fleetwood Mac

"I've seen Stevie's show, I've seen Christine's show. To me, they both bordered on being lounge acts, simply because they were resting so heavily on Fleetwood Mac's laurels." (Lindsey Buckingham, on the solo careers of Mac bandmates **Christine McVie and Stevie Nicks**)

Generation X

"Hear it first thing in the morning and you'd want to go straight back to bed." (Elton John)

Genesis

"Groups like Genesis and Yes are about as exciting as a used Kleenex. It might as well be Tony Bennett." (Nick Lowe)

The Grateful Dead

"We want to be one of the great bands—not like the Grateful Dead." (Clem Burke, Blondie)

George Harrison

"George is very paranoid about the press. There's a lot of anger in him. I don't know why. He's got his guard up before he begins. But the worst they can say is that he's a boring old fart." (Eric Clapton)

"If you see George Harrison, you can tell him I think he's a load of old rope." (Cliff Richard)

Billy Idol

"The Perry Como of punk." (Johnny Rotten)

LaToya Jackson

"She had a tit job for sure. This is desperation. Well, maybe she'll get a job out of it." (Madonna, after seeing Jackson's *Playboy* layout)

Michael Jackson

"I can't fathom Michael Jackson at all." (Morrissey)

"I really wanted to be Michael Jackson when I was growing up. But if I met him today, I'd unplug his oxygen tent, rip off his surgical mask, and spit in his face." (Mike D, The Beastie Boys)

"Billy Idol was the
most stunning man in
the world at one point.
He now looks like an
extra from Michael
Jackson's video
Thriller."
(Boy George)

Mick Jagger

"He moves like a parody between a majorette girl and **Fred Astaire**." (**Truman Capote**)

"He's not unlike **Elton John**, who represents the token queen, like **Liberace** used to. He represents the sort of harmless, bourgeois kind of evil that one can accept with a shrug." (**David Bowie**)

"I think Mick's a joke, with all that fag dancing." (**John Lennon**)

"It really bothers me that a twerp like that can parade around and convince everybody that he's Satan." (**Ry Cooder**)

"Mick flirted with me unbelievably, and told me I was pretty and that I should be with him and not **Todd**. But you know, Mick said that to all the girls. He's like the little pixie that runs around causing trouble with all the females, and that's what I love about him—his boldness. He was relentless. He also kept telling Todd what a great ass he had. He'd say, 'God, Todd Rundgren, you've got a great ass,' which was absolutely true." (**Bebe Buell**)

"Mick Jagger loves to humiliate people, but he was nice to me because he needed the music." (**Ry Cooder**)

"That cunt is a great entertainer." (**Bill Graham**)

"Every minute has to be filled. He's not a big one for self-reflection or inner reflection at all." (**Keith Richards**)

Sir Elton John

"Poor old fatty has finally got his Lordship, which he's been after for years. But look, he went through the back door—literally—to get it." (**Johnny Rotten**, on Elton's knighthood)

"Elton's already a queen, so isn't this a bit of a comedown?" (**Boy George**, on Elton's knighthood)

John Lennon

"I think his greatest achievement was recognizing that he was a macho asshole and trying to stop it." (Sean Lennon, on his father)

"If you want to hear pretentiousness, just listen to John Lennon's 'Imagine.' All that 'possessions' crap." (Lou Reed)

"John Lennon ain't no revolutionary—he's a fucking idiot." (Todd Rundgren)

Courtney Love

"I met her in New York at this party after the MTV awards, and she just jumped on me like she was my best friend. I'd never met her before in my life. She was like, 'Oh my gawd, **Boy George**, I loooooove you.' We chatted for about ten minutes, and then she looked at me like a mad person and said, 'Would you mind? I was in the middle of a conversation with my friend.' " (Boy George)

"Courtney never bothered to say 'hi' to me until I sold a million records." (Marilyn Manson)

"Is there any lower valley of vulgarity that one can plummet to? I don't know. She's really a pioneer in that area. I'm glad there are Courtney Loves around to give us a barometer of just how worthless man can be." (Ted Nugent)

John Lydon (Johnny Rotten)

"Johnny Rotten is a paranoid clown." (Hugh Cornwell, The Stranglers)

Madonna

"[Madonna should] be a little more magnanimous and a little less of a cunt." (Cher)

"All of [Madonna's] aloofness and star stuff . . . it's just bullshit." (George Harrison, who financed *Shanghai Surprise*)

"Desperate womanhood." (Morrissey)

"It would be my guess that Madonna is not a very happy woman. From my own experience, having gone through persona changes like that, that kind of clawing around to be the center of attention is not a pleasant place to be."
(David Bowie)

"I love [Madonna's song] 'Frozen.' I love the line, 'You're so concerned with how much you get.' I thought, 'Really? You can say that, with sixty million pounds in the bank?' " (Boy George)

"I *acted* vulgar. Madonna *is* vulgar." (Marlene Dietrich)

Marilyn Manson

"Marilyn Manson's okay—but look at me. I'm not sitting here with my eyes blacked up, chomping on a dead animal. I'm just having a chat. But he walks around the street with his full makeup and stage gear on. If you're Coco the clown in the circus, you don't go home with your big boots and your red nose on, shout, 'Hello, darling, I'm home!' and sit down dressed like that to watch *EastEnders*. I met his father—he came backstage after my show and said, 'You are the Antichrist; my son is the Antichrist Superstar.' I just wanted to say, 'Oh, shut the fuck up. . . .' " (Ozzy Osbourne)

"The guy's got a girl's name, and he wears makeup. What an original idea." (Alice Cooper)

"I'm not into being controversial and despised like Marilyn Manson or something. I would never walk around with a sign that says 'Please kick me; I'm the hated one.' " (Ozzy Osbourne)

"I think they're very creative. I think their work is very powerful, but I think it's very naive—sort of, if you like, a petulant young child out of control." (Peter Murphy, Bauhaus)

Paul McCartney

"I'd join a band with **John Lennon** any day, but I wouldn't join a band with Paul McCartney." (**George Harrison**)

Mark McGrath, Sugar Ray

"Mark chooses to live the lifestyle. He parties every single night of the week. He's the most Hollywood guy of all time. He's gotta be seen." (**DJ Homicide, Sugar Ray**)

George Michael

"Imagine having sex with George Michael. It would be like having sex with a groundhog." (**Boy George**)

The Monkees

"Oh god, I hate them. Dishwater!" (**Jimi Hendrix**)

Alanis Morissette

"[*Jagged Little Pill*] would make a dog's ears hurt." (**Tori Amos**)

Morrissey

"He sometimes brings out records with the greatest titles in the world, which somewhere along the line he neglects to write songs for." (**Elvis Costello**)

The New York Dolls

"The Dolls are all right if you want a good laugh, but they're so very camp and silly. I mean, one of them is quite pretty, but he can't sing." (**Mick Jagger**)

"The Dolls scared the life out of me. I took one look at them and I thought, 'If they can play anything like they look, we've had it.' Fortunately, they couldn't." (**Ian Hunter, Mott the Hoople**)

Nirvana

"I'll match the power of my ballads with anything Nirvana are doing." (Barry Manilow)

Oasis

"Oasis are definitely not the Beatles. They're a mediocre pop band." (Sean Lennon)

"Someone went to introduce us. I went to shake [Liam Gallagher's] hand, and he put his nose in the air. So I put my middle finger in his face. We started yelling at each other. But we wound up doing cocaine until ten o'clock in the morning. Blame it on the drugs—I think that was the only reason we were talking to each other." (Twiggy Ramirez, Marilyn Manson)

"A complete knobhead." (Noel Gallagher, on Liam)

"Liam is so vain that if he went into hospital he'd insist on having the X rays retouched." (Paul Gallagher, Liam and Noel's brother)

"I don't have much respect for Oasis. They're just a group who copied the behavior and marketing campaign of the Rolling Stones and the Beatles (Geri Halliwell, former Spice Girl, who has a pretty firm grip on that subject herself)

RAVING BEAUTIES

Divalicious!

Mary J. Blige

Mariah Carey

The Eurythmics (an engineer who worked with them says, "They had a feudal system. They were the king and queen, and you were the serfs. Despite their image, they treated everyone badly, especially the musicians.")

Sammy Hagar

Whitney Houston

Mick Hucknall

Elton John ("I could be unbelievably horrible and stupid. On tours, I'd get on a plane then get off it maybe six or eight times. I'd walk out of a hotel suite because I didn't like the color of the bedspread. I remember looking out of my room at the Inn on the Park one day and saying, 'It's too windy. Can someone please do something about it?' ")

Courtney Love

Babs Streisand

Ozzy Osbourne

"Ozzy Osbourne is a moron. He couldn't carry a tune around in a suitcase." **(Ronnie James Dio)**

"Ozzy has the attention span of about two seconds. He has all these nervous habits that he's totally oblivious of. We were at [son] Jack's school for a parent-teacher meeting recently, where there were these five ladies around this table, and Ozzy's yawning loudly with his hand in front of his mouth. Then he lifts his shirt up and down, showing everybody his bare chest and belly. I'm like, 'Ozzy!' and he says, 'What? What have I done?' After we had been there for five minutes, he says, 'All right, can we go now?' " **(Sharon Osbourne)**

"From what I've seen, Sharon [Ozzy's wife] is in charge. Ozzy may be Ozzy, but he may only be Ozzy because he's in the body of Ozzy. His wife is really Ozzy as well." **(Marilyn Manson)**

Iggy Pop

"Very sweet, but very stupid." **(Lou Reed)**

Lou Reed

"Lou isn't my friend, though. Because he wouldn't share his drugs with me. He was taking Octagell, which is the strongest form of speed. You know of it? It makes your teeth clench together. Also, I had to leave his house because he was beating his girlfriend." **(Nico)**

William Reid, The Jesus and Mary Chain

"You think about killing each other, then you think, 'Nah, I don't want to go to jail over him. It's not worth it.' " (**Jim Reid**, on his brother and bandmate, **William**)

Keith Richards

"He's the only dirty man I know who doesn't smell." **(Ron Wood)**

"I wouldn't piss on him if he were on fire." **(Sid Vicious)**

The Rolling Stones

"I despise those cunts. The Stones should have quit in 1965." (**Sid Vicious**)

"Them touring at their age is like Evita going on tour stuffed in that glass case of hers." (**Lemmy, Motörhead**)

Axl Rose, Guns N' Roses

"Axl is a magnet for problems." (**Slash, master of understatement**)

"On the average, Axl is pretty unreliable. He's always been that way. It's no big deal." (**Slash**)

"Without the other four of us around, I wouldn't even *want* to imagine what the fuck would go on in his head. Or his life." (**Izzy Stradlin**)

Diana Ross

"She is a piece of licorice in shoes. She walks into a pool hall and they chalk her head." (**Joan Rivers**)

The Sex Pistols

"I think the Sex Pistols have copped out. Now they're on the cover of *Rolling Stone*. That's a real cop-out." (**Mick Jagger**)

"They're not the brightest people on God's earth." (**Johnny Rotten, on his ex-bandmates**)

Grace Slick

"Fuck Grace Slick? I wouldn't even let her *blow* me." (**Marty Balin**)

Patti Smith

"All I could think about was her B.O. She wouldn't be bad looking if she would wash up and glue herself together a little better." (Andy Warhol)

"I think she's so awful . . . a poseur of the worst kind—intellectual bullshit. Trying to be a street girl when she doesn't seem to be one. A useless guitar player, a bad singer, not attractive." (Mick Jagger)

Sonny and Cher

"Sonny and Cher are a drag. A guy gets kicked out of a restaurant and he went home and wrote a song about it." (Bob Dylan)

Spandau Ballet

"Spandau Ballet . . . amateur hour! Stuff like jamming at rehearsals which you'd chuck out and wouldn't consider putting on plastic. To them, that's a tour de force." (Johnny Rotten)

"You can't drink on an eight-hour flight, pass out, then go onstage . . . well, you can, but then you're Spandau Ballet." (Robert Smith, The Cure)

The Spice Girls

"The Spice Girls aren't a dignified creation. I mean, they're fun, but I wouldn't want to be in them." (Damon Albarn, Blur)

"The Spice Girls are like heroin. You know somebody's doin' it, but nobody is willing to admit that it is them." (Chris Rock)

Bruce Springsteen

"We used to eat guys like him for breakfast." (Patti Smith)

Sting

"Somebody should clip Sting around the head and tell him to stop singing in that ridiculous Jamaican accent." (Elvis Costello)

Michael Stipe, REM

"He's like, 'Oh God, man, I suffer for my art.' And I'm like, 'Oh, fuck off. Go and suffer somewhere else, but don't do it on MTV when I got to watch you, you cunt." (Noel Gallagher, Oasis)

Babs Streisand

"She said she wondered if [TV] shows like *South Park* are responsible for all the negativity in today's culture. She doesn't realize that *she's* responsible." (*South Park* creators/writers Matt Stone and Trey Parker)

The Supremes

"All the old Supremes fans are winos with false teeth." (Rick James)

Tiffany

"She hasn't got a look, and she's got a dumpy body and no talent that I can see." (Dave Mustaine, Megadeth)

Van Halen

"Classic Van Halen made you want to drink, dance, and fuck. Current Van Halen encourages us to drink milk, drive a Nissan, and have a relationship." (David Lee Roth)

Frank Zappa

"Frank Zappa is probably the single most untalented person I've heard in my life. He's two-bit, pretentious, academic, and he can't play his way out of anything. He can't play rock 'n' roll, because he's a loser. And that's why he dresses so funny. He's not happy with himself, and I think he's right." (Lou Reed)

If You Don't Know Me by Now

I just gotta be me

"I have always preferred people to bottle things up—which, of course, you're not supposed to do these days—because I can't stand vomitous eruptions of emotion." (Damon Albarn, Blur)

"You have to be a bastard to make it, and that's a fact. And the Beatles are the biggest bastards on earth." (John Lennon)

"I'm just bursting on the scene like a pathetic, gold-plated sperm." (Beck)

"I don't mind being thought of as a moody bastard. That's my thing. I wear black and don't give a fuck." (rebel sans cause Ritchie Blackmore)

"My persona is so confused it even confuses me." (David Bowie)

"Most artists are insecure, I suppose—insecure overachievers." (Lindsey Buckingham)

"We're fucking forty-four-year-old men, and we're behaving like children. It's silly—absolutely fucking idiotic. Retarded." (Eric Burdon)

"There's a party in my mind, and I hope it never stops." (David Byrne)

"We're just normal people." (Karen Carpenter)

"I was always the seven-stone weakling." (Eric Clapton)

"I'm absolutely despicably boring." (Elvis Costello)

"I'm a pacifist until you come into my house, and then I'll kill your children." (Elvis Costello)

COMPROMISING POSITIONS

"I'd rather not compromise. I'm in it for the musical adventure."
(Joni Mitchell)

"I'm sick of musicians saying, 'I don't care what you wanna hear, I'm gonna play whatever I want 'cause I'm an artist.' You're an artist? Paint my house, bitch!"
(Gene Simmons, Kiss)

"I'm like a suburban housewife, taking the occasional Valium, doing the dishes, putting on my *Texas Chainsaw Massacre* video." (Evan Dando, The Lemonheads)

"I'm the guy who does the 'live' thing." (Peter Frampton)

"I'm just an ordinary guy who likes to get through life on an even keel." (Justin Hayward, The Moody Blues)

"If I seem free, it's because I'm always running." (Jimi Hendrix)

"In most artists there's a self-destructive streak. Drugs, sex, and doomed liaisons were my form of destruction." (Elton John)

"I can't think of any other group that turns up to a gig, spends a couple of hours talking to the fans outside a fish-and-chip shop, and then goes home." (Mick Jones, The Clash)

"You know, people think I'm all cuddly and lovely and beautifully pop-starrish. I'm not, really I'm not." (Elton John)

"If a painter is doing a painting, he does it by himself. I just paint my picture with sound." (Lenny Kravitz)

"Mild barbarians is how we were once described, and I can't really deny it." (Jimmy Page, Led Zeppelin)

"I'm a different type of asshole. I'm an *intentional* asshole." (Marilyn Manson)

"I'm just a very well-paid juvenile delinquent." (Al Jourgensen, Ministry)

"If this was a slightly more primitive time, I would already be burning at the stake. I expect there is still time for that." (Morrissey)
Hopefully you're right.

"If we moved in next door, your lawn would die." (Lemmy, Motörhead)

"In a word, I'm boring." (Randy Newman)

"I've always wanted to be a drum machine." (Stephen Morris, New Order)

"I am a dork." (Iggy Pop)

"I cry at Walt Disney movies when the dog is defending the child against an enraged bear." (Lou Reed)

"I am the field marshal of rock 'n' roll." (Patti Smith)

"I'm equal parts **Brando** and **Balenciaga**." (Patti Smith)

"If we were all devastatingly handsome and actually liked one another, we'd probably be **Duran Duran** or the biggest band on earth. As it is, I'm actually quite a decent chap, and the rest of the group are wankers." (Jools Holland, Squeeze)

"I'm so tight, I don't spend a penny. I don't mind buying a round, but I can't stand buying two." (Rod Stewart)

"Given the choice of friendship or success, I'd probably choose success." (Sting)

That's an enlightened viewpoint, Mr. Buddha.

"I probably embody that whole idealism/cynicism conundrum that my generation and people younger than me carry." (Michael Stipe)

"I was always a freak. Never a hippie, but always a freak." (Frank Zappa)

"Someone once described me as the original hippie, and that's because of the flowery lyrics, you know, and also because of the buzz we give out."
(Robert Plant)

Dumb and Dumber

"The majority of pop stars are complete idiots in every respect."
(Sade)

"Being intelligent is not a prerequisite for being a rock star."
(Sting, who should know)

Fiona Apple's speech at the MTV Video Music Awards in 1997 reached new heights of inanity *(partially excused by the fact that she's only eleven years old or something):*
"I'm not going to do this like everybody else does it. . . . This world is bullshit. . . . It's just stupid that I'm in this world, but you're all very cool to me."

"I am a mess and you're a mess too. Everyone's a mess—which means, actually, that no one's a mess."
(Fiona Apple)
Except you.

"I'm not very mental at all, believe me." (Sammy Hagar)
That's hard to believe—I thought "I Can't Drive 55" was a cogent and searing indictment of our society.

"The biggest misconception people have about me is that I'm stupid." (Billy Idol)

"The ramifications of death are final." (Cyndi Lauper)

"My brains are oatmeal." (Mick Mars, Mötley Crüe)

"I don't think about deep things." (Ted Nugent)

"In my heart I feel Mexican-German. I feel if I were to organize it correctly, I would try to sing like a Mexican and think like a German. I get it mixed up sometimes anyway. I sing like a Nazi and I think like a Mexican, and I can't get anything right." (Linda Ronstadt)

GAY PRIDE

"I started being really proud of the fact that I was gay even though I wasn't."
(Kurt Cobain)

"Everyone thinks I'm queer. And I kind of am—except for the dick part."
(Jonathan Davis, Korn)

"I'm a bisexual man who's never had a homosexual experience."
(Brett Anderson, singer, Suede)

"I want to be an artist who is appreciated. Maybe I should do something for cancer research or something." (Diana Ross)

"Sometimes I get bored riding down the beautiful streets of L.A. I know it sounds crazy, but I just want to go to New York and see people . . . suffer." (Donna Summer)

Diana Ross stomped out of a meeting with execs from Revlon after one of them said he felt "certain that [she] could do quite a bit for the black women's market of cosmetics." Sniffed one of her handlers, "Miss Ross is not black. Not in her mind, and not in the mind of anyone who works for her."

"I've never in my life succeeded in reading a book from cover to cover." (Posh Spice [Victoria Addams])

"I want an Internet. Can I have one . . . ?" (Scary Spice [Mel B])

"You can write a book on each of my thoughts." (Vanilla Ice)
See Dick play. See Jane run.

"Sometimes you might want to take your brain out of your head and wash it to make you clean, but you can't." (Mark Wahlberg)

Regarding his star turn in *Boogie Nights*, **Mark Wahlberg** worries, "I just hope God is a movie fan or at least understands that the movie is just a movie. I think it's okay. But I don't know if any of it is okay."

Philosophy Majors

Rockers ponder weighty matters

"In these high-charged moments, where time and history are supposed to come to a cross point, it's not a time to soberly step back and consider all the questions in the universe. It's a time to stick your dick in the gopher hole. It's time to head-butt a eunuch." (Beck)

"A day at a time. That serves me very well. I think it's the greatest principle of all. When I first heard that phrase, I couldn't believe how close it was to the Buddhist principles." (David Bowie)

"Keeping up with the times is just a matter of living every day." (Judy Collins)

"Make a bigger place in the universe for your head to live in and it will grow to fill the space." (David Crosby)

"In England, kids are disillusioned with having too little. In America, they're disillusioned with having too much." (Dennis de Young, Styx)

"A man is a success if he gets up in the morning and gets to bed at night and in between he does what he wants to." (Bob Dylan)

"I know in my own mind what I'm doing. If anyone has imagination, he'll know what I'm doing. If they can't understand my songs, they're missing something. If they can't understand green clocks, wet chairs, purple lamps, or hostile statues, they're missing something too." (Bob Dylan)

"I haven't really got a home anywhere. The earth's my home." (Jimi Hendrix)

"Everyone in the world is getting fucked one way or the other. All you can do is see that you aren't fucking them directly." (Paul Kantner)

"All love is lucky, even when it breaks your heart." (Madonna)

"Turn the other cheek too often and you get a razor through it." (Johnny Rotten)

"You can't entertain a man who has no food." (Bob Marley)

"People are interested in bridges. I guess I've always been interested in what goes on beneath bridges."
(Bono)

SOUND ADVICE

Good advice for musicians . . . by musicians!

"To get your playing more forceful, hit the drums harder."
(Keith Moon)

"Don't eat at McDonald's."
(Trey Anastasio, Phish)

"Don't use speed! It'll mess up your liver, your heart and kidneys, and screw your mind up, and in general will make you just like your parents."
(Frank Zappa)

"If you feel like singing along, don't."
(James Taylor)

"Don't get a canvas [guitar] strap. Get something smooth so it doesn't leave a brush burn on your shoulder. And make sure it's colorfast so it doesn't bleed all over the slick new shirt you bought to look smooth at your gig."
(Johnny Rzeznik, Goo Goo Dolls)

"I am interested in anything about revolt, disorder, chaos—especially activity that seems to have no other meaning." (Jim Morrison, who specialized in meaningless activity)

"I'm still searching for an angel with a broken wing. It's not very easy to find them these days. Especially when you're staying at the Plaza Hotel." (Jimmy Page)

"I love people. I love life. I'm happy to be alive. I'll never grow old. We're all brothers and sisters in one big family. We all have power. We're all full of beauty just waiting to explode. It's always springtime." (Jonathan Richman)

"There is no light so full of hope as that of the dawn." (John Squire, guitarist, Stone Roses)

"Fuck the whole fuckin' world, you know? Let's just keep movin'." (Izzy Stradlin)

"You have to keep busy. After all, no dog's ever pissed on a moving car." (Tom Waits)

"One of my favorite philosophical tenets is that people will only agree with you if they already agree with you. You do not change people's minds." (Frank Zappa)

96 Tears

Or, Why life is difficult because I'm a rock star

"I'm only twenty-two, and I feel I've seen everything. It makes it very difficult sometimes." (Johnny Rotten)

"My body is damaged from music in two ways: not only has my stomach inflamed from irritation, but I have scoliosis. . . . It gives me back pain all the time. That really adds to the pain in our music. It really does. I'm kind of grateful for it." (Kurt Cobain)

"It's against the law to destroy Jews, blacks, people for religious causes. All we have is celebrity, and every society has to kick a dog, someone to raise and someone to burn." (Michael Hutchence)

"I didn't laugh for about two years. I was just very overwhelmed by a lot of it. For a long time I didn't see the beauty in being in the public eye." (Alanis Morissette)

"You don't have to be perfect to be Christ. All you have to do is stick your neck out and say the system sucks. They'll find a way of nailing you to the cross." (Eric Burdon)

"People see rock stars when they're onstage or on TV or on album jackets and it looks glamorous. They don't see the Holiday Inns and Howard Johnsons and the plane rides and the six hours to get to a gig in West Virginia or the twenty hours in a bus to drive from Austin to Iowa City. They don't see the eight months a year away from home. There are times when I don't know what town I'm in." (John Hall)

"Having waited so long to be successful, I found out it was a terrible anticlimax." (Rod Stewart)

"The only thing I ever got out of fame was a better table in a restaurant." (David Bowie)

"If you were a normal person walking down the street, they wouldn't come up to you and say, 'Cor, I think you're ugly.' If you're famous, they think it's a right." (Gary Numan)

"I don't want to spend the rest of my life changing my phone number every thirty days." (**Van Morrison**)

"Having seen more of what's around me and what's going on in this country, I can't really be happy about it. I can't really kick back and sing about how life is good and everything is good while all I see is tragedy around me." (**Eddie Vedder** explains his tendency to whine)

"Rock 'n' roll, in comparison to motor racing, is so much more dangerous. I've known so many more people who have been really awful casualties of the music business and drugs. It's higher-risk than people realize." (**Nick Mason, Pink Floyd**)

"We really are shit magnets. I don't know why that is. Maybe we are just spoiled brats that need attention, but the shit just follows us." (**Tommy Lee, Mötley Crüe**)

"Everything about the romantic notion of being the biggest rock band in the world was blown to shreds. I'd gotten everything I'd ever dreamed about from the time I was a teenager, and it felt terrible. . . . It was a time of major alcoholism, major depression." (**Jon Bon Jovi**)

"I was totally miserable. Partying like a fiend but depressed as hell. But you know, it's sex, drugs, and rock 'n' roll, baby. What do you want? That's the way it is." (**Mick Hucknall**)

"It's not commonplace for people to get to the top of this profession when they're very young and then to live happily ever after." (**George Michael**)

"In the end, you become part of everything you hate, basically." (**Ray Davies, The Kinks**)

"I *am* crazy. I mean, you have to be crazy to put yourself through this all the time." (**Janet Jackson**)

"Onstage, I make love to twenty-five thousand different people, then I go home alone." (**Janis Joplin**)

"Once I was doing a commercial with **Tina Turner** in the south of France and I had the top suite of the Carlton Hotel and I was flying birds in from everywhere and shagging them. I was so fucking unhappy." (**Rod Stewart**)

"If I had the capabilities of being something other than I am, I would. It's no fun being an artist." (John Lennon)

"Being a Beatle was a nightmare." (George Harrison)

"I remember at one point glancing in the mirror and once again saying to myself, 'Will I have to sit in front of this mirror and spend hours putting on makeup for the rest of my life?' This is what I have been doing since I was a child—putting this stuff on my face, then going onstage for two or two and a half hours, maybe three at the most, and then having to undergo the misery of taking it all off again." (Diana Ross)

"Somebody told me that I don't make small talk and that's why men hate me." (Yoko Ono)
That must be it.

"Just because I have my standards, they think I'm a bitch." (Diana Ross)

"When I travel, I love to be invited to use someone's private plane, because that way I can look funky—I don't have to dress up at all. But that isn't always possible. Sometimes I have to walk through public airports where people see me, and there is this expectation that I look a certain way. I have to be Diana Ross, the performer, the star—not Diana, the human being, the mother, the weary traveler." (Diana Ross)

"I always dreamed of being famous and rich, but when it happened it was a nightmare. . . . By 1993, things were turning sour. Sure, I'd blown a fortune on partying and wild living. But nothing compared to the millions my records earned. Quite a few people from my former management team are millionaires today thanks to me. When I finally took stock of what I had left, there was virtually nothing left." (Vanilla Ice)

"For every dollar I make, there's a pool of sweat on the floor." (Bob Dylan)

"Because of who we are and what we represent, if we were ever in a car wreck, they'd leave us to die." (Ozzy Osbourne)

"One thing that depresses me is that there are so many successful people that are fucking *miserable* with it. It's so important to have fun with your success." (Elton John)
That's right, Mr. Bulimia.

LIFE
IN
THE
FAST
LANE

Life's Been Good to Me So Far

"For me, a rock star's not necessarily a musician in a popular band, but some coke-sniffing, supermodel-fucking, Learjet-riding freak."
(Dave Grohl, Foo Fighters)

As Elton John reminds us (see page 156), you've got to have fun with your celebrity status. After all, if you can't enjoy the spoils of success, what's the point of trying so hard to get it?

Rock stars are divided about evenly into two opposing camps: the ones who eschew the trappings of fame and whine about wanting to be left alone, and those who revel in their newfound positions as gods of the musical stratosphere. Case in point: Marilyn Manson's likable dim-bulb Twiggy Ramirez, who says, "It's all about money, girls, and drugs. That's what it comes down to. Money, girls, drugs, and music last. If you have money, then you have the freedom to be able to do the drugs and get away with it and not be a loser. And, well, girls are always there. And also, if you have money and you're a rock star, no one looks down on you if you're on drugs. You're allowed to. That's one of the status symbols of being a rock star. And I guess if you have all those other things, then you have the freedom to keep on being able to make music." Another very good point, as voiced by paragon of decadence Dave Navarro: "Extreme artists are an avenue—people live vicariously through us." So true.

"Now it's a whole asexual, 'we don't want to be stars, we stare at our shoes' kind of thing. I sort of feel sorry for guys now, because they're missing out on how wonderful, how glamorous, and how goofy being a rock star used to be."
(Jon Bon Jovi)

Life of Illusion

The celebrity lifestyle, while providing large rewards, also promotes insularity and an inevitable distancing of oneself from reality. Anyone even on the periphery of fame knows how hard it is to keep one's feet on the ground. "They all crack up over that—end up believing their own publicity themselves. Completely out of it," noted Johnny Rotten. Bret Michaels, of eighties hair-band Poison, would tend to agree—because he's lived it: "[I] was partying and becoming everything I swore I would not become. I swore I would never try to satisfy myself by surrounding myself with a bunch of 'yes' people telling me I'm the greatest thing on earth. It's what I vowed I wouldn't become. And you can't help but become it when you have too much time off the road and you're not being creative."

"I like rock stars. I'm a rock star. I'm glad rock stars and supermodels are becoming popular again. They are the only superheroes we have. Because life is painful, life sucks, you want things that seem fun, exciting."
(Scott Weiland)
Like heroin addiction?

Sex and Drugs and Rock 'n' Roll

"You read about the excesses of the rock 'n' roll stars of the seventies—driving Rolls-Royces into swimming pools. Well, that's better than *polishing* them."
(Bono)

"I don't think interviews oughta be done unless you've just driven a Rolls-Royce into a Holiday Inn pool."
(Grace Slick)

"It was a strange experience, flying around the world in a private plane and getting boozed. An interesting way to make a living, but definitely strange."
(Robbie Robertson, The Band)

"Basically, as a rock star, your nearest equivalent in history is a Roman emperor. You have enough money to fill a room with cocaine and women and drink. You can debauch yourself to death."
(Sting)

"The slogan in the sixties was sex, drugs, and rock 'n' roll. The slogan now is drugs and sex and rock 'n' roll."
(Mick Jagger)

"Being in control, snorting coke, having fabulous sex, having friends over in your hot tub, doing crazy things, finding some cool, confident woman who looks so hot you never have to look for one again."
(Courtney Taylor, Dandy Warhols front man, on his goals in life)

"ROCK STAR FEVER"

"When I think about those records, I remember the time we had when we were making them. That's why I like *Volume Four* [1972]. We'd got the rock star fever by then—limousines everywhere, groupies sucking our dicks, dealers dropping by with bags of white powder. By the time we did *Sabotage* [1975], we were all fucked up with drugs. . . ."
(Ozzy Osbourne, on his stint in Black Sabbath)

"A photograph of Keith Richards at his most wasted says more than anything just exactly what rock 'n' roll is all about."
(Ian Hunter)

"I think if you take sex, drugs, and rock and roll, let your imagination run wild, and then multiply it by ten, then you'll have an idea of what our life has been like."
(Vince Neil, Mötley Crüe)

"I just can't figure out why you need to have something to do. I'd rather stay in bed and grab a handful of oatmeal and put it in my mouth and have some broad give me a blow job and grab the syringe and jab it in."
(Richard Hell, The Voidoids)

"We don't want to be known as some fucking spaced-out Mancunians who've got nothing better to do than take drugs and make music."
(Ian Brown, Stone Roses)

The High Life

How Marilyn Manson and company lead
their lives of excess

"I was . . . coke, blow job . . . coke, blow
job . . . "
(Madonna Wayne Gacy, a/k/a Pogo)

"If you take a break from the excesses of
sex and drugs every once in a while, you
can turn your odometer over and start
again."
(Marilyn Manson)

"Sex and drugs and rock 'n' roll: too
much of any one fucks up the other two."
(Madonna Wayne Gacy)

"This whole past year, my house has
become a real Hollywood Babylon, Studio
54 type of place. It's a magnet for the
where-are-they-nows and the they're-not-
doin'-real-good-nows. I started a project—
usually at about six or seven in the
morning—of taking these
unlikely individuals and putting them
together to sing karaoke in my living
room. So at any given moment you may
have found Leif Garrett or Corey
Feldman singing the theme from
Grease. I've also been painting these
ten-minute portraits. Sometimes I
trade them for drugs, so there's a lot
of portraits of drug dealers going
around town."
(Marilyn Manson)

Money Honey

"My goal was riches in the uppermost strata."
(Harry Nilsson, who used to bathe in Brandy Alexanders)

Money—particularly the kind of ultralarge infusion of cash received by a successful rock star—changes everything. Suddenly, the kid who couldn't afford to buy a hot dog at Kmart is now dining in five-star style and hiring private chefs to tour with him (not to mention learning how to use all those different kinds of forks). Private planes and limos replace more mundane forms of locomotion, and he can blow big wads on anything that strikes his fancy—leading to some fun examples of conspicuous consumption (like Liam Gallagher, who once spent £1,800 for ten pairs of designer sunglasses in one shot—as far as I know, he only has one set of eyes).

"People say I'm a millionaire, but that's not true—I only spend millions."
(Robert Plant)

SPREADING THE WEALTH: THE COLLECTOR

Mick Fleetwood: vintage sports cars, handmade pinstripe suits

Graham Coxon, Blur: rare hardcore punk albums

John Entwistle, The Who: armor, antique guns, brass instruments, teapots, porcelain, guitars (owns 230), animals (nine Rottweilers, an Irish wolfhound, three Labs, two parrots, a tarantula, six horses, twelve goats)

John McVie, Fleetwood Mac: Nazi memorabilia (David Bowie, too, during his "Thin White Duke" phase)

Morrissey: vintage jeans, '50s wrestling magazines

Peter Gabriel: Robert Mapplethorpe photographs

Dave Stewart, The Eurythmics: art (Salvador Dali, Damien Hirst)

Rick Wright, Pink Floyd: Persian and Turkish carpets

SPREADING THE WEALTH: THE COLLECTOR (CONTINUED)

Ian Anderson, Jethro Tull: guns, musical instruments, landscape paintings by Sir William Russell Flint and the Newlyn School

Noel Gallagher, Oasis: Beatles memorabilia

Jimmy Page: Aleister Crowley memorabilia, occult antiques and trinkets

Rod Stewart: art collection (worth £15 million), cars (Ferraris, Porsches, Lamborghinis)

Eric Clapton: guns, art

David Bowie: art (Basquiat, Egon Schiele, Graham Sutherland, William Tillier)

Mick Jagger: art (gave Bill and Mandy Wyman a £200,000 Picasso as a wedding gift)

Elton John: photography, Erte, Magritte, Picasso, also owns more than fifty thousand albums

Simon LeBon, Duran Duran: yachts, racing bikes

Elton John owned fourteen cars at one point in time, and blew gazillions on his trademark oddball shades and fancy clothes (he dropped £150,000 for Versace garb to outfit his pudgy frame during one tour). Says the notorious spendthrift: "You can't become a slave to money. If money dictates your life and you spend years trying to save money—for what? You could die. You could have a heart attack. You could be knocked over by a bus. You spend all your life trying to save money, being unhappy, and living in a place you don't want to, and all of a sudden, pow, you're dead. Great fun. That's ridiculous."

"If you don't go for as much money as you can possibly get, then I think you're stupid."
(Mick Jagger)

Like Elton John, Keith Richards has champagne taste: between April and November of 1971, Richards's weekly bills were £1,000 for food, £1,000 for booze, £2,500 for illegal substances, and £2,500 rent for a Cote d'Azur villa. Sound like a lot? Well, he was actually living well within his means—this rather significant outlay wasn't even a third of his weekly income at the time!

SPREADING THE WEALTH: GARAGE BANDS

Paul Arthurs, Oasis: £85,000 Aston Martin, Jaguar, Rolls-Royce Silver Shadow

Nick Mason, Pink Floyd: among other very high-end autos, owns a £1 million Ferrari 250GTO (one of only forty made) and a £414,000 Jaguar XJ220

Rick Parfitt, Status Quo: a speedboat, his own plane, six Porsches, and a load of classic American cars

Tommy Cunningham, drummer, Wet Wet Wet: Ferrari Testarossa

Noel Gallagher, Oasis: a Rolls-Royce, six miniature Jaguars

George Michael: £3 million Cessna airplane

Robert Plant: hot pink Chrysler Imperial Crown convertible

"Rather than living in five-star hotels—which I think would be much more extravagant—we have very beautiful homes. The only embarrassment is that it draws a big line between the haves and have-nots. . . ."
(Trudie Styler, spouse o' Sting)
Yes—we must leave the little people their illusions.

Don't think this life of privilege is taken for granted. Stevie Nicks says, "I totally appreciate being able to buy, say, this thousand-dollar cashmere blanket. . . . Because if I couldn't, I would hate the fact that I would have to go back to real, regular blankets."

"I've been living on [the royalties from] 'Sister Morphine' for ten years, which is really bizarre—don't tell me drugs don't pay!"
(Marianne Faithfull)

One good way to make money is by doing what David Bowie did: mortgaging the rights to ten years' worth of future royalties by floating himself on the stock market. (The thin white kook picked up a very cool $55 million for his "Bowie bonds," which were expected to return about eight percent annually to investors.

We'll see.) Other rockers have since followed suit, although they attempt to distance themselves from Bowie and his crass "investment package"; said Rod Stewart about *his* six-million-dollar deal: "It's totally different to David Bowie. Bowie sold his master tapes, his touring, his publishing, everything. I just sold my publishing for the next twelve years. . . . It's a good way to take money on a loan, and you don't have to pay taxes on it." (Yeah baby—that's far superior.)

"The guy who said money can't buy you happiness didn't know where to go shopping!"
(David Lee Roth)

Spreading all this new wealth around can sometimes be a chore, especially if superannuated shopkeepers have no clue who you are. Def Leppard guitarists Steve Clark and Phil Collen, both completely inebriated, once wandered into a posh shop, where a snobby salesman looked down his aquiline nose at the ragamuffin rockers. This so incensed the two that they plunked down £17,000 for Rolex watches (what does that buy you—one-and-a-half?).

SPREADING THE WEALTH: GARAGE BANDS (CONTINUED)

Eric Clapton: £40,000 speedboat (never even taken out of its packing case!), £400,000 1957 Ferrari

Keith Moon: lilac Rolls-Royce, hovercraft

Gary Numan: Ferrari, three airplanes, bought a Daimler for his dad and a Tiger Moth plane for his brother

Elton John: purchased a tram in Melbourne, Australia, and had it shipped home to England

Jason Kay, Jamiroqui: a Lamborghini, two Mercedes, two BMWs, three Ferraris, an Aston Martin, a Ducati minimotorcycle

Keith Richards: Nazi staff car (a Mercedes he totaled the day after he got it), Bentley (fell asleep at the wheel and wrecked this car too)

"Bro, I was spending money as quick as I could make it. Clothes, rented jets, a boat, going to the Palm and ordering four-and-a-half-pound lobsters, leaving $500 tips at bars—man, my credit card bills ran from $70,000 to $150,000 a month."
(Mark Wahlberg)

Why one should always keep an eye on one's bank account: Sting was defrauded by his accountant, Keith Moore, in 1995—to the tune of nine million bucks! (Moore was jailed for his crimes.) Commented Gary Numan, "I'm not sure that I'm that stupid. How much must that guy have to not even notice losing so much money?" Of course, with the kinds of fees Sting commanded at the time (two million dollars for a private show for the Sultan of Brunei; £300,000 for a concert appearance for Nomura Asset, a Japanese company), maybe he can afford it. What's a few million among friends?

BANKABLE STARS

"They had to act like stars so they would be treated like stars. They had to learn to spend money, and spend it in the right way."
(Tony Defries, on management client David Bowie and band)

"Most bands don't make money—they just squander it on producers and cocaine and lots of other bullshit, and it's disgusting. There's so much idiotic excess."
(Sting)

"If I seem to be the new messiah, fantastic. My aim is to make a big pile and get out while the going is good."
(Nick Lowe)

"I have one basic drive on my side that they can't defeat: greed."
(Frank Zappa)

"The more you get, the more you get."
(Tom Petty)

"No, that's The Who."
(Ron Wood, when asked if The Stones were touring for the money)

Stung!

Gary Glitter used to live in a very sparsely furnished dwelling, so when he learned of an impending visit by family members, he rented the entire set of furnishings (including light fixtures) from the BBC television show *Duchess of Duke Street*. The cost? A mere £4,000—a week!

"You mean you can actually spend $70,000 at Woolworth's?"
(Bob Krasnow, Blue Thumb Records, after taking a gander at Ike and Tina Turner's house)

One of the biggest wad-blowers in pop is increasingly strange Michael Jackson, who has purchased various bizarre extravagances in his time, including his own private zoo at his sprawling "Neverland" complex in California. Jackson currently has big plans to construct a mega-casino/amusement park, the "Majestic Kingdom" (to include the "Thriller Theme Park"), in Detroit. The reason he wanted to go into the theme-park business in the first place, according to Jackson himself, was not for selfish material gain—noooooo, in the words of Jackson himself, it was so that "children will always have a bright and exciting future to look forward to." Discuss.

SPREADING THE WEALTH: HOUSES OF THE HOLY

"After reading Tolkien, I just had to have a place in the country."
(Robert Plant)

Brian Jones bought A. A. Milne's manor ("Pooh Corner"); Pete Townshend bought Alfred, Lord Tennyson's estate; The Who's John Entwistle has an eighty-six-room mansion (with seven cottages and a recording studio scattered about its forty-two acres) in Gloucestershire; Ian Anderson (Jethro Tull) bought an entire town (Strathaird, on the Isle of Sky), along with its associated salmon farm and processing factory; David Bowie has mansions in Dublin and Lausanne, and on Mustique, plus apartments in New York, Beverly Hills, and London; Noel Gallagher, half of Oasis, paid £1.2 million for a mansion in Belsize Park, which he named Supernova Heights (just so you can't miss it, the name is embedded in stained glass over the front door), plus an eight-bedroom house in Bucks; Robert Plant had a sheep ranch near Kensington; and Jimmy Page purchased Aleister Crowley's old Loch Ness mansion, Boleskine House.

"**We would rather be rich than famous. That is, more rich and slightly less famous.**"
(*John Lennon*)

"Somebody said to me, 'But the Beatles were antimaterialistic.' That's a huge myth. John and I literally used to sit down and say, 'Now, let's write a swimming pool.'" (Paul McCartney)

"Paul handed me a big parcel and I opened it and it was a picture of a horse. So I said, 'Very nice,' but I thought, 'What do I want with a picture of a horse?' Then Paul must have seen my face, because he said, 'It's not just a picture, Dad, I've bought you the bloody horse.'" (James McCartney)

"Nobody believes me that I came into music just because I wanted the bread." (Mick Jagger)

"Of course we're doing it for the money as well . . . we've always done it for the money." (Mick Jagger)

"Like I've said before, the Moodys are a Communist band run by a capitalist board." (Ray Thomas, Moody Blues)

"They're always saying I'm a capitalistic pig. I suppose I am. But it's good for my drumming." (Keith Moon)

GOING FOR BROKE

Rock 'n' roll bankruptcies

Toni Braxton

George Clinton

Mick Fleetwood

Gary Glitter

Isaac Hayes

After his monster hit "Theme from Shaft" hit the top of the charts in 1971, Hayes went out and bought himself a Cadillac fit for a king, complete with gold-plating and ermine lining, and a couple of mansions in Memphis. Amazingly, by 1976 he was millions in debt.

Meat Loaf

Tom Petty

Andy Rourke, XTC

Sly Stone

"**If you've got a mind-shattering talent, you want a million dollars for it.**"
(*Elton John*)

Political Animals

From the dopey peace-love-and-meditation diatribes of sixties rockers to Sting and his unrelenting "save the rain forest" campaign and Don Henley's tireless, tiresome "Walden Woods" efforts, rockers have always felt it was their place—nay, their God-given right—to expound on the issues nearest and dearest to their little bleeding hearts. Political action is all right if it's tongue-in-cheek, like Jello Biafra's 1979 San Francisco mayoral campaign (he actually placed fourth) or Joe Walsh's 1984 and 1988 U.S. presidency bids (his slogan? "He has never lied to the American public"). But in general, politics and music don't mix—let's just get that straight right now. Then maybe we won't have to hear the next generation sounding off other than in concert. Hey, I can dream.

"Think of us as erotic politicians." (Jim Morrison)

"Messages become a drag, like preaching. I think one of the worst possible beliefs is that pop stars know any more about life than anyone else." (Nick Mason, Pink Floyd)

"You can't trust politicians. It doesn't matter to me who makes a political speech. It's all lies . . . and it applies to any rock star who wants to make a political speech as well." (Bob Geldof)

He's really taken that one to heart, huh?

"[Al Gore] goes, 'I'm a really big fan,' and I was like, 'Yeah right. Name a song, Al.' 'I can't name a song, I'm just a really big fan.'" (Courtney Love)

"I hope you don't have anything in your past that's going to come back and haunt me." (Courtney Love, posing for photos with L.A. mayor Richard Riordan)

TELL IT LIKE IT IS

Rockers speak out on the hot-button topics of our time

Captain Beefheart on racism: "Everybody's colored—or else you wouldn't be able to see them."

Hugh Cornwell (The Stranglers) on the women's movement: "I like women to move when I'm on top of them."

"I don't know fuck about the U.N. I'd rather sing about rock 'n' roll and chicks. I think I'm much more in touch with that." (Tom Petty)

"We're so sick of the goody-goody stuff. 'Save the farmers, save the starving Africans.' It's all so perverse. In times when culture is living in a dream world and looking for silly things to get excited about, rock 'n' roll seems like the only sanity left."
(Lux Interior, The Cramps)

Some political objectives have rather short shelf lives

In March of 1975, rock promoter extraordinaire Bill Graham sponsored the SNACK (Students Need Athletics, Culture, and Kicks) concert featuring the Grateful Dead, Tower of Power, Jefferson Starship, Graham Central Station, Joan Baez, Neil Young, and Bob Dylan. The organization raised a few bucks for the San Francisco school system, then was never heard from again.

In December of 1970, Eric Burdon kicked off a "Curb the Clap" campaign (I use the term loosely—it was just a bunch of bumper stickers) to combat what he called "the number-one sickness in the record business today—VD [venereal disease]." Explained his manager, Steve Gold, "It's because Eric has the clap. He says from age fifteen to twenty-six he only had it once, but it's happened three or four times since."

John and Yoko staged an oh-so-sixties "bed-in for peace" (hair peace, bed peace, pillow peace, room peace, floor peace, ceiling peace, ad nauseam) in Amsterdam, the week after their wedding in 1969. In the eight days their asses were parked in bed, they only got up to use the bathroom. And world peace never happened.

"Starvation in India doesn't worry me one bit. No one iota, it doesn't, man. And it doesn't worry you, if you're honest. You just pose. You don't even know it exists. You've just seen the charity ads. You can't pretend to me that an ad reaches down into the depths of your soul and actually makes you feel more for these people than, for instance, you feel about getting a new car."
(Paul McCartney)

I'm a Believer

"I have a lot of faith. I don't believe in any kind of religion, though, 'cause religion is complete and total control through fear. My god is the god of the Christians, the god of the Jews, the Hindus, Muslims, Mormons, Martians—I believe in an energy of love which transcends all individuals, 'cause that's what keeps me and you alive. Let music and art connect us all by one universal energy, and let that be love."
(Scott Weiland)

The quest to find meaning in our trivial lives: It has stupefied the minds of far more intelligent beings than rock stars. Inexplicably, that doesn't stop 'em from trying. (Yes, you'll notice the same names on some of these lists. Enlightenment can be *so* confusing. And chances are, by the time you read this they'll all be on to something completely new.)

"I used to move in with people and fuck them because I thought they'd give me their powers. And they did." (Courtney Love)

"I sometimes speculate that [the human race] will evolve, temporarily at least, into machines." (Roger McGuinn)

"If you offered me a passionate love affair and you offered me a high priestess role in a fabulous castle above a cliff where I can just, like, live a very spiritual kind of religious-library-communing-with-the-stars, learning kind of existence, I'm going to go for the high priestess." (Stevie Nicks)

In February of 1971 (before Stevie and Lindsey's time), Fleetwood Mac was booked to do an L.A. gig at the Whisky a Go Go. On the afternoon of the gig, Jeremy Spencer ran out to do an errand— and never returned! A massive search was launched: the errant guitarist was hunted by Interpol, the FBI, and even psychics before finally being found hanging out with the Children of God cult—to whom he has devoted his life.

SHOUT AT THE DEVIL

Repent, ye sinners! Rock stars the Christian Right doesn't like, and why

Ozzy Osbourne: Worships the Dark Lord, wrote the song "Suicide Solution" (which has caused the deaths of so many innocent young men), and geez, he sometimes dresses up as an evil, hairy werewolf

The Rolling Stones: Had the bollocks to name one of their records *Their Satanic Majesties Request,* their blasphemous song "Paint It, Black," Brian Jones's recordings of African devil-worshipers

W.A.S.P.: The song "Animal (Fuck Like a Beast)," the pentagram in the group's logo, the live shows that featured front man Blackie Lawless simulating the drinking of blood

Mötley Crüe: The song "Shout at the Devil," the fact that they went on tour with Satan-worshipping Ozzy, the "devil horn" signs they make with their hands, the pentagrams in the band's artwork

Ronnie James Dio: The calligraphy in his logo spells "Devil" when turned upside down.

The Devil Inside

"When we came out of *The Exorcist,* we had to all stay in one room together—that's how black magic we were."
(Ozzy Osbourne, on Black Sabbath)

"Do what thou wilt shall be the whole of the law" was a philosophy espoused by **Jimmy Page** (who took it from infamous amoral mystic Aleister Crowley, who took it from Rabelais), well known for dabbling in the black arts (and thereby starting the persistent rumors about **Led Zeppelin** having sold their souls to the devil). But most Satan-worshiping rockers are mere poseurs—like Black Sabbath. Confesses Ozzy Osbourne, "The devil-worship thing was a marketing invention of the record company. We played along to put dough in our pockets."

Marilyn Manson is an ordained minister of Anton LaVey's Church of Satan.

"I don't worship the devil, but magic *does* intrigue me."
(Jimmy Page)

THE RECORD PLANT: VEGETARIANS

Bryan Adams

Damon Albarn

Joan Armatrading

Jeff Beck

Michael Bolton

Boy George

Belinda Carlisle

Peter Gabriel

Kevin Godley

Whitney Houston

Chrissie Hynde

Billy Idol

Joe Jackson

LaToya Jackson

Michael Jackson

Wendy James

Knockin' on Heaven's Door: Jehovah's Witnesses

Michael Jackson

Rock writer/singer Lester Bangs

George Benson

Ornette Coleman

Janet Jackson

Van Morrison

Heaven Is a Place on Earth: Muslims

Rap star Everlast

Ice Cube

Big Daddy Kane

Peter Murphy

Cat Stevens

Blinded by the Light: Eastern Mysticism

"I don't wanna take no year's sabbatical and go see some guru in the Himalayas to learn the secret of life. I don't think there's too many secrets to life, really."
(Charlie Daniels)

The Record Plant: Vegetarians (Continued)

Howard Jones

Martin and Gary Kemp (Spandau Ballet)

Nik Kershaw

Gladys Knight

Lenny Kravitz

Paul McCartney

Morrissey

Stevie Nicks

Ozzy Osbourne

That Thing Once Known as Prince

Seal

Siouxsie Sioux

Ringo Starr

Michael Stipe

Tanita Tikaram

Charlie Watts

Pete Townshend: Meher Baba

Seals and Crofts: Baha'I

Beatles: Maharishi Mahesh Yogi

Carlos Santana (took a new name—Devadip Carlos Santana—in September of 1973; "Devadip" translates as "the lamp of the light of the Supreme"): guru Sri Chinmoy

Gary "Dream Weaver" Wright: Paramahansa Yogananda (Wright and the guru were introduced—surprise, surprise—by George Harrison)

Think It Over: Transcendental Meditation

"If you really want to get it permanently . . . be healthy, don't eat meat, keep away from those nightclubs, and *meditate*."

(George Harrison)

Marianne Faithfull

Brian Jones

Donovan

Ray Manzarek

Beach Boys (used the Maharishi Mahesh Yogi as their opening act in 1968)

Eric Burdon

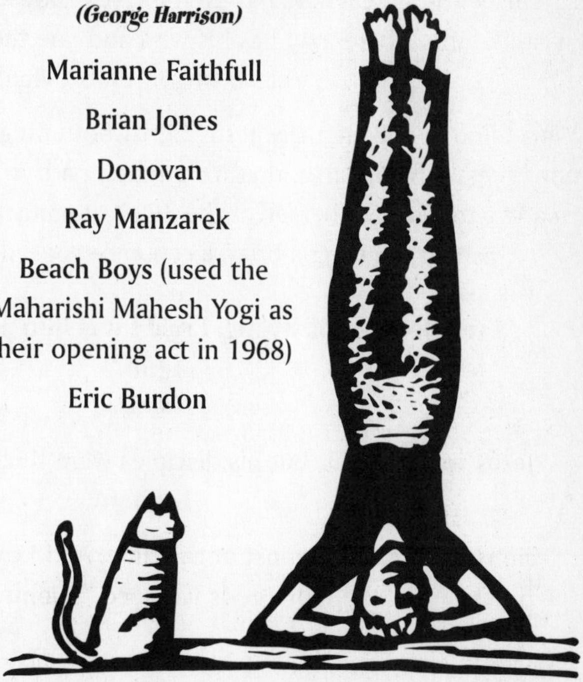

Livin' on a Prayer: Christian Mystics

"I hate Christmas. I like to go around and replace the Baby Jesus in the nativities with a boiled ham."
(Marilyn Manson)

Backstreet Boys

"Most people think we got kicked out of the Garden of Eden. I'm not so sure. I think we kicked God out of it." (Bono)
Bono, if you were in it, I think God would have turned tail and run.

Bob Dylan (Tried everything—Buddhism, Hinduism, psychics, Hasidism—then converted from Judaism to Christianity, celebrating this milestone by releasing the execrable album *Saved* in 1980)

"Satan is the ruler of this world." (Bob Dylan)

"This world is scheduled to go for seven thousand years, six thousand years of this where man has his way, and one thousand years when God has his way." (Bob Dylan)

"Nina Simone and, actually, Jesus Christ both taught me that your thanks is not necessarily on earth, that it's a rough path to tread." (Lauryn Hill, who made a total ass of herself at the 1998 Grammy Awards ceremony when, instead of giving a brief acceptance speech, she read a psalm)

"Everybody got it wrong. I said I was into porn again, not born again."
(Billy Idol)

"Jesus was all right, but his disciples were thick and ordinary." (John Lennon)

"Pain is what we're in most of the time. And I think the bigger the pain, the more gods we need." (John Lennon)

"I just can't picture Jesus doing a whole lotta shakin'." (Jerry Lee Lewis)

"I gave up rock 'n' roll for the rock of ages. If God can save me, an old homosexual, he can save anybody." (Little Richard, who left the music business at the peak of his popularity in 1958 to enter a four-year program at a college of evangelism)

Van Morrison

Roger McGuinn

Maria Muldaur

"I have dreams of angels holding notes indefinitely in perfect pitch, and you don't want it to stop because if it does, you're dead." (Prince, who announced he was going to "look for the ladder" in 1985, and therefore would be unable to perform live anymore)

"Anyone who thinks a Christian is soft can think again." (Cliff Richard)

Puff Daddy (reportedly making a gospel album)

Will Smith

Donna Summer

"I've been checking out churches—Catholic, Baptist. I haven't decided on any religion yet. But definitely, God is in my life." (Vanilla Ice)
But not vice versa.

"I thank the Lord for all the blessings he's brought upon me. I readily acknowledge him as my creator and beg him to be my savior. I let him know that I realize I am weak but that I want to be strong, and that my heart is open to being filled with nothing but the Lord's love." (Mark Wahlberg)

Papa Don't Preach: Buddhists

Boy George
Paula Cole
Mike Diamond, The Beastie Boys
Annie Lennox
Courtney Love
Lulu

Madonna: Searching . . . searching . . . is also a follower of Deepak Chopra, and was a part of his ridiculous *A Gift of Love* album, which featured his celeb pals reciting Persian poetry over a hokey New Age soundtrack), Ashtanga Yoga, Kabbalah (Judaism), and so on and so forth. Why? "I started asking myself, 'What's really important about life? Why am I here?' " Madonna explains. *We're all wondering the same thing.*

Alanis Morissette
Chris Novoselic
Sting
Tina Turner
Adam Yauch, Beastie Boys

Space Oddities

"I feel songs coming from across the galaxies to find me sometimes. They're busy doing something, disagreeing with Jabba the Hutt somewhere, and then they tear across the universe when I am really in a bad way." (Tori Amos)

"We are older than the sun and older than the moon. And now that we've released our new album, UFOs will no longer be able to crash on this planet." (Ol' Dirty Bastard/Big Baby Jesus, Wu-Tang Clan)

She Talks to Angels: Reincarnation

"I think all that afterlife thing has been invented because people can't accept that they're not too important to be finished with."
(Bill Wyman)

The **Beatles** made a pact that the first of them to die would send a message to the others from "beyond." **Paul McCartney** says, "**Stuart Sutcliffe** was the first to die, and I didn't have a message. When **John Lennon** died, he knew the deal—but I never had a message from him."

Terence Trent D'Arby claims **Marvin Gaye** sings to him from beyond the grave.

"What comes after [life]? The next thing. I don't believe in reincarnation, but I believe in the next life. I won't be coming back as a goat or anything." (**Lenny Kravitz**)
No, not when you're so highly evolved in this lifetime.

"In my next incarnation, I want to become a dolphin. . . . They've always got an undefinable glint in their eye, and the way they carry on I find very appealing." (**Robert Palmer**)

"I definitely feel that **Mick** [**Jagger**] and I knew each other in another lifetime." (**Tina Turner**)

Sundry Superstitions

After consulting a southwestern mystic before his second divorce, **John Denver** said, "The shaman found three pieces of me that had been missing."

"I have friend I talk to, a cowboy. Yeah, I met him in the desert. I was looking for spirituality, searching my butt off, and happened to run into this guy. He's older, very wise, works with horses, but he's experienced practically everything. And within thirty minutes of us talking, he knew my shit like he'd lived with me my entire life. I was like, *Fuuuuck*." (**Janet Jackson**)

Communication Breakdown

Fabulous rock 'n' roll feuds

Boy George vs. Jon Moss, Culture Club

> *"I always felt sorry for the rest of the band, having to suffer our fighting. No one was meant to know about me and Jon."*
> *(Boy George)*

> *"Our relationship was built on power-tripping and masochism. Our love, however diseased, was the creative force."*
> *(Boy George)*

Bandmates Boy George and Jon Moss had a decided difference of opinion when it came to Moss's sexual orientation. Although the pair were having a tempestuous affair, Moss insisted he was hetero, and would also sleep with female groupies. This didn't sit well with jealous George, and the boys had regular heated rows. Their fights, according to the Boy, got pretty vicious—they regularly threw whatever was at hand at each other, and put broken bottles to each other's throats. To no one's surprise, the affair ended bitterly. Says Jon now, "George has always harangued me publicly. In fact, the last time he was in [British rock rag] *Q*, he called me a 'No-dick dwarf.' "

> *"Sit down and have a chat together? Us? Not in this lifetime, darling."*
> *(Boy George)*

> *"We were never friends. We just fucked."*
> *(Boy George)*

Boston (the group, not the city) vs. CBS Records

Boston mastermind **Tom Scholz** compares his perfectionist streak to Mozart's—and while that may be pushing it a little, Boston's albums are certainly certifiable hard-rock classics. However, they each were years in the making due to Scholz's quest for perfection (he had a litany of excuses for not finishing, according to the president of the group's record label, CBS,

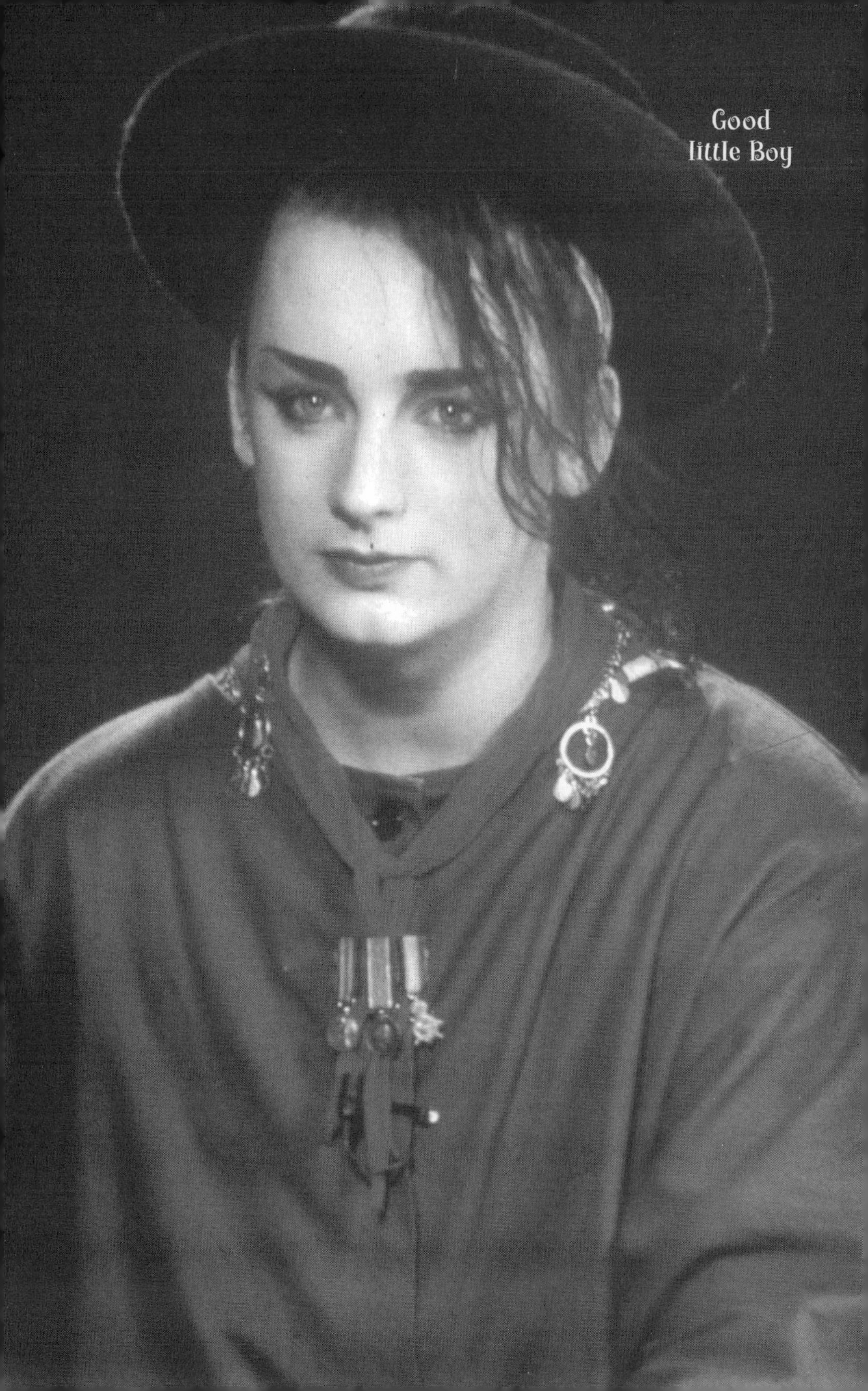

Good
little Boy

Walter Yetnikoff: "He told me from time to time I could go fuck myself. He'd complain about the color of the sky, all sorts of things"). The powers-that-were at CBS finally decided enough was enough—and decided to drop Boston from their roster. Yetnikoff put Scholz's royalties in suspense and demanded an almost one-million-dollar buyout from the group. A nasty lawsuit ensued when Scholz, furious at Yetnikoff, made a behind-the-scenes deal with MCA to release future Boston albums—*while the band was still signed to CBS.*

Stephen Stills vs. Neil Young

"Things got pretty hot onstage, and when Neil and Stephen got into the dressing room they started swinging at each other with their guitars. It was like two old ladies going at it with their purses." (Dewey Martin, Buffalo Springfield)

Paul Stanley and Gene Simmons, Kiss, vs. former bandmate Ace Frehley

In response to public aspersions from Stanley and Simmons, Frehley huffed, "They want me to become a drunk again and disappear into the fucking mist. But that's not gonna happen—in fact, I'm only gonna get bigger. I'm like a bad rash that won't go away." Like Kiss.

Mariah Carey vs. Celine Dion

There is a pretty serious rivalry going on between chart-topping songstresses Mariah Carey and Celine Dion—both prima donnas of the first order, which made them perfect for MTV's televised Save the Music benefit, *Five Divas* (the others were saint-on-earth **Gloria Estefan**, country twit **Shania Twain**, and sassy soul legend **Aretha Franklin**). Over-emoter Carey initially refused to sing on the same stage with ultraham Dion *at all* during the 1998 event (who could blame her?), but was ultimately persuaded by the diplomatic efforts of Ms. Franklin (during the taping, Carey stuck to her side of the stage and Dion to hers). A crew member remarked, "There was a bit of tension—but then again, they are divas."

Rod Stewart vs. Elton John

"I don't think he was ever born to be a rock 'n' roll star. He was probably born to be chairman of Watford Football Club, and now he's beginning to *look* like the Chairman of Watford Football Club as well." (Rod on Elton)

"I am capable of being a rock 'n' roll star and the Chairman of Watford Football Club, and I sell more records throughout the world than Rod Stewart. Anyway, he should stick to grave-digging, 'cause that's where he belongs—six feet under." (Elton, on former grave digger Rod)

Mick Jagger vs. Rod Stewart and Elton John

"I don't like people like Rod Stewart and Elton John, and I don't like the way they carry on. I get very upset at being identified with that kind of person. I also don't talk to anyone who's a better singer than I am." (Mick Jagger)

Julian Lennon vs. Yoko Ono

Yoko Ono gave Apple Computer Corp. permission to use a photo of herself and John Lennon for the company's grammatically questionable "Think Different" advertising campaign in 1998. Selling out? Why no—she professed to have given the rights away in exchange for Apple's promise to provide free computers to schools. "He was not about commercialization," protested son-of-John-not-of-Yoko Julian, bitterly. "The one last thing that upsets me is what Yoko Ono does with the estate."

Peter Murphy, Bauhaus, vs. Marilyn Manson

Peter Murphy was quoted in the *Los Angeles Times* as saying that "bands like Marilyn Manson" were merely goth-rock wannabes, whereas his band, Bauhaus, was the real deal. Sneered Manson in response, "I wanted to say to Pete Murphy, 'I'm pretty sure I got it all *right* and you got it all wrong—because I have a successful career, and you're going bald.' "

Metallica vs. Pantera singer Phil Anselmo

During Pantera's 1996 tour, Phil Anselmo spouted off publicly about how Metallica were "selling out" because they'd shorn their trademark long locks. Jason Newsted, Metallica's bassist, retorted, "He's got a big mouth for somebody who ODs on heroin [Anselmo had recently overdosed, and had issued a press release about his experience]. I used to think we were pals, I really did. I'm kind of disappointed, but I'm not going to waste my hate on him." Metallica drummer Lars Ulrich chimed in: "Phil Anselmo means nothing in my life. Anybody who ODs and, because nobody notices, has to write his own press release about it . . . well, that tells you a bit about their character. Like, 'I just ODed and nobody cares!' "

Keith Richards vs. Elton John

"All I said was I thought [Elton's **Princess Di** tribute 'Candle in the Wind 1997'] was a bit tacky and said 'songs for dead blondes.' He went apeshit. I thought Elton liked me. But I did say that he *will* regret it one time, one day. Apart from that, I've forgotten all about it. I mean, the spite in that old faggot's mouth! Oh man, what an old bitch." (Keith Richards)

"He's Sir Brown Nose to me. And he looks like my grandmother on a bad day." (Keith Richards)

Rod Stewart vs. Sting

Sting chartered an airplane for his 1991 U.S. tour, and upon boarding the craft, spied a hand-carved message in one of the jet's tables: "Sting, you pompous bastard, when are you going to get a sense of humor?" The nasty note had been etched into the tray by the aircraft's former lessor,  Rod Stewart, who'd learned that the onetime **Police**-man would be using the plane after him. Sting decided to get even, so during his tour's L.A. leg, he cruised over to Stewart's abode, only to learn the rooster-haired rocker was in Reno. Sting chained and padlocked the front gate, forcing Rod, upon his return, to wait for hours while handymen attempted to pry it open. When he finally got in, Stewart placed an irate call to Sting, who blithely replied, "Come along, Rodney, where's your sense of humor?"

ADDICTED
TO
LOVE

Strange Bedfellows

Why do most men get into rock 'n' roll in the first place? Love of music? Hunger for fame? I think not—as most of them freely admit, it was the desire to *get laid, man.* And music does allow one to live out one's deepest, darkest fantasies—which tend to get deeper and darker as time goes by.

What do they like?

J. J. Burnel, The Stranglers

"For me, cannibalism is sexually erotic. When I was really young, I started getting interested in women's legs and thought, 'I just wanna eat them,' you know, as you do. Then I read some interesting things about castaways and people eating each other. Apparently human flesh tastes a bit like pork."

Brian Burrows, Spider

"We're into motorbikes and women who ride motorbikes; we're into rock 'n' roll and women who like rock 'n' roll; and we're into women and women who like women."

Hugh Cornwell, The Stranglers

"Hugh happens to have this thing toward underage girls. He'll get arrested for it one day, but that's his quirk." (J. J. Burnel)

Chico DeBarge

Keeps panties in his refrigerator (nope, don't wanna know why)

BREAST STROKES

"I truly believe that when men are looking at women they can't see past their hooters. You could get the stupidest woman imaginable, but if she's got a beautiful pair of hooters, a man is gonna want to fuck her. Whereas if I have a stupid man in front of me, I don't give a fuck how big his dick is, I want him out of my life!"
(Shirley Manson, Garbage)

"I'm thirty-two now, and I think, shit, I must be a bit more mature. But I'm not. Still gullible for long legs and a big tit."
(Rod Stewart)

"I've met so many girls— 'Here, feel these, they're brand new.' You grab 'em and they're like bolt-ons— really hard. It's like anything—it's got to be done just right."
(Steven Tyler, on breast implants)

Martin Gore, Depeche Mode
Bondage

Janet Jackson

"There are certain things that I love . . . candle wax or ice or having a blindfold on and anticipating your lover's every move."

Brian Jones and Anita Pallenberg
Whips

Tom Jones

"Okay, if you want to get down to the nitty gritty . . . let's say I'm watching a porno, for instance—and I've analyzed it, to see what makes me tick—I do like to see two women together. It turns me on more than anything else. That's what rings my chimes."

Mandy Lion, World War III

"I'm not afraid to tell you that I like a little bondage and sex. I don't do drugs, I don't drink—fucking is what I'm into."

Little Richard

Liked to watch others having sex (such as his girlfriend and Buddy Holly). Confessed Richard, "I would pay a guy who had a big penis to come and have sex with these ladies so I could watch them."

Madonna

A little spanky

NUMBERS RACKET

"I've fucked seventy-two women in the past three months."
(Bam, Dogs D'Amour)

"I love chicks! I've got quite a little harem at Huntington Beach, full of sixteen-year-old nymphets. When I visit them I call it frolic time."
(Don Costa, short-lived Ozzy bassist)

"We were five heterosexual, good-looking men. We competed against each other for the sexiest girls . . . I won."
(Simon LeBon, Duran Duran)

"If I choose to go and fuck five girls in a bedroom, I can do it, it's my right to do it, and I'm going to enjoy doing it. It's my fucking job."
(Notorious—if hard-to-fathom—sex symbol Mick Hucknall)

"We worship [women]."
(Kiss's Paul Stanley)
"Repeatedly."
(Kiss's Gene Simmons)

"Vince—he loves chicks, man! Vince is definitely the sultriest person I've ever met."
(Nikki Sixx, on Mötley Crüe bandmate Vince Neil)

NUMBERS RACKET
(CONTINUED)

"Having a hundred girls isn't any different from one girl—except I like it a whole lot better."
(Ted Nugent)

"The offers to fill my bed would keep it full for a fortnight."
(Jimmy Page)

"We used to booze and fuck ourselves blind every night."
(Poison guitarist C. C. DeVille; the band, to facilitate their sexual profligacy, had a condom machine installed on their tour bus)

"From the start there were a lot of ladies, and that escalated."
(Noel Redding, The Jimi Hendrix Experience)

"I can't get enough of women. I have sex as often as possible. . . . It's really hard to maintain a one-on-one relationship if the other person is not going to allow me to be with other people."
(Axl Rose)

"I started getting so screwed up that getting fucked up was more important than getting fucked. Part of me is still bummed out that I didn't have all of the sex I could have had in the seventies."
(Steven Tyler)

Shirley Manson, Garbage

"Spontaneous sex in spontaneous places—in fact, spontaneity of all kinds—helps to keep the fire alive. I've enjoyed cars, empty building sites, and bathrooms that weren't mine. I love trains because they are unbearably sexy.

However, I draw the line at airplanes. They turn me off completely. I associate them with impending death and everything hideous about the world. So even if Brad Pitt came up to me on a plane and said, 'I need you immediately,' I'd have to say, 'Not right now, dear.' "

Keith Moon

Role-playing and dress up

John Phillips

Spanking, tying women to bedposts, whipped cream

Elvis Presley

Young women wrestling in white cotton underpants

Prince

Put honey in his lady friends' navels

Linda Ronstadt

"My big fantasy is to seduce a priest."

Gavin Rossdale, Bush

"The two-girl fantasy is the one I've been waiting for."

GENE POOL

"One night, Liz Derringer and I were hanging out with [Gene Simmons], and as we were saying good night he asked, 'Do you girls want to see my cock dance?' We looked at each other and said, 'Sure.' So he pulled his pants down and proceeded to do this complicated muscle thing he can do. And it danced. I told him he should get it tap shoes."
(Bebe Buell)

Simmons Says: Gene gives us his thoughts on one of his favorite subjects

"People often ask me what I look for in women. I look for me in women!"

"You can be as ugly as I am and still get laid more than the best-looking guy. 'Cause I'm in Kiss."

"If you wear perfume and you're not in jail, we're game."

"Thank god I'm in a band. Because I'm the ugliest guy on the face of the planet—but my goodness, do I get a lot of puss."

"It's long enough to make you my very closest friend."
(Gene, on his famous tongue)

WHOLE LOTTA LOVE

"It's not the size of the ship, it's the size of the waves."
(Little Richard)

"Someone said, 'It's not the size, it's the magic of the wand.' And I said, 'What's wrong with a *big* magic wand?' "
(Janet Jackson)

Rock 'n' roll's "A" list

Jeff Beck

David Cassidy

Julian Cope

Noel Gallagher

Levon Helm

Jimi Hendrix

Chris Isaak

Jim Kerr

Tommy Lee

Huey Lewis

Robert Plant

Iggy Pop

Todd Rundgren

Peter Tork

Paul Young

"I can apologize for my inadequacies. What are you going to do? God made me as God made me. I didn't say it was broken, just small."
(Mark McGrath, Sugar Ray)

Groovy Kind of Love

Since the subject matter is so important to them, rock stars tend to devote an inordinate amount of time to thinking and writing about sex (not to mention doing it). This has a couple of results: firstly, a large percentage of rock songs are about this one limitlessly entertaining topic, and secondly, the men and women of music seem to have no problem divulging their truest, bluest yearnings. From the ridiculous to the sublime, herewith rock stars' maunderings on this most interesting topic:

"If I was a Jewish girl in Hitler's day, I would become his girlfriend. After ten days in bed, he would come to my way of thinking." (Yoko Ono)

Yes, because he would have been driven insane.

"That's all I can remember—thinking about getting laid, getting blown. . . . I was twenty-one years old, my dick was always hard, and they were so willing." (David Cassidy)

"Girls usually fall over themselves to go out with me." (George Harrison)

"You can't just go to bed with a cup of hot chocolate." (John Bonham)

"I had sex on the set of the next *Star Wars* film, where we got to play at the wrap party. It's probably on a security camera somewhere." (Tim Wheeler, Ash)

"Ad-Rock would try to get the older, sophisticated girls. Yauch would fuck anybody—he'd fuck the fish if they were in the fishbowl. Then he'd act like he was the holiest man—that's what would kill me." (Dr. Dre, on touring with the Beastie Boys)

"My inspiration is right below my waist and in between my legs." (Jon Bon Jovi)

"Bill Clinton's gorgeous. I'd love to sleep with him." (Boy George)

"If I find myself in bed with another living thing, I tend to treat it as a sexual object." (J. J. Burnel, The Stranglers)

"If I wrote about sex, Jackie Collins's efforts would look like nursery rhymes." (Morrissey)

"C. C. DeVille is the epitome of what rock 'n' roll is all about. He is the sex, the drugs . . . the violence." (Bret Michaels, Poison)

"It was a hilarious time. We had fabulous, much-publicized affairs with a string of obscenely beautiful women." (Simon LeBon, Duran Duran)

"Sex is about as important as a cheese sandwich. But a cheese sandwich, if you ain't got one to put in your belly, is extremely important." (Ian Dury)

"You can squirt me anywhere but in my face. You'll ruin my mascara." (Jackie Fox, The Runaways)

"The great thing about being thirty is that there are a great deal more available women. The young ones look younger and the old ones don't look nearly as old." (Glenn Frey)

"[Liam Gallagher] would never have to look for a girl. They throw themselves at him. . . . Girls needed two qualities to get Liam into bed: they had to be beautiful and patient. They had to be able to sit up in a bar all night and be ignored while he got plastered. Then, at 4 A.M., if they were lucky, he'd grab them by the hand and take them to his room. Even when he was completely out of his head he found the stamina for sex. Then the next day the girl would be discarded like an old newspaper." (Ian Robertson, Oasis's former tour manager)

"I've never tried to hide the fact that I'm a chick. I like whorey-looking shoes with little stiletto heels. I love perfume. I love guys, man." (Chrissie Hynde)

During the seventies, says **Elton John**, "I would walk into a club and see someone I hadn't even met, and I would already have them on the conveyor belt. They'd come out with a Versace shirt and a Cartier watch at the other end."

"I can't understand being with only one woman. As soon as you declare yourself to one, all these beautiful women appear as if by fucking magic—they never showed up when you were looking." (**Lemmy**)

"People say to me, 'Lemmy, don't you realize that chick only wants to get hold of you because of who you are?' I say, 'Huh, like I care?' " (**Lemmy**)

"Strong women leave big hickeys." (**Madonna**)

"I'm saving the bass player for Omaha." (**Janis Joplin**)

"You never really know a guy until you ask him to wear a rubber." (**Madonna**)

In October of 1978, **Queen** threw the party to end all parties in New Orleans. The invitees were entertained by nude female dwarf mud-wrestlers, among other circus-type acts, and there was a hooker in the back who was hired to supply blow jobs on demand. Is that rock 'n' roll or what!

"Tell the young ladies to get themselves in gear. Have them tell their mothers they're staying with a friend, and then let them come knock at my door." (**Bon Scott**)

"I don't think anybody ever made it with a girl because they had a Tom Waits album on their shelves. I've got all three, and it never helped me." (**Tom Waits**)

"You know how Americans are—when it comes to sex, the men can't keep from lying and the women can't keep from telling the truth." (**Robin Zander, Cheap Trick**)

"I think pop music has done more for oral intercourse than anything else that ever happened—and vice versa." (**Frank Zappa**)

I Like Boys

Gay or bisexual rockers

Marc Almond, Soft Cell

"I thought Marc was more gay than straight. He had no hang-ups about sex, and all the figures he admired were men—to the point of finding them sexually attractive." (Soft Cell manager Simon Napier-Bell)

Joan Baez

Roddy Bottum, keyboardist, Faith No More: The only Metal personality besides Judas Priest's Rob Halford to come out publicly. Gee, could anyone get just a tiny hint about his sexual orientation from his name?

David Bowie calls himself a "trisexual" ("I'll try anything once").
When Bowie came out of the closet in the seventies, guitarist Mick Ronson remembered, "It wasn't a very good thing to say, especially up north. My family took a lot of flak for it. I gave my mother and father a car—somebody threw paint all over it. With so many people around being bisexual, you got used to it for yourself. But it shook me up."

"I'm pretty much over my affection for men. The only time I get halfway wistful for those old days is in Japan. All those little boys are so cute—I just want to take them all up to my room." (David Bowie)

I WANT TO KNOW WHAT LOVE IS

"The idea of sex with a man doesn't turn me off, but I don't express it. I satisfied my curiosity about that fifteen years ago . . . strange experiences with older boys. But men don't particularly turn me on."
(Daryl Hall)

"Me and my mate tried once. We were about fifteen, and we sat on this couch trying to masturbate each other but we couldn't do it. And the poor lad whose house we were in was freaking out. He was like, 'I can't believe you're doing this in my house!' I think we did it to shock him. But we couldn't get erections, so we concluded that we probably weren't gay. But we did try."
(Mick Hucknall)

Boy George: Was taken to court in England for "malicious falsehood" in 1997 by an alleged ex-lover, **Spear of Destiny** guitarist **Kirk Brandon**, who denied the Boy's assertions that they'd been more than close friends—while Brandon had a wife and child at home. A judge dismissed Brandon's writ, having decided in favor of George's version (Brandon had admitted to sharing a bed with Boy, but swore nothing happened), concluding that the evidence showed they'd had "a brief, passionate, and turbulent affair."

Melissa Etheridge

Simon Fowler (Ocean Colour Scene) was "outed" by a British tabloid. Because he had been in the closet, his family and fans had no idea of his sexual orientation until the allegations were published, on an occasion he called "the worst day of [my] life."

Rob Halford (Judas Priest): "I have formally walked out of the closet. Coming out is a freeing experience."

Janis Ian

Mick Jagger: "When I was thirteen, all I desperately wanted to do was have sex. I did it with boys at school. I think that's true of almost every boy."

Elton John

"Give me a couple of drinks and *I'll* be the bitch." (Elton John)
"I haven't met anybody I'd like to settle down with—of either sex." (Elton John)
"The whole world was amazed when Elton got married." (**Rod Stewart**)

Holly Johnson and Paul Rutherford, Frankie Goes to Hollywood

k.d. lang

Little Richard: "I'm twenty-four years old and beautiful . . . pink hanging down my legs, sequins all round my bottom, and pearls hanging 'round my neck. I'm the bronze **Liberace!**"

Madonna

George Michael: "I spent the first half of my career being accused of being gay when I hadn't had anything like a gay relationship. In fact, I was twenty-seven before that happened to me."

"It's hard when you know someone's gay and they know you know they're gay, and you're talking to them—it's really unreal. George Michael has always said, 'I don't care.' Well, if he doesn't care, why doesn't he just say it in the first place?" (Boy George)

Me'Shell Ndegéocello

Amy Ray and Emily Saliers, The Indigo Girls

Lou Reed: "I remember always noticing these faggy-looking types hanging around the apartment. It took me quite a while before I realized what was going on. . . . It wasn't until he gave me a few sexual nudges that it finally clicked that Lou was gay, or at least bisexual. When I told him that I was not interested, he mumbled, 'They make them differently in Scotland,' quickly adding that anyway I was not suitable material for a marital partner." (John Cale, on his Velvet Underground bandmate)

Jimmy Somerville, Bronski Beat

Michael Stipe, REM

Pete Townshend

"It was the first time I realized that I wanted to fuck a man." (Pete Townshend, after seeing a Rolling Stones performance—and Jagger's dancing—during the 1960s)

"Yes, it's true. I fancy Vince." (Andy Bell, on Erasure bandmate Vince Clarke)

Sid Vicious: "Before meeting me, he was a homosexual." (Malcolm McLaren, on Sid Vicious)

"I didn't like fucking then and I still don't—it's dull."
(Sid Vicious)

CLOSET CASES

"Maybe I'm a latent homosexual—who knows? Make me an offer I can't refuse."
(J. J. Burnel, The Stranglers)

"People are really surprised when they meet us and find out that we're all straight."
(Alice Cooper)

"I've lived for years with people saying I'm a poof, but I don't give a damn."
(Cliff Richard)

"As far as I'm concerned, being any gender is a drag."
(Patti Smith)

"I have no preferences—I don't limit myself. I'm all sexes. I don't know what a homosexual is or a heterosexual is or a monosexual. I don't understand the differences."
(Nona Hendryx, LaBelle)

In Marilyn Manson's colorful "autobiography," *The Long Hard Road Out of Hell*, he writes that max-tattooed alterno-rocker Dave Navarro once attempted to give him a blow job. Protests Dave, "I didn't see it that way at all, but it didn't really matter because to me the whole thing was really fucking funny. . . . Put it this way— he was sucking on my fucking nipples that night. The reason it even came out in the book was more of a spiteful stab at me based out of fear and rejection. Why would he feel the need to lash out at me with homophobic rage? I think he felt rejected. . . . There was a point where we had discussed how amusing it might be to spread a rumor wherein we were homosexual lovers. I think that might have been his moving forward with that plan. But I got mad at him about something else, so I put a halt to the plan."

Model Behavior

"It's not much of a stretch from wearing the fanciest leather jacket or driving the flashiest car to squiring the cover girl of the month—they all prove that the boy has arrived. And if rockers are living out their fans' fantasy lives by remaining in a state of extended adolescence, what could be more ego-satisfying than dating the adult equivalent of a homecoming queen?" (rock writer Jon Pareles)

"We're the meat in the supermodel sandwich."
(Terence Trent D'Arby)

Supermodels: one of rock's major status symbols—don't leave home without 'em

David Bowie and Iman

Eric Clapton and Patti Boyd and Naomi Campbell and Carla Bruni Patti Boyd, of course, is "Layla" (the name is taken from a book of Persian poetry, *The Story of Layla*, given to her by Clapton), the love of his life. Married at the time to Beatle George Harrison, she met Clapton through his friendship with her then-husband. Clapton fell quickly for the comely lass, then confronted George: "I'm in love with your wife," Clapton told Harrison. "What are you going to do about it?" "Whatever you like, man," was George's cosmic reply. It didn't take long for Patti to switch camps. But, "after the spiritual life with George, within a few weeks of going to live with Eric, I seemed to be surrounded by mayhem. I drank like a fish, too," admitted Patti. Clapton and Boyd split in the eighties, due in large part to his substance abuse.

Adam Clayton (U2) and Naomi Campbell

Harry Connick Jr. and Jill Goodacre

Elvis Costello and Bebe Buell

Bob Dylan and Edie Sedgwick

Bryan Ferry and Jerry Hall

George Harrison and Patti Boyd

Michael Hutchence (INXS) and Helena Christensen and Elle MacPherson

Chris Isaak and Helena Christensen

Mick Jagger and Chrissie Shrimpton and Jerry Hall

Billy Joel and Christie Brinkley The vows they took on their wedding day included a promise to "honor and respect each other's goals and ambitions"; the happy couple allegedly split because he couldn't forsake his party-animal ways.

Brian Jones and Anita Pallenberg

Lenny Kravitz and Vanessa Paradis
"He's such a genius," Paradis gushed. "He thinks about music all the time. Sometimes we'll be in a restaurant and I'll be talking to him and he won't reply. He's in a trance. And I'll say, 'Are you okay?' and he'll reply, 'I'm just thinking of some lyrics.' He's amazing."
Ever get the feeling it doesn't take much to impress a supermodel?

Simon LeBon (Duran Duran) and Yasmin

Madonna and Tony Ward

Steve Marriott and Chrissie Shrimpton

John Mellencamp and Elaine Irwin

John Oates and Nancy Hunter

Ric Ocasek and Paulina Porizkova

Keith Richards and Anita Pallenberg and Patti Hansen (He invited her to his birthday party; she went home with him that night and never left. Says he, "I couldn't have made it without her. I ain't letting the bitch go.")

Axl Rose (Guns N' Roses) and Stephanie Seymour

Todd Rundgren and Bebe Buell

Seal and Tyra Banks and Tatjana Patitz (and many other lesser names)

Bruce Springsteen and Julianne Phillips

Ringo Starr and Barbara Bach

Rod Stewart and Britt Ekland ("I'm the most unavailable woman that you ever met") and Bebe Buell and Alana Hamilton-Stewart (once dumped a flute of champagne down Britt Ekland's dress when Britt got a little too friendly with her ex, Rod) and Kelly Emberg and Rachel Hunter

Britt, who once said, "I'm so happy. It's so nice to go with a man whose clothes you can wear," unsuccessfully sued Rod for $15 million in palimony in 1978.

Alana: "If he wants to go out with a series of mindless, moronic young models rather than being with me and the children, I don't think I'm losing anything."

"I'm a Jekyll and Hyde. I live with Kelly Emberg. I have three kids and I enjoy a family life . . . for a couple days a week. I also have a lion inside me that wants to go out. So I do that, too." (Rod Stewart)

"I've always been the one to push and shove and say, 'Sorry, that's it, darlin', it's all over, good-bye. Take twenty Valiums and have a stomach pump and that's the end of it.' " (Rod Stewart, who now knows how it feels—dumped by model-wife Rachel Hunter, brokenhearted Rod can't help crying while performing certain of his more sentimental songs.)

John Taylor (Duran Duran) and Renee Simonsen and Amanda De Cadenet

Tico Torres and Eva Herzigova (divorcing)

Alex Van Halen and Kelly Carter

Ron Wood and Jo Howard

Honky Tonk Women

"I'll be with one, and then we'll go inside to get a beer or something and then someone else will say, 'Well, when's my turn?' Or 'Let's go out. How about me now?' You know, if it's someone's birthday or they're new to the road, I initiate them. And . . . it's a tradition. That's the thing. When they come to Little Rock or whenever I'm at a show, it's basically a tradition."

(Supergroupie Connie Hamzy, on how she always gets her man)

Dirty Diana

The Groupie Hall of Fame

"It's really maddening to us as women to see young girls just lay themselves at the feet of any male who happens to be involved with rock 'n' roll. It's a really sad sight—like sheep to the slaughter."

(Ann Wilson, Heart)

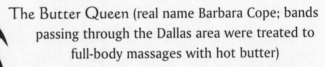

The Black Widow (dressed in black from head to toe and had a spider tattoo on her thigh)

The Butter Queen (real name Barbara Cope; bands passing through the Dallas area were treated to full-body massages with hot butter)

Patti Cakes: "You get to ball the prettiest boys, smoke the best dope, and meet all the most far-out people."

Cherry Vanilla: "I was hysterical last night as I sat with Poppy, Mandy, and Alicia—the ladies—being royally entertained by [a famous band] in their hotel room. Since we were with [a musician] from the royal family of [another famous band], they assumed we were Ladies of Quality, and they spent hours putting down this whole decadent orgy scene that [a band] and their roadies had held the night before with some cheap nympho hussy who had been fucking them all in the shower. Little did they know that the very same cheap nympho hussy was right there, all prim and proper. Guess who?"

"Never do with your hands what you could do better with your mouth."

(Advice to fellow groupies from Cherry Vanilla)

Suzy Creamcheese, real name Pamela Zarubica: Lived for a while in Frank Zappa's guest house

Pamela Des Barres: Also resided with the Zappas, and later wrote a best-selling book—*I'm with the Band*—on her adventures as a groupie

Linda Eastman

Jenny Fabian: Cowrote a novelization of her life, *Groupie*, and married a tour manager

"Sweet Connie" Hamzy has been with 1,500 men, "give or take a hundred or two"; a few of the bands she's been with had T-shirts made up that said, "I kissed Connie and lived," and "I choked Connie."

"I'd wake up in the morning thinking, 'I don't know your name, I don't know where you're from, and I know I'm not the first guy you've done this week.' "

(Ozzy Osbourne)

"I cover a lot of ground. But I don't look at it as who's most important or who's the most famous. To me, at this point in my life . . . these people are my friends because I've been doing this for so long." (Connie Hamzy)

Courtney Love

Lori Maddox, a.k.a. Lori Lightning: Got her start at a very tender age (fourteen, to be exact) with Jimmy Page

"Down there [in Texas] they've got the richest groupies in the world. Some of the groupies followed our jet in their private jet."

(Jimmy Page)

"The really famous groupies were extremely tough and unpleasant. These conniving, loveless little girls really affected my whole concept of femininity for a while. Talk to the bass player from the Sweet and he would probably say those were the best months of his life. But to someone with a bit of taste, who wasn't just hopelessly addicted to pussy, it was pretty sordid. It was a period when, if you were skinny and English and dressed like some horrible Biba* girl, you could have anything you wanted."

(Rock writer Nick Kent)

*A trendy English department store of the sixties

Cynthia Plaster Caster, real name Cynthia Albritton: led a ragtag group of willing women who, using dental alginate, made casts of rock stars' aroused members. The Plaster Casters were financially supported by Frank Zappa and his business partner, Herb Cohen—whom Cynthia later sued for the return of twenty-five of the "sculptures" (including those of Jimi Hendrix and Eric Burdon), claiming she'd loaned them to him, and that he'd never returned them. The court ruled in her favor, ordering Cohen to return the castings, and awarding Albritton $10,000 in damages. So what's she going to do with them? Geoff Glass, her attorney, was a bit evasive: "There are definite commercial possibilities, but she doesn't want to talk about it. She doesn't want an exhibit. Her mother still doesn't know about this."

Nancy Spungen: Prohibited by the Heartbreakers' manager from seeing or being around band member Jerry Nolan—because he knew she'd encourage Nolan to do drugs, thereby rendering him unable to perform

Sable Starr: Hit her peak at age fifteen, and limited her conquests to the very top of the superstar heap. Starr settled down for a while with New York Doll Johnny Thunders, who said, "She got out of the whole groupie scene. Changed a lot. . . . She's crazy, but, uh, she's cool, ya know?"

"If you don't have any groupies hanging around, then obviously you're not really making it."

(Frank Zappa)

Suzy Suck
Wonder what her specialty was.

"They're just so sleazy—they'll do it anywhere, you know? Take them in the bathroom, you know? They just want to beat you, they want to, you know, fuck their brains out, and that's what they're there for."
(Vince Neil)

Devon Wilson: Exotic black beauty who spent time with Mick Jagger, Duane Allman, Miles Davis, Quincy Jones, and especially Jimi Hendrix (he called her "Dolly Dagger"). Two years after Jimi's death, Devon jumped or fell out of a window at New York's Chelsea Hotel. "[There were] four or five sort of famous groupies and Devon was one of them, but she never lasted long with anybody. She didn't want to live with anybody—it was just a real status thing." (Pat Hartley, friend of Devon)

"The last time I was in L.A., there was this incredible groupie feud which was getting down to razor-blade sandwiches. The competition thing out there is incredible."
(Jimmy Page)

Paula Yates

Frank Zappa said his wife, Gail, used to be a groupie, "and an excellent groupie, too." Admits Gail, "Well, we knew the Byrds and the Beach Boys—I'd say Brian Wilson, as a matter of fact." And, "There were a lot of girls who were in it for the castle in England. That was a prevailing dream: I must have an English pop star and retire to one of those great houses in England."

"As a rule, they're the most incredibly warm people. If making love to you was going to make you happy, they'd make love. If you were tired and didn't want to make it, they'd cook you a meal and make you feel at home. They really were ports of call."
(Eric Clapton)

What's Love Got to Do with It

Road dogs of rock

Jon Bon Jovi

"We come to a town, do a show, try to pick up women, take the money, and you don't see us again." (Jon Bon Jovi)

Aerosmith's Joe Perry and Steven Tyler

Bang Tango

"We're not gonna take some chick up to our room and do her. We've got a road crew for that!" (Joe Leste)

Jeff Beck

Black 'N' Blue

"We hear that there aren't many chicks at the concerts in Britain, so we're bringing over sixteen hundred wicked bitches with us." (Jaime St. James)

Blood, Sweat, and Tears

"You ought to see our groupies. We have the funniest groupies in the world—real bottom-of-the-barrel stuff. We're the ugliest band ever born. When we play, I expect to find puke in the aisles." (Bobby Colomby, drummer)

CREW CUTS

Rock 'n' roll road crew dudes get all the girls

"I have a girlfriend, but when I was single it was crazy with groupies. Sometimes it was like being a pimp. You give backstage passes to the prettiest ones. It was like herding cattle."
(Jeff Mittelman, roadie)

David Cassidy

"English girls demand a lot more of you. They're strong, positive, and very physical, and will go to any length to get at you." And, "On the road, there was this one room where we'd corral a hand-picked dozen of the most beautiful. After the show, I'd go up to this room, pick the one I wanted, and let the band divvy up the rest. I was an animal."

Evan Dando, Lemonheads

Faster Pussycat (especially Taime Down)

Mick Fleetwood

Describes on-the-road groupie encounters individually as an "attack of veal viper"

ROTH & ROLL

David Lee Roth gives us a lesson in his favorite subject

"Women are great. When they dig you, there's nothing they won't do. That kind of loyalty is hard to find—unless you've got a good dog."

"I feel sexy a whole lot of the time. That's one of the reasons I'm in this job: to exercise my sexual fantasies. When I'm onstage, it's like doing it with twenty thousand of your closest friends."

"Is it possible to insure my dick?"

Greg Guiffria, Guiffria/House of Lords

"After the show, [I would] go back to the hotel, go to the lobby and go, 'You and you and you.' And then go upstairs, then go back down, have a drink, go, 'You, you, you,' all night long, until I just passed out."

Guns N' Roses

Jimi Hendrix

Don Henley

Kiss

"You have to do something to keep your mind busy, and I took up photography as a hobby," says Gene Simmons, who has amassed a large collection of Polaroid portraits of his on-the-road conquests. How does this affect his off-the-road love life? "The very first thing, if I'm going to get into a relationship, I sit the young lady down and say, 'Look, I really care about you. . . . Here's everything you need to know about me.' And I bring the books out and I say, 'Here they are.' "

A snippet of dialogue between **Gene Simmons** and **Paul Stanley**:

Paul: "You know what we've been getting a lot of lately? Letters from sixteen- and seventeen-year-old girls with little Polaroid pictures of them naked. That's amazing. That's great. There's nothing like knowing you're helping the youth of America—"

Gene: "Undress."

Paul: "Sometimes it says, 'My girlfriend took this,' and then there's another picture she took of her girlfriend. We really appreciate that."

Led Zeppelin (especially Jimmy Page)

"Girls come round and pose like starlets, teasing and acting haughty. If you humiliate them a bit, they tend to come on all right after that."
(Jimmy Page)

"You get bored. Anything that's ever happened has been in a spirit of fun. We've never hurt anybody . . . well, no one who didn't dig it." (Robert Plant)

"I saw Jimmy's whips curled up in his suitcase as if they were taking a nap, and pretended I didn't. He came up behind me and put his hands around my throat and said, 'Don't worry, Miss P, I'll never use those on you.' "
(Pamela Des Barres)

"All he did was chew me and slap me a little." (Pamela Des Barres)

Brian Jones

Fathered two illegitimate children by age sixteen, and had a total of nine by the time of his death at age twenty-seven.

Huey Lewis

Loverboy

"God, I'm just glad I didn't get married in the last couple of years. . . . Girls are starting to pull their clothes off in the middle of our set!" (Scott Smith)

Manowar

"It's an honor to be a pleasure slave for this band because we give 'em money to go out shopping or do their hair." And, "We have no problem in stopping the show if we see a hot chick out there. And we make sure we grab her attention and invite her to come backstage." (Joey DeMaio)

The Monkees

"I'd be kissing one girl, going to another, saying, 'Wait a minute—I'll be with you in a second.' " (Davy Jones)

Jim Morrison

Mötley Crüe

"That's the reason most people get into rock bands, for the groupies." (Vince Neil)

LOVE CHILD

"I've got a son who played in a band in Sweden. He's Swedish. Had him by a Swedish girlfriend I had. He played in a band, but he wasn't brilliant. He's my boy, but I have to be honest. There are a million as good as him out there."
(Roger Daltrey)

"He sure left his mark, that cat. I know of five kids, at least. All by different chicks, and they all look like Brian."
(Keith Richards, on Brian Jones)

"I thought everybody in rock had illegitimate children."
(Rod Stewart)

"If there ever is a time that a person should be on drugs, it's when they're pregnant, because it sucks."
(Courtney Love)

"I don't want children. I hate kids. I don't want to have a baby who might be like my brother."
(Noel Gallagher, Oasis)

"If I had a little girl, I wouldn't want my girl at any rock concert—not at all."
(Vince Neil)

Poison

"Basically, if you're in town with a girl one night, you know, and you want to fool around, it's pretty ridiculous to start talking about, you know, Shakespeare."
(Rikki Rockett)

Iggy Pop

"One time in D.C., this chick—this biker chick, about 250 pounds—was with three of the Stooges; I wasn't involved. But they told me to come over and look. And I cracked up. They took this girl, and, using their belts, tied her arms and legs to the four corners of the Sealy Posturepedic. Then with these big Magic Markers they divided her entire body into amazingly accurate illustrated butcher cuts, like shank, prime rib, spare rib—just like the charts on the wall at the butcher shop, only with arrows pointing 'This way to beaver,' with little slogans and everything. She had been unconscious, and when she woke up she was so *desperate* to have a good time—party at any cost—that as long as we would ignore the fact that she was covered with graffiti, she could accept it. The fact that she happened to be tied down and couldn't move didn't bother her and her groove. She had arrived with an ounce of angel dust and was smoking plenty."

Ratt

The Rolling Stones (especially Bill Wyman)

"I think a tour makes it easy on a chick. She doesn't have to bother putting the make on anyone. She's just there to say yes." (Renée, groupie, in the unreleased Stones tour documentary, *Cocksucker Blues*)

Rick Springfield

"Rick Springfield collects naked pictures that groupies and fans send him, and keeps them in a gigantic photo album. He also likes taking sexy videos; the two times he's traveled to Little Rock, we've made videos in his dressing room." (Connie Hamzy)

Rod Stewart

"We used to take pictures of birds with no clothes on—nothing wrong with that. . . . I think it was about 1972—I was doing an interview and I thought the tape machine was off and I told this guy and it ended up in the *Sun*. The 'Polaroid Kid,' they called me. My dad was really disgusted."

Sugar Ray

"We sort of come from the seventies ideology of road work. I think, in some instances, we've had what Van Halen had on the *Women and Children First* tour. But I don't want to incriminate myself." (Mark McGrath)

Van Halen

"[David Lee Roth] gets a lot of girls. He likes blondes. He likes tall blondes. And he goes—he picks them out, out of a line backstage. And those he doesn't like, he sends them off with a beer. 'Go home. Bye.' " (famed groupie Cinnamon)

When asked if he had any other interests besides guitar playing, **Eddie Van Halen** replied, "The chicks, man. The chicks on the road. Whew!"

Vanilla Fudge

" 'You want a backstage pass?' And they'll go, 'Yeah.' And I go, 'Well, this is what you got to do for it.' And they'll do it." (Carmine Appice)

Warrant

"We're the horniest fucking band in the world!" (Erik Turner)

The Who (especially Keith Moon)

Winger

Frank Zappa

"It's amazing what you run into on the road. These chicks are ready for anything. They'll give head without thinking about it—anyplace: backstage in the dressing room, out in the street. Anyplace, anytime." (Frank Zappa)

"Sex on tour—

how empty can you get?"

(Gavin Rossdale, Bush)

Work Mates

The band that plays together, er . . . plays together. Some of rock's notable personal~slash~professional couplings:

Pat Benatar and her guitarist, Neil Geraldo

Cocteau Twins: Elizabeth Fraser (vocals) and Robin Guthrie (keyboards)

Culture Club: Boy George and Jon Moss (see page 180)

The Fall: Mark E. Smith (vocals) and Brix (vocals, guitar)

Fleetwood Mac: Lindsey Buckingham and Stevie Nicks, Mick Fleetwood and Stevie Nicks, Christine and John McVie, Christine McVie and sound engineer Martin Birch

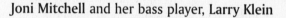

Joni Mitchell and her bass player, Larry Klein

No Doubt: Gwen Stefani (vocals) and Tony Kanal (bass)

Pretenders: Chrissie Hynde and Pete Farndon

Siouxsie & the Banshees: Siouxsie Sioux (vocals) and Budgie (drums)

Smashing Pumpkins: D'Arcy Wretzky (bass) and James Iha (guitar)

Style Council: Paul Weller (vocals, guitar) and D. C. Lee (vocals)

Talking Heads: Tina Weymouth and Chris Frantz

Ike and Tina Turner

"A metal shoe stretcher, shoes, phones, wire hangers, fists, walking canes. Once he threw boiling coffee in my face. He gave me black eyes and swollen lips. He broke my arm and my ribs and busted my jaw."

(Tina Turner, on how [and with what] Ike abused her)

X: Exene Cervenka and John Doe

Star-Crossed

Matches (some long-lived, some not so lengthy) made in celebrity heaven

Damon Albarn, Blur, and Justine Frischmann, Elastica (they had an open relationship wherein he slept with groupies, and she slept with other musicians—including her ex, Brett Anderson of Suede. Says Justine, "[Marianne Faithfull] balanced Mick [Jagger]'s togetherness with her own self-destruction. Which is something that people do in relationships. If your boyfriend is getting up and going for a run at eight in the morning, then you lie in bed till midday and get up and do some heroin.")

Cher and Gregg Allman (he insisted she call him "Mr. Allman")

David and Angela Bowie (his ultraromantic proposal was: "Can you handle the fact that I don't love you?")

"When we met, we were both laying the same bloke."
(David Bowie)
The "bloke" was record executive Calvin Mark Lee.

ANIMAL HUSBANDRY

"Even if you have only two seconds, drop everything and give him a blow job. That way, he won't really want sex with anyone else."
(Jerry Hall)

Eric Clapton and Sheryl Crow

Natalie Cole and producer Andre Fisher

Elvis Costello and Cait O'Riordan, The Pogues

Evan Dando and Julianna Hatfield

Adam Duritz, Counting Crows, and Jennifer Aniston and Courteney Cox (no, not at the same time—but he sure must've been a fan of *Friends*)

Liam Gallagher (Oasis) and sometime actress/full-time rock-star-magnet Patsy Kensit

Chrissie Hynde and Jim Kerr, Simple Minds (just one year prior, she'd had childhood idol Ray Davies's baby out of wedlock; a city official had refused to wed Hynde and Davies because of their constant arguments)

EVERY TIME YOU GO AWAY

"Marriage is worse than dying. Why stay with one person for fifty years?"
(Joey Ramone)

Bob Geldof and Paula Yates: She kicked off divorce proceedings against Geldof on the grounds of adultery—kind of funny, considering she was already quite publicly seeing Michael Hutchence

"He had some new girlfriend and we were all supposed to go [to the premiere of Perry Farrell's film *Gift*] together. It was like, whatever. Go with the flow with Perry. Then we got into a big fight, so I smoked a bunch of crack and went to the premiere. Perry had decided that he didn't like the typeface on the titles and he changed all that and spelled my name wrong. I freaked out. I had been with this guy for eight years, and he can't spell my name."
(Farrell's former girlfriend, Casey Niccoli)

Janet Jackson and **James DeBarge**

Mick and **Bianca Jagger** (they had an "open" marriage—see below) and **Jerry Hall** (she lived with their "open" marriage for years, but finally decided to end it all when a model showed up and announced she was pregnant with Jagger's child—see below)

"Domesticity is death."
(Mick Jagger)

Mick Jagger's marriage to Bianca Macias was, according to her, an "open" one (she admitted to an affair with golden-boy Ryan O'Neal). Presciently, Mick had made her sign a pre-nup before their 1971 marriage, so it didn't cost him much when the pair decided to split up.
"I know people theorize that Mick thought it would be amusing to marry his twin. But actually he wanted to achieve the ultimate by making love to himself." (Bianca Jagger)
For the longest time, onetime supermodel Jerry Hall seemed to have reconciled herself to her mate's philandering ways—although that's not to say it didn't bother her: said Jerry in a 1998 interview with Brit mag *Harpers & Queen*, "[An unnamed supermodel "friend" of Hall's] doesn't know I know she slept with Mick, but I do, and she's just a little tramp." It

wasn't the first time this had happened . . . or the last. Shortly after Hall's interview, South American model Luciana Morad claimed she was pregnant with Jagger's child (she had the baby, a boy, in May of 1999, and DNA test results proved the little nipper was Mick's), and the Jagger-Hall union finally imploded. "Mick is quite a tricky man. But my theory is, the more you let 'em go, the more they come back. You can't take anything for granted in a relationship. The thing with rock stars is that women keep chasing after them—they're not like normal guys. With normal guys it's bad enough, but things calm down. My girlfriends are always saying, 'I could never do it. I don't know how you stand it.' Because after all these years, all these girls are still chasing after him." (Jerry Hall)

"I'm thinking about entering politics. I'd love to do it. But I haven't got the right wife."
(Mick Jagger)

Third Eye Blind singer Stephen Jenkins and actress Charlize Theron

Rickie Lee Jones and Tom Waits

Lenny Kravitz and *Cosby* star Lisa Bonet and Natalie Imbruglia ("Torn")

Tommy Lee and Heather Locklear (by way of introduction, he said, "Hi, I'm Tommy—nice to touch you") and Pamela Anderson

John Lennon and Yoko Ono ("Intellectually," he said, "we didn't believe in getting married. But one doesn't love someone just intellectually.")

EVERY TIME YOU GO AWAY
(CONTINUED)

When Rod Stewart and Rachel Hunter split (she evidently got bored with her sports-obsessed, superannuated spouse), *People Weekly* ran the story under the headline "Not-So-Hot Rod."

"For the first time in my life, I'd rather have my dick cut off than be unfaithful."
(Rod Stewart, on model [in the noun sense] wife Rachel Hunter)

"I was so sure she was the woman I was going to spend the rest of my life with. I hope and pray with all my heart that she will eventually come back."
(Rod, after the split)

"Sometimes a woman can really persuade you to make an asshole of yourself."
(Rod Stewart)

> "As usual, there's a great woman behind every idiot."
> (John Lennon)

Courtney Love and Kurt Cobain

"We bonded over pharmaceuticals. I had Vicodin extra-strength . . . he had Hycomine cough syrup." (Courtney Love)

"Kurt makes my heart stop. But he's a shit." (Courtney Love)

Madonna and Vanilla Ice

He appeared in her book *Sex* (about which he said, "It kind of cheeses me out, makes me look like I'm like all the other people in there—a bunch of freaks. I'm no freak," and about which she said, "It is a work of art—underlining the importance of irony and provocation in an artist's life"). She is reportedly the jealous type, and would phone him in the middle of the night to make sure he was alone.

CRAZY LITTLE THING CALLED LOVE

> "It's always interesting when new girls come on the scene. It must be the most stressful thing that they can go through, because not only do they have to get to know and go out with the particular guy, they also have to go out with the other five guys as well—and their girlfriends and wives—and get along with them all. I really pity that sort of situation."
> (Kirk Pengilly, INXS)

> "There's really no reason to have women on tour unless they've got a job to do. The only other reason is to screw. Otherwise they get bored. They just sit around and moan."
> (Mick Jagger)

Marilyn Manson and actress Rose McGowan (they're engaged)

> "It's very dysfunctional. Every reason for someone to leave the relationship has existed. She's no angel either. It's beyond compromises. Two normal people would have been gone a long time ago. Yet we can't leave. I think it's a product of low self-esteem on both our parts. I really do."
> (Mark McGrath, Sugar Ray, on his relationship with his girlfriend)

CRAZY LITTLE THING CALLED LOVE
(CONTINUED)

"I wanted to be an actress and a scholar too. My first move was to get a Rolling Stone as a boyfriend. I slept with three, then decided that the singer was the best bet."
(Marianne Faithfull)

"Mick had me on a pin and he couldn't let me go. He had me on a pin and he was watching me flail and writhe, but it was something that fascinated him as an artist."
(Marianne Faithfull)

"Love is what you feel for a dog or a pussycat—it doesn't apply to humans, and if it does it just shows how low you are. It shows your intelligence isn't clicking."
(Johnny Rotten)

"Men have an unusual talent for making a bore out of everything they touch."
(Yoko Ono)

George Michael (?) and Brooke Shields: "We went back to her apartment for what I thought was going to turn into the real McCoy. We walked into her bedroom . . . then her mother and security guard jumped out going, 'Surprise!' Next day I told her we wouldn't be seeing each other anymore. She was really upset." (George Michael)
Yeah right. Shields went on to date (?) Michael Jackson.

Ozzy Osbourne and manager Sharon Osbourne (nee Arden)
"When Ozzy drank too much he started to get violent, but I could deal with that. I was never one of those women who go, 'Oh god, he slapped me—I'm going to call a policeman.' He would hit me and I would hit him back three times. And if Ozzy would throw something at me, I would destroy the fucking room. Our fights are legendary in this business." (Sharon Osbourne)

"I got a bouquet from that actor— what's his name . . . Nick Nolte—but I couldn't accept them. Mind you, he's just a sad old man."
(Nina Persson, The Cardigans)

Gavin Rossdale (Bush) and Gwen Stefani (No Doubt)

Richie Sambora (Bon Jovi) and Heather Locklear

Gene Simmons (Kiss) and Cher and Diana Ross

Paul Simon and Carrie Fisher and Edie Brickell

Patti Smith and former MC5 guitarist Fred "Sonic" Smith

Paul Stanley (Kiss) and topless model/pop star–wannabe Samantha Fox

Peter Wolf, J. Geils Band, and Norma Desmond–like actress Faye Dunaway

Neil Young and actress Carrie Snodgress

Girls, Girls, Girls

"I've never bought that open marriage thing. I've never seen it work. But that doesn't mean I believe in monogamy. Sleeping with someone else doesn't necessarily constitute an infidelity."
(Carly Simon, formerly married to James Taylor)

"I didn't get married under the premise or the deceit . . . that my ex-husband was anything closely resembling monogamous. . . . So I cultivated and knew and was very friendly with the groupies that were involved. And when I could, I employed them."
(Angie Bowie)

" 'You just go and have a good time,' my wife says—and she means it. If I went and had a really good time with a lot of chicks or whatever, if she didn't know about it she'd not be worried about it in the least."
(Roger Daltrey)

"Unless you're married to a very suspicious partner, going out and having a drink with a friend—a female friend—is not a problem. Being seen at a club with someone isn't a problem. Being seen leaving their house at dawn, however, would be a problem. Fortunately, I've never been in that situation."
(Simon LeBon)
Eyewitnesses suggest otherwise—like more than one affair with much-younger-than-his-supermodel-wife (Yasmin) models.

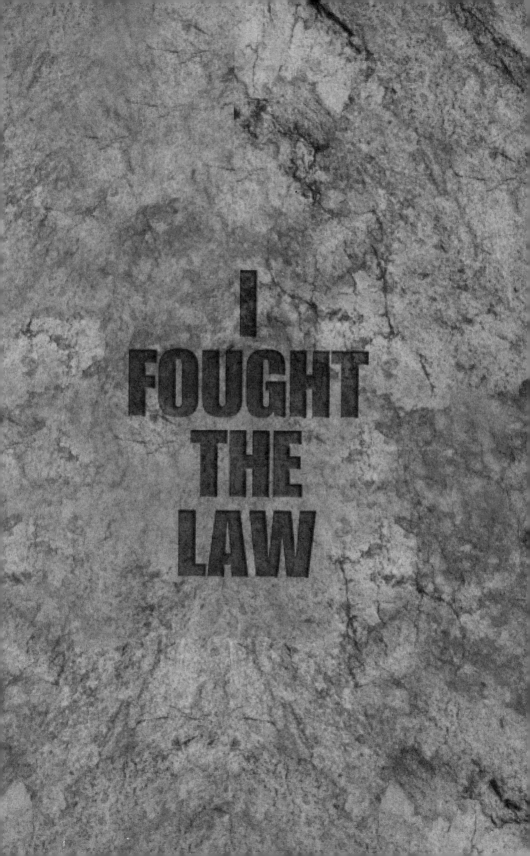

Flying
high
again

Wild Thing

Trashing backstage dressing rooms, throwing TV sets out windows, "doing" groupies, threatening flight attendants, chainsawing through motel-room walls, drinking bars dry . . . it's all in a day's work for a rock star—who, after all, has the one career where juvenile behavior is not only allowed, but encouraged.

"Whatever else I do, my epitaph will be 'Ozzy Osbourne, born December 3, 1948. Died, whenever. And he bit the head off a bat.'"
(Ozzy Osbourne)

(The first known warmblooded victim of Ozzy's choppers was a dove, one of a pair he and wife Sharon brought with them on a visit to their record company as a goodwill gesture. When the birds were released, one landed on the cognac-drenched rock star, who picked it up, and—chomp! Off with its head! The second animal Ozzy bit was a dead bat a fan threw to the stage during a 1982 concert. Ozzy "thought it was plastic," he said. This miscalculation cost him a painful rabies treatment, in addition to a whole lot of unwanted infamy.)

The Beatles

In 1965, the Beatles were awarded MBE (Member of the British Empire) medals at Buckingham Palace (still in their rebellious-rocker stage, they smoked some pot in the rest rooms at the palace while they were waiting for the ceremony to begin). A Canadian member of Parliament returned his MBE in protest, not wanting to be lumped together with "a bunch of vulgar numbskulls." But, retorted **John Lennon**, "Lots of people who complained about us receiving the MBE received theirs for heroism in the war—for killing people. We received ours for entertaining other people. I'd say we deserve ours more, wouldn't you?" A few years later, however, Lennon returned his medal with a strange little note addressed to Her Royal Highness: "Your Majesty, I am returning this MBE in protest against Britain's involvement in the Nigeria-Biafra thing, against our support of America in Vietnam, and against [Lennon single] 'Cold Turkey' slipping down the charts. With love, John Lennon of Bag." Whatever.

Björk

Photographer Julie Kaufman accused former Sugar Cube Björk of assaulting her at a Bangkok airport in February of 1996.

Kaufman said she "was waiting to welcome Björk and film her arrival. We got a message that she was willing to do a five-minute interview. But then her security said the interview was off as Björk was in a bad mood. She came out from the VIP area wheeling a trolley with her son on it. I approached her, and with my camera turned to her and said, 'Welcome to Bangkok.' She paused, looked at me for a few seconds, then she lunged." Björk allegedly knocked Kaufman to the ground and smacked her head against the ground repeatedly. Later, the Icelandic singer called to apologize, saying "she had been under a lot of strain for the past three weeks because people had been filming her son."

John Bonham, Led Zeppelin

During a flight in May of 1974, wild-man-of-rock John Bonham got absolutely pissed, and urinated in his first-class seat. He then staggered back to the coach section, where the band's roadies were parked, and magnanimously offered his premium seat to his unsuspecting personal assistant—who gladly took him up on the invitation, not realizing there was a small catch. John happily snored through the remainder of the flight in dry comfort, while the hapless assistant was forced by turbulence to remain in Bonham's old sodden seat. During another flight, this time on Zep's private jet (a Boeing 720 named the *Starship*, which included among its amenities a full bar, video screens, showers, bedrooms with "fireplaces," and an organ), Bonham, three sheets to the wind as usual, grabbed a stewardess and was just barely prevented by burly Zep roadies from sodomizing her on the spot. The band's scarily mountainous manager/handler, **Peter Grant**, advised all outsiders along for the ride (which included a few journalists) to forget what they'd witnessed.

David Bowie

In the late seventies, Bowie, in the throes of a heavy cocaine addiction, began answering interview questions in monosyllables—all the while carrying a stuffed monkey he called "Asshole." Aladdin Sane, indeed!

Jarvis Cocker, Pulp

Cocker crashed a **Michael Jackson** performance at the 1996 Brit Awards and made a mockery of the once-black singer. Jackson was in the middle of performing his insipid "Earth Song" to a cast of children when Cocker and a pal snuck past security and rushed the stage, where Cocker stuck out his butt and minced around in a grotesque parody of Jackson's moves, making mincemeat of Michael's pious performance. Cocker later explained, "It was just off the top of my head—seeing him with those kids under his outstretched arms, setting himself up as the messiah." A bravura performance! (By Jarvis, not Jackson.)

Billy Corgan, Smashing Pumpkins

Billy Corgan didn't handle his first brush with fame very well. "Here I am," he'd scream at nonplussed journalists. "Everything's great and I'm suicidal, completely depressed, I hate myself and I hate my band!" "The rage came out," he later confessed. "I imploded. It about killed me."

Elvis Costello

Angry young man Elvis Costello got himself into trouble in March of 1979 while sitting in a bar with members of **Stephen Stills's** band and **Bonnie Bramlett**. Costello was off his rocker after a long night of drinking, and started shooting off his mouth, calling former cocaine addict Stills "steel nose." Then, in response to Bramlett's assertion that black American artists were a lot "deeper" than any English artist you'd care to name, Costello called legend **Ray Charles** a "blind, ignorant nigger" and **James Brown** "another dumb nigger." Bonnie's response? She knocked ol' four-eyes to the floor with a quick one-two punch.

Fleetwood Mac

After **Lindsey Buckingham** and Stevie Nicks's romance fizzled, the tightly wound guitarist began acting out his anger at Stevie during their performances. In the middle of a concert in Australia, he cruelly mimicked her "witchy" dancing during "Rhiannon" by jerking his jacket over his head and whirling madly about the stage. "Lindsey was angry—just mad at me," says Stevie. But, she adds, "That wasn't a one-time thing. Lindsey and I had another huge thing that happened onstage in New Zealand. We had some kind of a fight and he came over . . . might have kicked me, did something to me . . . and we stopped the show. He went off, and we all ran at breakneck speed back to the dressing room to see who could kill him first. **Christine** [McVie] got to him first, and then I got to him second—the bodyguards were trying to get in the middle of all of us." Remembers McVie, "I think he's the only person I ever, ever slapped. I actually might have chucked a glass of wine, too. I just didn't think it was the way to treat a paying audience. I mean, aside from making a mockery of Stevie like that. Really unprofessional, over-the-top. Yes, [Stevie] cried—she cried a lot." The quarrelsome couple have since kissed and made up—at least professionally.

The Go-Go's

"I had sex at the [defunct L.A. club] Masque; everybody had sex at the Masque. You just did. It was great. Everybody was making out with each other in the bathrooms—lots of girls with girls. Everybody was on acid. My thing was acid or MDMA." (Belinda Carlisle)

"The whole thing was just out of control. I used to smoke angel dust, and I can't believe it now. There was a lot of drugs and a lot of drinking and a lot of puking." (Jane Wiedlin)

"We could freak our crew out, which is pretty amazing because you know how bad road crews are. We were so mean. We would spend hours trying to drive our road manager crazy. We would take pictures of our crotches and then slip them underneath his hotel room door and write, 'Guess whose is whose.' " (Jane Wiedlin)

"We'd take naked pictures of each other in England in the woods, we were so bored. We looked like wood nymphs. We'd say to our road manager, 'We have naked pictures of us,' and he'd go, 'Yeah right,' and we'd give them to him and he'd start shaking and then we'd snap them out of his hands." (Belinda Carlisle)

"The most disgusting thing we got up to was the Corner Cleaners. Kathy started this thing where we would go into rest stops on the freeway and say, 'Let's be corner cleaners,' which involved getting into the corners and sucking up the filth with your mouth. It was always in dirty bathrooms with shit everywhere. Just repulsive." (Gina Schock)

"This is how bad things got by 1984: Charlotte got thrown out of Ozzy Osbourne's dressing room. That pretty much sums up the height of our drug intake." (Gina Schock)

"Belinda, you were a major coke fiend." (Jane Wiedlin)
"Yeah." (Belinda Carlisle)

Guns N' Roses

"We're like a fuckin' grenade, and it's like everybody's struggling to hold the pin in."
(Slash)

Charm-school dropout **Axl Rose** once beat up a man in a hotel bar for saying the Guns N' Roses star bore a marked resemblance to poodle-rocker **Jon Bon Jovi**. (Can't blame Axl at all under those circumstances.) Axl also had an argument during the 1992 MTV Video Music Awards with **Hole** star **Courtney Love** and her better half, **Kurt Cobain**—which got so heated that Rose told Cobain to "shut your bitch up or I'm taking you down to the pavement."

Why Axl caused $100,000 worth of damage to a brand-new mansion he'd built: "I'm standing in this house going, 'This house doesn't mean anything to me. This is not what I wanted. I didn't work forever to have this lonely house on the hill that I live in because I'm a rich rock star.' So I shoved the piano right through the side of the house."

Billy Idol

When Billy moved to the West Coast in 1986, he paid frequent visits to (and occasionally trashed the offices of) his record company, Chrysalis, once adorning their walls with that weighty question we've all pondered: "Why are there no 'Rebel Yells' here?"

The Kinks

The American Federation of Musicians called a halt to U.S. concert tours by the Kinks for a while in the late sixties because of their out-of-hand onstage boozin'-and-brawlin'. In fact, **Ray** and **Dave Davies**, the two brothers who form the nucleus of the band, were constantly picking on each other (much like **Oasis's Gallagher** brothers today) . . . once, during a dinner the duo were having together in a Manhattan restaurant, Dave reached for one of Ray's french fries, prompting Ray to stab Dave in the chest with the nearest sharp object: a fork.

Every Rose has its thorn

Led Zeppelin

"Of course, it's usually one of our roadies that rides along with us and then gets us a bad reputation with his shenanigans." (Robert Plant)

That "bad reputation" was caused in large part by wild man **Richard Cole**—tour manager and prankster extraordinaire, who penned a must-read tome *(Stairway to Heaven)* about his wild years with the best rock 'n' roll band in the world. Sex-mad, always-good-for-a-larf Cole and his crew were well known for their insatiable appetites and willingness to try anything, particularly when it came to shagging.

"Nothing exciting ever happens to me."
(John Paul Jones)

John Lennon

Everyone's heard about the time when a very inebriated John Lennon was ejected from L.A.'s Troubadour club (for unruly behavior, which included assaulting a waitress while wearing some very strange apparel—he had a Kotex stuck to his pate). *Jackie Brown* star **Pam Grier** was there that night, and remembers that the incident started when the scheduled act, the **Smothers Brothers**, were late in taking the stage. So Lennon decided he'd try to amuse the crowd in the Smothers' stead—even after the brothers

finally showed up and began their show. Remembers Grier, "Everyone tries
to quiet him down but the guys are bombing out—no one's listening to
them. I said, 'John, they wouldn't do that to you.' He said, 'They don't
fucking need to—I'm John Lennon. I'm a Beatle.' So the manager comes
over and says, 'I told you to fucking get out of here.' So John says, 'Fuck
you!' Next thing you know, there's nine guys duking it out, and I'm
underneath the table, holding it like an umbrella, kicking and screaming.
Then we all got kicked out. But hey, he was the best company ever."
Sounds like it.

Marilyn Manson

During their 1998 tour, trash-goth rocker Marilyn Manson and his merry band got a little rambunctious in Poughkeepsie. First, Manson and crew lit a T-shirt and some carpeting on fire and trashed some lighting equipment at the venue, the Poughkeepsie Civic Center; then, after the concert, the bad boys wrecked four rooms at the local Sheraton, again burning carpets, ramming a telephone through the wall, and staining the bathroom fixtures with hair dye. *Rock 'n' roll, man!* A very *un*-rock-'n'-roll Marilyn immediately, contritely offered to pay for all damages. Wimp!

Metallica

The members of Metallica had a run-in with the bobbies for vandalizing a movie theater when they first visited London. "We climbed on top of the marquee, kicking the lights down on people," remembers vocalist/guitarist James Hetfield. "It was just one of those things we had to do when we were drunk."

THE KING AND I

Bruce Springsteen and Jerry Lee Lewis were both caught in 1976 attempting to gain entry to Graceland to see the King. Bruce was halted by security men (who were unmoved by his argument that he'd been on the covers of both *Newsweek* and *Time* that week), and Lewis was arrested after he showed up, brandished a hog-leg, and demanded entry. Though Springsteen escaped unscathed, Lewis was dinged for public intoxication and weapon possession. And neither one of them got to meet the King.

Keith Moon

"I suppose to most people I'm probably seen as an amiable idiot—a genial twit. I'm a victim of me own practical jokes." (Keith Moon)

"[Keith Moon's girlfriend] Annette turned 'round one day and said, 'Where's Keith? Keith's missing.' So we went looking for him. It was ten miles from his house to Malibu, two o'clock in the afternoon and there's Keith in his gold Sha Na Na suit and odd socks, wearing Annette's sunglasses and a buffalo coat, directing the traffic on the Pacific Coast Highway. Out of it." (Dougal Butler, Moon's minder)

"In eighteen months we had £148,000 of insurance claims, and I always said I was driving." (Dougal Butler)

POP PSYCHOLOGY

"I think of myself as an intelligent, sensitive human being with the soul of a clown, which always forces me to blow it at the most important moments."
(Jim Morrison)

Keith Moon was well known for his overweening fondness for practical jokes and his reckless willingness to try anything—*anything* (even the most dangerous stunts—which resulted in many injuries, including a broken collarbone, spine, wrists, and ankles, and the loss of the use of two of his fingers, at various times throughout his checkered career). These incidents included:

*Moon renting a helicopter to take him down to his local pub—all of three hundred yards away (he also bought a bar once so that there was at least one place where he couldn't be refused service).

*Almost being shot by a security person as he attempted to play a prank on **Mick** and **Bianca Jagger** by crawling along a ledge outside the window of their eleventh-story hotel room.

*Then there was the **Steve McQueen** incident. Moon was the actor's Malibu neighbor, and according to Moon's onetime business manager, Bill Curbishley, "I kept getting calls when I was in Canada from a lawyer who kept stressing that he had a woman client who used to run along the beach every morning, and she was interested in Moon's house. So I said to Moon, 'Keith, do you want to sell this house? As it is, I think you'll make a very good profit.' . . . I don't think it was a woman client at all. Steve McQueen lived next door and he wanted to get rid of Moon. I told Moon this, so he drove Steve absolutely fucking crazy. He built a ramp and bought a motorcycle, which was going to go over the wall like Steve McQueen in *The Great Escape*. He got dressed up as Hitler and knocked on McQueen's door, and when McQueen opened it, he got down on his hands and knees and bit McQueen's dog."

"If you're sitting around after a show and there's something you don't like, you just switch it off by throwing a bottle through the screen."
(Keith Moon)

Nirvana

"One of the funniest things was when Nirvana got thrown out of their own record-release party for starting a food fight. I think it was with ranch dressing. I turned up after the fact and saw Kurt standing outside of the club on the street with salad dressing all over his shirt and hair." (Kim Thayil, Soundgarden)

After a 1988 gig, **Kurt Cobain** and **Chris Novoselic**, who didn't get along with their drummer, **Chad Channing**, got so mad at him that they completely trashed his drum kit.

At the Reading rock festival in August of 1992, recalled promoter Harold Pendleton, "Kurt Cobain was a theatrical loony, totally out of it. At the last minute, he insisted he wouldn't go on without a wheelchair. Can you imagine, trying to find a wheelchair backstage at a rock festival? Chaos."
Note: Cobain—wearing a white dress and a lady's wig—got his wheelchair, and performed the entire show sitting in it.

Oasis

The bad boys of Oasis, **Noel** and **Liam Gallagher**, never cease to amaze and amuse with their ongoing series of monkeyshines, to wit:

In February of 1996, the boozed-up brothers attended the Brit Awards, where they infuriated most and sundry with their shitfaced shenanigans. First, Noel bad-mouthed presenter **Michael Hutchence** (called the INXS rocker a "has-been"), along with host Chris Evans (labeled him "Ginger Bollocks"), and simulated the insertion of one of the award statuettes up his booty, then sniffed it. Ee-yew. Then the Gallaghers refused to leave the dais, challenging anyone who felt he was "hard enough" to take them off by force. No takers. Later, a Brit Awards spokesperson said of the planned telecast of the event, "We'll have to cut out a few expletives and a few incidents because rock stars like Oasis insist on being very rock 'n' roll."

In August of 1996, temperamental Liam, on the eve of a major North American tour, stalked out of Heathrow and went home—reportedly because of yet another serious row with his brother. "I don't care about the tour," huffed Liam, who had just sold the house he shared with actress-wife **Patsy Kensit**. "I'm sick of living my life in hotels. I need to be happy. We'll be out of here in a week's time, and I've got to sort something out. The band are going to have to see if they can do it without me because I've got to find somewhere to live. If they can't do it without me, I guess I'll come back. I'm fucking sick of it. I've got to be happy—that's why I am not there. I've got to get my life sorted out. I have got to get a house and I'm not going to play for silly bloody Yanks before I've found a home." (Liam did end up rejoining the Oasis tour for a brief time, but then flew back home less than a month later.) He now admits he "was doing it to be a fuckin' moody cunt, and I apologize for that."

"All the rows that ever started, we've been drunk. 'Look at your shoes, you dickhead.' 'Who are you calling a dick?' 'Calling you a dick.' 'Who's a dick?' And before you know it, you're hailing a Concorde."
(Noel Gallagher)

1997 was a busy year for Liam. Early in the year, he received an official warning for possession of cocaine, and in July, he got an official caution for grabbing a bicyclist through the window of his Mercedes in London. Then, in December, angered at the disparaging comments former **Beatle Paul McCartney** had made about the band (such as this snide statement: "I figure I've probably got a better chance of coming up with a good Paul McCartney song than Oasis has"—referring to the band's Beatles-influenced sound), Gallagher destroyed a copy of *Many Years from Now*, McCartney's autobiography, at a Scottish airport after an Oasis performance, ripping the book apart and flinging it off a balcony. The badly behaved brothers then flew into Cardiff, where Liam overturned a few drinks on a hapless journalist, who was sitting in the lobby of a hotel doing nothing more offensive than drinking his tea.

In March of 1998, looped Liam became instantly besotted with a comely lass he spotted outside Sydney, Australia's Criterion Hotel. "I didn't recognize him at first," said the victim, Julia Kerrigan. "I just thought he was another drunken idiot who'd been at the pub. I told him to piss off, and he asked if I knew who he was. I replied, yes, I did know who he was, but that I thought he was a dickhead regardless." Liam's response? He followed her across the street, said, "Here, I have something for you," deposited something down the front of her blouse, then ran off. What was it? A used Kleenex. (Gag.) Kerrigan said, "I'm going to lodge a harassment complaint with the police just for the record, but I don't want to file any charges because I think it's the wrong time of my life to be going to court over a snotty tissue." Well, how about a snotty rock star?

In February of 1998, the band wore out their welcome with Cathay Pacific airline after belligerent Liam threatened to stab a crew member during a flight from Hong Kong to Australia. (Liam's explanation: "One panhead told me to shut up—some panhead who needs stabbing through the head with a fucking pickax.") The band and their entourage also reportedly caused nonstop disturbances on the flight after they'd had a snootful o' booze: they'd thrown things all over the plane, swore loudly, and lit up (both ciggies and "the herb") in the cabin. An airline spokesperson said, "We made the decision to ban Mr. Gallagher and those known to have caused nuisance on the flight from Hong Kong to Perth. We want to put the safety of our crew and passengers as a priority." Added another, "They were unruly, using foul language, trying to smoke on a nonsmoking flight, and above all upsetting other passengers. We feel that we don't want to carry Oasis again unless they can give us some kind of guarantee of adult behavior." Yeah. That'll happen.

> **"Abusive."**
>
> **"Disgusting towards the air crew."**
>
> **"Destructive."**
>
> *(Pissed-off passengers aboard the Cathay Pacific flight)*

Sinéad O'Connor

"Troubled pop star" might be an understatement if you were trying to describe Sinéad O'Connor. The incident for which she's most notorious is the time she tore up a picture of the pope during an appearance on *Saturday Night Live*. "Fight the real enemy," the bald beauty cried—then looked as if she expected the audience to clap (they didn't). Said *Saturday Night Live*'s **Lorne Michaels**, "We were sort of shocked, the way you would be at a houseguest pissing on a flower arrangement in the dining room," and banned the problematic Irish pop star from the show for life. Why'd she do it? She explains, "The photograph was a picture of the pope in Ireland. It was a picture which belonged to my mother, so there was a whole subconscious personal thing going on there. It was myself I was tearing apart. Just before that, I was ostracized by my father and my brother. So the pope is the symbol of the father, and my family always says that I don't care about anyone but myself and I wanted to show them that I did care so much that I would kill myself to prove it."

Ozzy Osbourne

Ozzy Osbourne had a wild time on tour with **Mötley Crüe**, what with all the substances being abused (birds [or bingers] of a feather)—too wild for manager-wife Sharon. Because there were so many temptingly illicit ways to get in trouble, she decided to take matters into her own hands in San Antonio and ensure he got a good night's rest—so she deposited him in their hotel room and locked up his clothing. Well, Ozzy wasn't going to let a little thing like that stop him from enjoying the lovely Texas countryside. When she departed the room, he promptly donned one of her dresses, plus a pair of fashionable high heels, downed a bottle of brandy, and went wandering about town. Right about the time he approached the Alamo, he felt an urgent need to heed Ma Nature's call—and relieved himself on one of the landmark's walls. Security men were decidedly unamused, and Osbourne was thrown in the clink for public intoxication and defiling a national monument.

Iggy Pop

Iggy Pop was dropped by MainMan, his management company, after he reportedly stripped down and masturbated in public—albeit only over the radio waves (from a station in Detroit, where the jocks were attempting to conduct an interview). "I'm naked here!" he crowed to a less-than-thrilled audience.

Slade

Robbie Wilson, tour manager for Slade, among others (Led Zeppelin, The Eagles, Elton John), recounts a classic rock tour tale: "In Australia, I received a call very early one morning asking why I had parked a transit minibus on the eleventh floor of the hotel. I couldn't answer the question, but I was informed that the night before, after a party at a nightclub involving Slade, Status Quo, Lindisfarne, and Caravan, I had driven everybody back to the hotel—quite illegally, given the amount of alcohol I'd consumed. I discovered a service lift at the back of the hotel and, to assist everybody in the minibus, I decided to drive us onto the eleventh floor. I parked this vehicle in the service lift, took it up, drove it onto the landing, and we all just popped out." Wilson spent a few days in the pokey and coughed up about a thousand bucks in fines. "It was fashionable," Wilson explains. "It was all caused by too much alcohol, bravado, and one-upmanship. People were vying to be the craziest group around. If Led Zeppelin threw a TV into the swimming pool the night before, we'd see if we could do the three-piece suite."

LEARNING BY EXAMPLE

"All you've got to do is delete the words 'punk rock' and write in 'Rolling Stones' and you've got the same press as you had fifteen years ago. . . . They've made the press play the same old games as they played with us. They puked at London airport, we pissed in the filling station."
(Keith Richards, on the Sex Pistols)

"If we puke in public, it's because we feel sick."
(Steve Jones)

"Sometimes I wonder what all the fuss is about. We're the nicest bunch of guys you'd ever want to meet."
(Johnny Rotten)

Snot

During **Limp Bizkit**'s performance at OzzFest 1998, Snot's (love these names, guys) singer **Lynn Strait** climbed atop the Bizkit's forty-foot porcelain toilet (a stage prop) on a dare, and was sexually, er, *gratified* by an anonymous vixen dressed up in bondage gear. Strait was having the time of his life, but was forced to flee the stage when security guards took notice of the salacious show-within-a-show. "I ran into a dressing room, slammed the door, and there's **Ozzy Osbourne**'s wife and daughter," he shamefacedly confessed. "They were really sweet about it." Strait was caught and cited by the long arm of the law—"But after that, the dominatrix chick finished it. I never knew her name. Man, it's *so* metal."

The Stranglers

The band were well known for having a very strong dislike of certain members of the press (probably due to years of bad reviews). Stranglers associate Alan Edwards recalled a time when the band was touring Iceland with a journalist in tow. "That bloke was a twat, a real upper-class twit . . . he said, 'I can out-drink you punks!' So J. J. [**Burnel**] decided to teach him a lesson. We're coming back to the airport and J. J. physically holds him down and literally pours a bottle of spirits down his throat. The guy gets off the bus at the airport, and I'm not exaggerating—there's sick coming out of this guy's ears and he's passed out by now. But, being the Stranglers, instead of calling an ambulance, what they do is that they get this wheelchair. He's covered in puke, and they get all the press, and there's forty or fifty journalists and photographers, and they get him there for a photo-call and the band line up behind him. It's pretty sick stuff." (Not only sick, but also tragic—the journo-victim lost his job and became a Brighton Beach tramp.)

Van Halen

Yes, the "brown M&Ms" story: In 1980, after playing a smokin' set at the University of Southern Colorado, the band went ballistic upon discovering that the promoter hadn't followed their explicit instructions—to remove all the brown (ugly color) M&Ms from their backstage candy dish. The enraged rockers trashed the facility, causing $10,000 worth of damage—and begetting a rock legend.

Sid Vicious

A few examples of Sid's outrageous oeuvre:

In one very eventful short period (January 1978): At the Kingfisher Club in Baton Rouge, Sid attempted to have sex with a forward fan who'd made her way onto the stage during a **Pistols** performance. Later in the month, he overdosed on the corner of Haight and Ashbury in the City by the Bay, and was rushed to the hospital (he made a full recovery). A few days later, he fell into a drug-induced coma during a flight to New York and was again hospitalized. Also in that same momentous month, he fell in love with a pair of motorcycle boots owned by a photographer traveling with the Pistols. The man magnanimously loaned his cool footwear to Sid for a couple of performances, and Vicious decided they were so "him" that he just had to own them. One problem—the shutterbug wouldn't part with them. Trouble was brewing . . . one night on the tour bus, a member of the Pistols' road crew awoke to find Sid brandishing a Bowie knife at the slumbering photographer. The roadie leapt up and threw Sid to the floor before he could use the knife. Whew! "I would have woken him up before I slit his throat," Sid whined.

At a punk club in New York, Vicious got into an altercation with **Todd Smith** (Patti's brother). The dustup started because Sid propositioned Smith's girlfriend. The two men began arguing, and Sid whacked Smith in the face with a broken bottle, nearly blinding him.

During a concert in San Antonio, Sid took umbrage at a Texas audience who was pelting the band with food and beer cans. "You cowboys are all a bunch of fucking faggots," he yelled, and bonked one troublemaker over the noggin with his bass.

Paul Weller (The Jam, Style Council) once knuckle-dusted Sid "because he headbutted me. It ain't much of a story, to be honest. It was in the Speakeasy, down Marlborough Street. . . . He came up and nutted me, so I slapped him back. That was it; I got lobbed out of the club or whatever. I'm never proud of getting involved in anything like that." Bet Sid was, though.

Wearing and Tearing

"We don't smash hotels, we redecorate them."
(Graham Gouldman, 10CC)

"It's strange how success and room-wrecking seem to go together. For years we never destroyed so much as a toothbrush holder, and it was only when we were playing every night to sellout crowds of anything from twenty thousand to seventy-two thousand did we get in trouble."
(Bev Bevan, ELO)

The Continental Hyatt House (a.k.a. the Hyatt on Sunset, a.k.a. the Riot House), in the middle of L.A.'s famed "Strip," had a blind-eye attitude when it came to rockers, which is why so many rockers came to them. Led Zeppelin used it as their unofficial Los Angeles headquarters, and the band and their crew had many great and wild times there—because hotel employees routinely ignored shenanigans like the group's habit of racing motorcycles up and down the hallways. The Zepsters were also fond of using parked cars as target practice, once lobbing a series of drinks over their high balcony railings to see what they could hit.

One item they bull's-eyed was the immaculate interior of a parked convertible; when the irate owner complained, the boys responded by shoving an entire dining table over the balcony, *completely* wrecking the man's fine automobile.

The band didn't stop with the trashing of the Riot House:

At another hotel, the boys glued the carpets and all the furniture in one room to the ceiling.

ALIAS SMITH & JONES

Elton John's on-the-road hotel aliases

Sir Tarquin Budgerigar

Bobo Latrine Jr.

Sir Horace Pussy

Binky Poodleclip

At an establishment in Nantes, **Robert Plant** became incensed after learning there was no milk for his tea. His reaction? "Go to town, boys." Zep's rowdy roadies removed doors and hinges, flooded a couple of floors with fire hoses, stuffed various items down the toilets to stop up the plumbing, and smashed furniture into bite-size bits.

The band were barred for life from the Tokyo Hilton after **John Bonham** and tour manager **Richard Cole** decided to see just how much damage they could do with a couple of Samurai swords. (The answer was "a lot.")

In New Orleans, bassist/keyboardist **John Paul Jones** picked up a comely lass and took her back to his hotel. They smoked a little pot, then fell asleep—and were rudely awakened by firemen, who'd been alerted by other guests to a fire in Jones's room. Jones must've been surprised to see them—but not as surprised as he was when he learned that the "girl" he was in bed with was actually a transvestite!

Zep were so well known for their room-wrecking, TV-tossing high jinks that desk clerks came to expect a hefty payment for damages along with  the normal room-'n'-board charges. Recalled manager Peter Grant about a worker at Seattle's Edgewater Inn, "This clerk went into the whole rap about, 'Well, it's all right for you guys to take out all of your things on stuff like that, but how do you think I'd feel, never being able to do the same thing?' So I jeered him on a bit and said, 'You'd really like that, wouldn't you?' And he said, 'Oh yeah, I'd love to do it.' So I said, 'Well, have one on us. I'll treat you. Do whatever you want to do.' And he went in and he fucking threw all the stuff around and threw the stuff out the windows, and I went down to the desk and paid his bill: $490."

"I can't think of anything I fear more, except possibly a nuclear holocaust."
(A Fort Worth hotel manager, on Led Zeppelin's imminent arrival)

Aerosmith brought chain saws along on tour (all the better to destroy hotel rooms), together with extra-long extension cords.

Why the cords? So the TVs they threw out their windows would continue playing all the way to the ground!

"We had one mad night in New York, when I woke up the next morning covered in sick. That was a bit stupid. I don't want to die in my sleep, covered in puke. That would be the textbook rock death—a bit clichéd. When you're traveling around the world, you just want to have a laugh; and when you've got tons of free booze you think, 'What the hell.' One famous mate I've got is Chloe from *Home and Away*—Kristy Wright, her name is—and we were in her hotel room in Australia once, throwing stuff out of the window. They told us we were worse than any rugby team and we got banned, which was a real pisser because it was a nice hotel."

(Tim Wheeler, guitarist, Ash)

Rap star Dr. Dre, who toured with the Beastie Boys, remembers his fellow musicians fondly: "On the tour, Ad-Rock drilled a hole in the floor of the hotel and put a hose down into Yauch's room to see if they could fill it up with water. Another time, we were in London and MCA jumped off the third-floor balcony into the pool. We were banned from Holiday Inns for the rest of our lives. I *still* can't get into a Holiday Inn. I tried the other day and they said, 'We have your picture with those other guys.' "

"We were barred from so many hotels—the entire Holiday Inn chain—that we had to check in as Fleetwood Mac lots of times."

(Ron Wood, on playing with The Faces)

"I tell you what is the best thing to do. If you check into a hotel, go straight upstairs and empty your minibar into a holdall. Then phone reception and say, 'I've just checked into my room and there's no fucking booze in the minibar. Come and fill it up please?' Usually the maids get sacked for pinching the minibar, but there you go. That's life, isn't it?"

(Noel Gallagher, Oasis)

Mötley Crüe were banned from an entire country—Germany—because of their bad behavior at a hotel. What did they do? Chucked mattresses out their windows to watch them boing off the parked autos below.

Moon Rocks!

"You'd come offstage and still be buzzing. Then you'd get to a party and it would get out of hand. Things get broken. If you're sitting around after a show and there's things you don't like on telly, you just switch it off by throwing a bottle through the screen."

(Keith Moon)

All-time, Hall-of-Fame, Five-Star Hotel-Trashing Champeeeeeen: Keith Moon

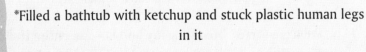

At various times, the king of hotel-room-wrecking:

*Blew doors off their hinges with homemade cherry bombs

*Blew up a toilet the same way ("This cherry bomb was about to go off in my hand, so I threw it down the bog to put it out," he explained.)

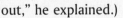

*Blew up a hotel manager's wife's room

*Filled a bathtub with ketchup and stuck plastic human legs in it

*Linked electrical fixtures together in odd ways—lights to radios to TVs, and so on

*Dropped several boxes of laundry detergent into a fountain from his twelfth-story room

More on-the-road Keith-and-hotel-room stories

*When a roadie borrowed a cassette player from Moon, then had the nerve to fall asleep without returning it, Keith tried to batter the man's door down with, variously, a bench and a fire ax. When it became evident that neither method was going to do the trick, Moon sidled into the roadie's adjoining room, which happened to be rented out to Pete Townshend, and had a go at the wall with a small knife. After an hour, he'd managed to

remove a single brick, and it didn't take long for him to work several more loose. Moon then backed up and ran madly at the wall, crashing through it like a cartoon character. The startled roadie, abruptly awoken and afraid there was an intruder in his room, whacked Keith over the head with a lamp. Moon, injured but victorious, returned triumphantly to Townshend's room, brandishing the cassette deck.

*At his twentieth birthday party, held at a Holiday Inn in Flint, Michigan, Moon got well and truly looped, then stood atop a table and threw bits of his birthday cake about—after divesting himself of his clothing (most of the partygoers, in similar states of intoxication, followed suit). The hotel manager soon arrived with the local gendarmes, and Moon attempted to flee—but fell onto a chair and knocked out his front teeth. Scrambling to his feet, Moon dashed outside, commandeered a Lincoln Continental parked nearby, and drove it straight into the hotel's swimming pool.

Roger Daltrey remembers an occasion when, "I don't know how and why they did such a mad thing, but the hotel management put Keith Moon in a fancy suite with a huge waterbed in it at the top of the hotel. Sometime around 2 A.M., he and a road manager for some unknown reason decided to remove the bed and managed to get it to the elevator—where it exploded and flooded twelve floors of the building. Gee, that was expensive. We'll never forget that, but hopefully they've forgiven. At least the bill was paid."

"I get bored, you see. When I get bored, I rebel. . . . So I took out my hatchet and chopped the Holiday Inn room to bits. The television. The chairs. The cupboard doors. The bed. It happens all the time."
(Keith Moon)

Jailhouse Rock

"I've been arrested for fighting and for breaking and entering. I broke into a shop for some cigarettes. I was arrested and put on probation. It wasn't a big crime or anything— nothing planned, just a spur-of-the-moment thing. I was a teenager, a kid."
(Lounge lizard Tom Jones)

Stars 'n' bars

Marty Balin, Jefferson Airplane/Starship

May 1970: With pal Terry Cost and sound engineer Gary O'Dell, Balin was found by cops in a Bloomington, Minnesota, hotel room with several underage girls (ranging in age from twelve to seventeen) after neighbors complained about a noisy party at five-thirty in the morning. Balin was charged with marijuana possession and contributing to the delinquency of minors, and was sentenced to a year's hard labor and a hundred-dollar fine (Balin only paid the fine).

Chuck Berry

Late fifties: Berry was convicted of a Mann Act violation involving an underage prostitute, Norine Janice Escalanti, who was employed at one of his nightclubs (Berry served two years); also, in 1979 Berry served four months for underpaying the IRS to the tune of a couple of hundred thousand bucks on his 1973 tax returns.

David Bowie

March 1976: Hanging out together at the Rochester Hotel in New York, Bowie and pal Iggy Pop were arrested on suspicion of marijuana possession. The pair were released on bail, and the charges were eventually dropped. In April of the same year, the Thin White Duke was detained for several hours on the border of Russia and Poland, where customs officers found and confiscated his stash of Nazi memorabilia (Bowie wasn't arrested).

Boy George

July 1986: Fined $400 for heroin possession

Ian Brown, Stone Roses

Getting cheeky with the help: In February of 1998, the singer was arrested after harassing a pilot and stewardess on a flight from Paris to Manchester, England (he allegedly threatened to chop the stew's hands off, then hammered hysterically on the cockpit door just before the plane touched down). In November of 1998, Brown lost an appeal to get a reduction in his four-month jail sentence, even though he insisted to the court it was all just meant to be a joke. (Hardy har—next he'll be telling the folks at check-in that he has a bomb.)

James Brown

1988: Brown allegedly shot at his wife, Adrienne, as she sped off in a car during a spat—then, to top it off, when she returned to the house, he beat her with a pipe. (He explained, "She was just mad because I wouldn't take her on my South American tour.") A few days later, Adrienne was arrested for receiving drugs (she was nabbed at an airport carrying some angel dust), but claimed she'd been framed by her volatile husband. Adrienne dropped her complaint against him a couple of weeks later. That summer, Brown was arrested and charged with drug possession (PCP), a weapons charge (illegally carrying a firearm), and resisting arrest. He was fined $1,200 and ordered to perform a benefit concert.

CLAIMED SHE WAS FRAMED!

Christian Death

Guitarist **Flick Fuck** and bisexual drummer **Steve** (a.k.a. Stephanie) **Wright**, April 1998: Charged with possession of narcotics, supplying narcotics, and statutory rape in Concord, New Hampshire, after cops found four fifteen- to nineteen-year-old naked girls, all under the influence of cocaine, in a hotel room with Flick and Steve. Fuck was sent off to jail, and Wright was remanded to rehab.

The Clash

(Bad boys, bad boys, whatcha gonna doooo . . .)

Joe Strummer and Topper Headon, June 1977: Arrested for painting "The Clash" on a wall in London

Joe Strummer, June 1977: Fined for the theft of some pillows from a Holiday Inn

Paul Simonon and Topper Headon, March 1978: Arrested for shooting birds from the roof of their rehearsal building in London

Joe Strummer and Paul Simonon, July 1978: Arrested in Glasgow for being drunk and disorderly

Joe Strummer, May 1980: In Hamburg, Strummer was arrested for whacking a concertgoer over the head with his guitar

Joe Cocker

October 1972: Police in Adelaide, Australia, say they nabbed the singer and six of his bandmates with marijuana, heroin, and "works" (syringes). Cocker was released on bail.

Harry Connick Jr.

December 1992: Connick was arrested for the oh-so-rock-star offense of gun-carrying-at-an-airport (JFK). Charges were dropped after Connick agreed to make a public service announcement warning folks not to carry unlicensed firearms in New York. Even most New Yorkers don't *need* to be told, Harry.

Hugh Cornwell, The Stranglers

January 1980: Sentenced to two months in a London jail for possession of heroin (90 mg), cocaine (1½ grams), some hallucinogenic "magic mushrooms," and pot (½ ounce). Cornwell served five weeks.

Elvis Costello

July 1977: Arrested and fined for an unauthorized street performance outside the Hilton in London—where there was a conference of CBS Records executives (it was worth it—he got a record deal shortly afterward)

Steve Cradock, Ocean Colour Scene

April 1998: Received an official warning by U.K. police for cocaine possession

David Crosby

March 1982: After passing out and crashing his car on a Southern California freeway, Crosby was arrested for possession of Quaaludes and drug "works," as well as driving under the influence (of cocaine) and carrying a concealed handgun (which, he claimed, he'd purchased in self-defense after hearing about the shooting of John Lennon by a crazed fan). The case was plea-bargained down to reckless driving, for which Crosby was put on probation. April 1982: Arrested in Dallas at a nightclub, where cops found him taking cocaine (Crosby was also in possession of a firearm). Crosby was convicted on drug and weapons charges and sentenced to five years.

Rick Danko

June 1997: In Japan, police raided Danko's hotel room, where they found a gram-and-a-quarter of heroin—which, Danko claimed, had been sent to him by his wife after he'd asked her for some "medication" (by which he said he meant codeine). "I'm just very surprised that she did something that stupid," he told officials. That's right, blame it on her. With his wife, Danko was found guilty of collusion to smuggle heroin into Japan, and received a two-and-a-half-year suspended sentence.

BLAMED INCIDENT ON WIFE!

Kevin DuBrow, Quiet Riot

January 1999: DuBrow was arrested for failing to pay off a female fan who won a lawsuit against him in 1994 for injuries she suffered at a Charlotte, North Carolina, concert. After his arrest, DuBrow told the judge he had no money (claimed he hadn't received a royalty check in years, and was living with his mom), which is why he hadn't paid the woman. DuBrow is now working out a payment plan.

Jerry Garcia, Grateful Dead

March 1973: Cops pulled him over for speeding in New Jersey, searched his car, and found illegal substances. Gee, they must have been really surprised.

Gary Glitter

November 1997: Nabbed upon his return from vacation after technicians at a Bristol, England, computer store found kiddie-porn pictures on a machine he'd brought in for repair (no one ever said rockers were Mensa material). Police ransacked his nearby abode, where they grabbed videos and more smutty pictures, and the tubby ex-glam rocker was arrested for suspicion of harboring child pornography (more than fifty counts), assaulting underage girls (four counts), and sodomy (four counts). The case is pending.

The Grateful Dead

October 1967: All six members were busted for pot possession at their Ashbury Street house in San Francisco (they spent just six hours in lockup—probably not even enough time for the drugs to wear off).

George Harrison and Patti Boyd

March 1969: Arrested in London for marijuana possession (they had 120 joints in their apartment) on the day of **Paul McCartney**'s wedding to **Linda Eastman** (Harrison and Boyd obviously couldn't make it). George claimed they'd been framed, but they both pled guilty anyway, and were fined £250.

CLAIMED THEY WERE FRAMED!

Jimi Hendrix

May 1968: Arrested on the Canadian border for possession of hashish and heroin. Hendrix claimed he'd been framed—and was in fact exonerated by a jury in December of the same year, even after admitting he'd taken pot, hash, LSD, and cocaine in the past.

Don Henley

November 1980: Paramedics rushed to the **Eagle**'s L.A. aerie in response to a 911 call, and found a nude, comatose sixteen-year-old who'd ODed. Cops called to the scene by the EMTs found a stash of illicit drugs, and charged Henley with possession of pot, cocaine, and Quaaludes, together with contributing to the delinquency of a minor. Henley spent a night in lockup, and was later sentenced to a mandatory stint in rehab plus a $5,000 fine. (He also penned "Dirty Laundry" in response to the media furor over this and other events in his life.)

Billy Idol

February 1987: Though he wasn't charged, Idol was allegedly caught in possession of (and arrested for) about a hundred bucks' worth of crack in Greenwich Village.

Rick James

August 1991: With girlfriend Tanya Ann Hijazi, the
Superfreak was arrested for the torture of a
twenty-four-year-old woman, who said he'd
suspected her of stealing some of his
cocaine, and, in retaliation, had burned her
body with a red-hot crack pipe, as well as forcing
her to perform oral sex on Hijazi. Ugh! Ick! James and
Hijazi were charged with assault
with a deadly weapon, aggravated
mayhem, torture, and forcible oral
copulation; James was also charged with
making terrorist threats and furnishing
cocaine. James spent a long stretch
in stir (he's now out, and he and
Tanya are still together—if anyone
cares).

CLAIMED THE VICTIM STOLE HIS DRUGS!!

Tom Johnston, The Doobie Brothers

December 1973: Arrested for possession of
marijuana. That's why they call him a *Doobie
Brother.*

Janis Joplin

November 1969:
Arrested for using
"vulgar and
indecent" language
during a performance in Tampa after verbally
lambasting a cop who'd instructed the crowd to
settle down. "Don't fuck with those people!" Joplin
screeched. "Hey mister, what're you so uptight about?
Did you buy a five-dollar ticket?"

Tommy Lee, Mötley Crüe

"He completely went blank. His eyes were glass. I didn't know who he was when he started . . . when he was doing that."
(Pamela Anderson)

February 1998: Lee was arrested and charged with spousal abuse, child abuse, and unlawful possession of a firearm. The charges stemmed from a panicky 911 call placed by Lee's wife, *Baywatch* bombshell **Pamela Anderson**, after a bad argument turned violent (possibly because Lee had gotten his paws on a video clip of Anderson having sex with former boyfriend **Bret Michaels**, Poison's lead singer). Explained Pammy, "He said, 'You know, my brain works too fast to be just looking after children.'

He had given Dylan a bath and played with Brandon. But he was like, 'I'm bored.' My therapist told me, 'Tommy's not your child. So when he's being needy, just walk away.' So I did. Well, it infuriated him. He was just throwing pots and pans around, rocking on the ground, and I wasn't catering to him. And then it exploded. I had to call 911. He could have done anything at that point. What really frightened me was that he had no regard for his children. The babies were crying and hyperventilating, and I was shaking and screaming and holding both the babies when he kicked me in the back. I thought, 'There's nothing I can do if he's not even listening to his children.' " Lee was hauled off to jail, where he cooled his heels overnight, and was later ordered not to contact Pamela or come within a hundred yards of their Malibu mansion. In May of 1998, he was sentenced to six months in jail, three years probation, and a court-imposed donation of $5,000 to a battered-women's shelter. (It's worth noting that in January of the same year, Lee had gone to court-ordered anger-therapy classes, as well as forking over a stiff fine and settling a lawsuit brought by a photographer who'd allegedly been injured by Lee in a scuffle outside a night-club in 1996.) Miss Pamela and her knight in shining tats are back together.

> **"He was sixteen when he became a massive rock star, and he's thirty-six now, and he's just used to having whatever he wants whenever he wants it. And he's just learning now that things have consequences. He's a thirty-six-year-old teenager."**
> *(Pamela Anderson)*

Paul and Linda McCartney

August 1972: Arrested for drug possession following a concert in Gothenburg, Sweden (Paul was fined $1,000, Linda $200, and drummer Denny Seiwell $600). March 1973: Local authorities found marijuana growing on Paul and Linda's farm in Scotland and immediately

arrested them. Paul claimed an avid interest in horticulture, and said a fan had given him some seeds—and that he'd had no idea what they'd grow. The pair were released after paying a paltry £100 fine. March 1975: Pulled over by a traffic cop when they ran a red light; loopy Linda's purse was searched by the policeman, who found a bit of marijuana and charged her with possession (Paul, who was driving, was not charged). 1980: Paul was busted in Tokyo after being caught at the air-port with half a pound of pot in his suitcase. He was deported to England after spending ten miserable days in prison. Through the efforts of the British consulate, McCartney was released and charges were dropped—but he was prohibited from reentering the coun-try for a year.

CLAIMED TO BE UNAWARE OF WHAT HE'D DONE!

George Michael

"He was quite tasty. They don't send Karl Malden in there—we're not talking Columbo with his dick out. . . . If you see a man playing with his penis in front of you, you don't think it's a cop."
(George Michael)

April 1998: Arrested in Beverly Hills' Will Rogers Memorial Park (a sign above the entrance reads "I never met a man I didn't like") and charged with "lewd conduct" for exposing himself. (Michael later pled no contest to the charge and was sentenced to perform eighty hours of community srvice.) Later in the month, he did an interview with CNN in which he admitted he hadn't been with a woman in the previous ten years.

CLAIMED THE COP WAS TOO "TASTY" TO RESIST!

"I won't even attempt to deny, I won't even say that it was the first time that happened. You know, I have put myself in that position before. I can try to fathom out why I did it, to understand my own sexuality a bit better, but ultimately part of me has to believe that some of the kick was the fact I might get found. You know, deep down, I truly believe that. 'Here I am, I got found.' "

"I am a very proud man. I want people to know that I have not been exposed as a gay man in any way that I feel any shame for. I feel stupid and reckless and weak for having allowed my sexuality to be exposed this way, but I don't feel any shame whatsoever and neither do I think I should."

You're right. What you should *feel shame about is your last few albums.*

Jim Morrison

December 1967: At a **Doors** concert in New Haven, Morrison was charged with breach of the peace and resisting arrest after an ugly backstage incident turned into an ugly onstage incident. Morrison had been smooching up a young lady before the show when the amorous pair were interrupted by an eagle-eyed cop, who ordered them to leave. Morrison, always resentful of authority, mouthed off, and the officer maced him into compliance. Jim recovered enough to go on, but when the Doors took the stage, he related the whole sorry story to the audience, whereupon pissed-off police turned up the houselights and arrested him for breaching the peace and resisting arrest.

March 1969: "Do you want to see my cock?" Morrison asked an audience in Miami, then proceeded to expose himself. He was arrested for lewd and lascivious behavior, public drunkenness, and profanity (and was later found guilty of indecent exposure and the profanity charge), and sentenced to sixty days in jail (plus a $500 fine). The sentence was on appeal when Morrison kicked the bucket.

> "I don't think anything of it, really. I suppose the show wasn't going too well, so Jim decided to pull out his prick and liven it up a bit. If he likes wanking, that's okay. I don't think he actually wanked off, though. Even if he did, I wish he'd done the whole thing and fucked some bird up there. Do the whole scene."
>
> *(John Lennon)*

November 1969: Harassed a couple of flight attendants on an L.A.–Phoenix flight and was charged with "interfering with the flight of an intercontinental aircraft" and public drunkenness. Charges were dropped after one of the attendants changed her testimony.

August 1970: Arrested for public drunkenness (do we detect a pattern emerging?) after he was found on a Los Angeles porch, passed out from drinking

Chuck Negron, Three Dog Night

July 1975: Arrested in his Louisville hotel room on the first night of a Three Dog Night tour and charged with cocaine possession (charges were dropped after the court learned the warrant had been obtained on the basis of inaccurate information)

Vince Neil, Mötley Crüe

December 1984: After a few days of hard partying, Vince and his pal **Razzle Dingley** (drummer for **Hanoi Rocks**) decided to cruise down to the liquor store in Vince's Pantera for some refills. Neil, who was legally drunk, sped down the street, hit a puddle of water, then hydroplaned the car across the road—and head-on into a Volkswagen coming the other way. Crrrrrrraaaaaaaaassssssshhhhhhh! Dingley died of his injuries almost immediately, and the two people in the Volkswagen were seriously injured, one suffering permanent brain damage as a result. Convicted of felony vehicular manslaughter, Neil spent twenty days in jail, played a few benefit concerts, spent two hundred hours doing community service, and paid $2.6 million in restitution. "I fucked up," admitted Vince. "I've always wanted to go out and have a good time, loved fast cars, loved to get drunk. I just fucked up."

Tam Paton, Bay City Rollers manager

May 1982: Sentenced to three years in prison in Edinburgh, Scotland, after pleading guilty of behaving "in a shamelessly indecent manner" (no specifics given) with ten teenage boys

John Phillips, The Mamas & the Papas

July 1980: Cops raided his capacious abode on Long Island, found amphet-amines and opiates, and arrested Phillips for conspiracy to distribute narcotics (e.g., dealing). His five-year prison sentence was ultimately reduced to 250 hours of community service and a few antidrug lectures.

Keith Richards

1967: After the infamous Redlands bust (you know, the "Mars bar" incident involving rug-wrapped Mick muse **Marianne Faithfull**), Richards was found guilty of allowing his residence to be used for pot smoking (ooh, naughty) and was fined £500.

October 1973: Fined and given a one-year suspended sentence in France on drug charges (as well as being barred from entering that country for two years) and given a fine and conditional discharges on three weapons offenses and four drug offenses in England.

July 1975: In Arizona, Richards was charged with reckless driving and carrying a concealed hunting knife after a cop pulled him over and searched his car; the case was later dismissed.

May 1976: Fell asleep at the wheel and wrecked his Bentley, in which cops (of course) found various drugs. Keith was fined £750 for cocaine possession (but found not guilty of LSD possession), and coughed up another £250 for court costs.

February 1977: Arrested by the RCMP at his room in the Harbour Castle Hotel in Toronto for drug possession: cops found twenty-two grams of heroin and five of cocaine, plus assorted narcotics paraphernalia. Richards was convicted of heroin possession with intent to traffic (a potential life sentence in Canada) and possession of cocaine. When the gavel fell, Richards got off lightly indeed—he was given a one-year suspended sentence, and ordered to perform a single charity concert.

Chris Robinson, Black Crowes

May 1991: Robinson strolled into a 7-Eleven to pick up some beer after a Crowes concert in Denver, but because it was after midnight (the witching hour when the state's blue laws kicked in), the cashier refused to sell him any brewskis. A customer pointed the famous person out to a friend, who looked baffled, then asked, "Who are the Black Crowes?" An enraged Robinson accused the ignorant friend of eating too many Twinkies, after which the pair put up their dukes. Robinson later pleaded no contest to charges of disturbing the peace. (He should plead guilty to that every time the Crowes play!)

USED THE "TWINKIE OFFENSE"!

Axl Rose, Guns N' Roses

July 1991: When Rose spotted a Kansas City audience member videotaping his concert—and saw that security wasn't doing anything about it—the enraged singer decided to take matters into his own murderous mitts: by stage-diving into the crowd to nab the evildoer. Axl's ill-advised actions caused a riot, and the melee caused over $200,000 worth of damage to the hall. Although the band beat a hasty retreat, a warrant was issued for Rose's arrest, and the group were forced to cancel concerts in Michigan because authorities were just waiting for the chance to grab Axl the second he set a Nike-shod foot in that state. Rose was ultimately arrested for the crime the following year (in July) at New York's JFK airport, and was charged with misdemeanor assault and property damage (the case was plea-bargained, and Rose was basically exonerated).

> **"I was looking for someone who wanted to get married, have a bunch of children and a station wagon."**
>
> *(Erin Everly, who probably now realizes that rock stars aren't the best candidates for this particular fantasy)*

Ah, poor Axl: the women in his life have caused the mentally scrambled singer nothing but grief. Former wife Erin Everly (daughter of Phil) says, "You never knew what would set him off," and claims he regularly smacked her around (sometimes so badly that she ended up unconscious), threatened her with firearms, and destroyed their possessions during their short, fiery marriage. He also, she said, kept very tight control over her, refusing to give her any money or even a key to their home, and once removed all the doors from the interior of her apartment so he could watch her every move. The relationship, as you may guess, ended on a less than high note.

> **"I was afraid when he came in, when he left, when he wasn't there."**
>
> *(Erin Everly, on Axl Rose)*

David Lee Roth

April 1993: In Washington Square Park in Manhattan, Roth was arrested after buying ten bucks' worth of pot. The charges were dismissed after Roth promised to stay out of trouble for a year. Man, don't New York City cops have anything better to do?

Johnny Rotten

January 1977: Spent a night in jail and paid a £40 fine for possession of amphetamine sulphate

October 1980: Sentenced to three months (but later acquitted) for disorderly conduct after participating in a barroom brawl in Dublin

Rich Stevens, Tower of Power

February 1976: The singer was arrested and charged in the murder of three men in San Jose, California. Motivation? Allegedly a drug deal gone south. Stevens and his partner in crime were each found guilty on two counts of murder, and are now serving lengthy stretches in the clink.

Ike Turner

1989: Arrested for the sale and possession of cocaine, and served eighteen months of a four-year sentence

Sid Vicious

February 1978: With punk-hag girlfriend Nancy Spungen, was arrested and charged with drug possession in their room at the Chelsea Hotel. (It wasn't until the following year that Vicious was charged with Spungen's murder.)

Scott Weiland, Stone Temple Pilots

May 1995: Arrested in Pasadena when cops stopped his car, searched it, and found crack and heroin. (Charges were dropped when he agreed to go to rehab—obviously worked like a charm.)

June 2, 1998: Busted for criminal possession of a controlled substance and criminal trespass in New York City. (When cops asked why he was in the notoriously druggy Lower East Side housing project where they found him, he replied blithely, "I just bought drugs.")

July 9, 1998: A Los Angeles judge issued a warrant for his arrest after he missed a court date. Weiland's attorney told the judge he didn't know where his client was.

August 1998: Sentenced to three years' probation and ninety days in rehab

January 1999: Weiland pled guilty to heroin posses-sion, and a judge put him on probation and sentenced him to a drug rehab program, four-times-per-week counseling sessions, and a guarantee that he'll stay out of trouble for one year. (And pigs will fly.) Sure enough, he was thrown in jail later that year.

Paul Weller, The Jam

November 1997: Arrested for destroying a room at the Warwick hotel in Paris. Weller was questioned by the gendarmerie, then released after promising to pay for the damage.

Wendy O. Williams, The Plasmatics

January 1981: Arrested for obscen-ity in Milwaukee after mimicking fellatio on a sledgehammer during her show. Classy lady.

Law of the Jungle

Sue the stars. Pocket some dough. Get some publicity.

Aerosmith

"Fan" Mark Nieto sued the band (the suit is pending) after attending a 1997 concert, during which he claimed to have suffered hearing damage. Nieto also named the venue, the Concord Pavilion (in Concord, California), saying he was "not aware of warnings for ear damage." Maybe he should stick to cello recitals, then.

Gregg Allman

In January of 1975, Gregg Allman gave up the goods on **Allman Brothers** road manager/drug supplier **John "Scooter" Herring** (who had saved Allman's life after a near-fatal OD in 1974) in return for amnesty regarding drug charges of his own. "I was scared to go in there and have them ask me those things," Allman said, "but it was either that or go to jail." Herring was sentenced to seventy-five years, and both band and fans were completely disgusted with cowardly Gregg. Singer/guitarist **Dickey Betts** huffed, "There's no way we can work with Gregg ever again. I mean, what can you do when a man who's worked with you personally for two years and saved your life twice is sitting there with his life on the line, and you walk into court and tap on the mic and say, 'Testing, one, two, three' like Gregg did?" (Well, he's an *entertainer*, after all.)

Mariah Carey

Mariah Carey was sued by limo driver Franco D'Onofrio in June of 1998 for

$1.5 million. D'Onofrio, Carey's personal driver in 1994, claimed she fired him without reimbursing him for major expenditures, including a GMC Suburban which she requested he buy, then refused to pay for after changing her mind a month later (a likely story). He also claimed she had an outstanding balance of $40,000 for his driving services. The suit is pending.

Guns N' Roses

In 1990, the members sued a toy store chain for using their names and likenesses in advertisements for a kiddie-size drum set. The Gunners claimed to have suffered "damage to their reputation, loss of goodwill, and mental anguish." I know *I* certainly think less of them now.

George Harrison

Harrison paid almost $600,000 to the publisher of the **Chiffons'** hit "He's So Fine" after successfully being sued for plagiarism for his hit "My Sweet Lord"— an almost note-for-note (unintentional, he insisted) copy of the original.

Michael Hutchence

After Michael Hutchence's death in 1998, his father, Kelland, filed for custody of Heavenly Hirani Tiger Lily, Michael's daughter by **Paula Yates**, because "I saw an apparition of Michael with tears rolling down his cheeks, holding Tiger Lily out to me. I felt he was telling me what to do."

Twiggs Lyndon, roadie, The Allman Brothers

When the band showed up late for a Buffalo gig, the venue's owner refused to pay them, prompting roadie Lyndon, a rough-and-tumble good ol' boy, to stab the man to death with a fishing knife. At his murder trial, Lyndon's attorneys put forth a most interesting argument in his defense: that living with the Allmans would drive anyone mad, and therefore Lyndon had been temporarily insane when he committed the murder. As proof, they called to the stand Allman Brothers member **Berry Oakley**—who was unable to put two sentences together, excused himself several times to go upchuck in the bathroom, and admitted taking drugs frequently— including in the hour before he'd appeared! The jury bought it, and Lyndon was acquitted.

Marilyn Manson

Spin magazine editor Craig Marks is suing Marilyn Manson for $24 million, stemming from an incident when Manson and his entourage yelled imprecations at the journalist ("I can kill you! I can kill your family! I can kill everyone you know!") and bodyguards shoved him against a wall and choked him—all because Marilyn had found out he wasn't going to be the cover boy on the magazine's January 1999 issue. Manson's attorney calls the accusations baseless: "The witnesses sharply dispute Mr. Marks's version of what happened." And Manson, in a statement published on his Web site, explained, "I had a conversation with Craig Marks expressing I was tired of *Spin*'s immature business behavior." (Evidently, Manson feels that roughing someone up is the mature way to handle disputes.) Manson has since filed a countersuit; neither action had been settled at the time of this writing.

George Michael

George Michael sent shock waves through the record industry when he sued his label, Sony, for restraint of trade, bitterly accusing them of being "a giant electronics corporation which appears to see artists as little more than software." Duh. Unfortunately for poor George, the judge sided with the big bad record company, determining the deal to be "reasonable and fair." George was left with a seven-million-dollar legal bill, and vowed never to record another album for the label. The standoff went on for a couple of years; then Sony said "See ya!" in return for a greatest-hits release by George, together with a big payoff from George's new labels (Virgin in the U.K. and DreamWorks in the States).

Bret Michaels, lead singer of Poison

Bret Michaels and **Pamela Anderson Lee** were caught having sex—on tape. The same Internet site that released the Pammy / **Tommy Lee** video somehow got hold of a raunchy flick of the dually bleached-out duo, and Michaels went to court (the case is pending) to keep it from being released, claiming his career would be "irreparably harmed" if the frolicsome flick were ever released. (What career?)

"Quite a few times, girls have been raped at our concerts. Some have claimed to have gone deaf while we were onstage. Someone lost their eyes in a fight, so we get assault charges because we were onstage when they got the shit kicked out of them. It goes on and on. We have a lawsuit pending from this guy who thinks he's me."

(Nikki Sixx)

John Phillips

John Phillips, the very picture of mental health, filed suit against Dunhill Records in August of 1973 for $9 million, citing Dunhill's "systematic, cold-blooded theft of perhaps up to $650 million, stolen from each and every artist who recorded for it during a seven-year period." So of course all the damages should go to John.

The Rolling Stones

In Feburary 1971, the Hell's Angel, David Passaro, that killed (and was acquitted for the murder of) Meredith Hunter at Altamont (see page 82) sued the group, charging that the documentary film *Gimme Shelter*, which showed some of the events that took place that day, was an invasion of his privacy.

Neil Young

In December of 1983, Geffen Records sued Neil Young for $3 million, claiming that his rockabilly-tinged album *Everybody's Rockin'* was "not commercial in nature and musically uncharacteristic of his previous albums." (Maybe that's a *good* thing.) The suit was settled out of court.

FIRING LINE

The Moody Blues

The Moody Blues were sued by their ex-keyboardist, Patrick Moraz, for £500,000 in 1991 after they'd dropped him from a tour. No word on the outcome of the suit, but it was reported that in 1995 Moraz was attempting to book private gigs (at $800 a pop) over the Internet.

Oasis

In 1997, former Oasis drummer Tony McCarroll sued his ex-bandmates for almost thirty million bucks, claiming he was owed twenty percent of the band's earnings since his alleged unwarranted firing by the group (due to a personality clash) in 1995. The case was settled out of court on the first day of the trial. "The way I look at it," McCarroll whinged, "is I had the dream of a lifetime taken away overnight." I don't know if I'd exactly call working with the Gallaghers a dream. . . .

Bark at the moon

The Devil (Well, Actually, Ozzy Osbourne) Made Me Do It

That Really Nontenuous Heavy Metal–Suicide Link

Ozzy Osbourne and Epic Records were sued after the October 1984 death of troubled nineteen-year-old John McCollum, who committed suicide with his father's handgun (the boy was found with headphones on and *Blizzard of Ozz* in the stereo). The family filed against Osbourne and the label a year later to "teach the record companies a lesson" (I guess the *record companies* needed the lesson despite the fact that the victim had a history of psychological problems and alcohol abuse). The suit was ultimately dismissed on First Amendment grounds. A few years afterward, the family of another suicide casualty, Michael Waller (an addict who abused booze, pot, and glue, and who shot himself to death in his van with the same *Blizzard of Ozz* album in the tape deck) filed a product liability suit. (The judge in the case dismissed the suit and refused to reinstate it later.)

FUNERAL FOR A FRIEND

Ozzy claims the lyric to the song "Suicide Solution" was actually intended as a eulogy for his friend Bon Scott, singer for AC/DC, who died after choking on his own vomit during an all-night booze binge.

"We were handed a writ claiming that our album *Stained Class* had been responsible for the double suicide, and we were being sued for $6.2 million. . . . Basically, the families claimed we had subliminal and hidden messages on *Stained Class*, but the First Amendment in America covers freedom of speech. In other words, you can say whatever you like, so the only way they could get it to court was to claim that you couldn't hear these messages, because then it wasn't protected by the First Amendment."

(Glenn Tipton, Judas Priest guitarist)

In 1986, Judas Priest were sued by the families of two Reno, Nevada, boys who had tried to commit suicide by blowing their heads off with a shotgun (one succeeded). The troubled young men had spent the day drinking brews, smoking pot, and listening to the Priest. In the action, the families alleged the band had intentionally inserted subliminal messages into their music, namely the command "Do it" (quipped guitarist K. K. Downing, "It will be ten years before I can even *spell* subliminal"), and added that the music's "suggestive lyrics, combined with the continuous beat and rhythmic nonchanging intonation of the music, combined to induce, encourage, aid, abet, and otherwise mesmerize plaintiff into believing the answer to life was death." (The fact that both boys had been abused by their parents and had long histories of behavioral problems had *nothing to do with it*.) The boy that survived, Jay Vance, endured a long series of plastic surgeries to repair the damage caused by the shotgun blast, then became a Christian—but eventually returned to his old religion (drugs) and was hospitalized for depression; he died not long afterward. A judge held Judas Priest not liable in the case.

"It's a fact that if you play speech backward, some of it will seem to make sense. So I asked permission to go into a studio and find some perfectly innocent phonetic flukes. . . . We bought a copy of the album in a shop, went into the studio, recorded it on tape, turned it over, and played it backward. Right away we found, 'Hey ma, my chair's broken,' and 'Give me a peppermint,' and 'Help me keep a job.' "

(Glenn Tipton)

STAIRWAY
TO
HEAVEN

Bad Medicine

The three categories of rock 'n' roll substance abusers: the Proud: Marilyn Manson; the Cured: Aerosmith; and the Lapsed (you know who you are)

"I'm sick of reading about all these different groups moaning about 'My Drug Hell.' Don't fucking do it, then!"
(Paul Weller)

The Needle and the Damage Done: Heroin Users

Have these habits been kicked?

"People who like smack also like Lou Reed, and that can't be anything in its favor."
(Lemmy, Motörhead, on why he refuses to try heroin)

Art Alexakis, vocalist for Everclear

Gregg Allman

Philip Anselmo, lead singer for Pantera: Made a postoverdose public statement that read, "I, Philip Anselmo, injected a lethal dose of heroin into my arm and died for four to five minutes. There was no light, no beautiful music, just nothing. My friends slapped me and poured water over my head, all basically trying to revive me. The paramedics finally arrived, and all I remember is waking up in the back of an ambulance. From that point on, I knew all I wanted was to be back on the tour bus, going to the next gig. Instead, I was going to a hospital, where I was released very shortly. You see, I am not a heroin addict. But I am an intra-venous drug abuser." We see, we see.

Boy George: Tried to deny his jones with the witty, "I'm a drag addict, not a drug addict"; was spending $750 a day on drugs for himself and his entourage; American keyboardist Michael Rudetsky, staying with George at his house in London, died of a heroin overdose one night while the Boy was out club hopping.

Tim Buckley

Nick Cave: Once got violent with a journalist who was trying to learn more about his addiction (threw a glass at him and punched him in the kisser)

Ray Charles

"None of us were drug-mad—we had enough trouble with beer and scotch."
(Chris Britton, The Troggs)

Eric Clapton: "I still feel that to be a junkie is to be part of a very elite club. I've also got this death wish. I don't like life. That's another reason for taking heroin, because it's like surrounding yourself in pink cotton wool. Nothing bothers you whatsoever. Nothing will faze you in any way." And, "The surprising thing about heroin is that you believe you can make yourself invisible. The minute your eyelids begin to droop, there is no one else in the room."

Kurt Cobain, Nirvana: "I've had this stomach condition for, like, five years. . . . I tried everything I could think of: change of diet, pills, everything—exercise, stopped drinking, stopped smoking . . . and nothing worked. I just decided that if I'm going to feel like a junkie every fucking morning and be vomiting every day, then I may as well take a substance that kills that pain."

Dion

"If you ask me, drug abusers give drug users a bad name."
(Marilyn Manson)

Dr. John

Mick muse Marianne Faithfull: In July of 1969, shooting the film *Ned Kelly* in Australia, Faithfull ODed on barbiturates and was fired. Two days later, she entered rehab for heroin addiction.

Perry Farrell, Jane's Addiction

Dave Gahan, Depeche Mode's singer

Debbie Harry, Blondie: "When [Blondie member] **Chris Stein** was very sick, I did some heroin then. I took it in the late sixties, then not at all through the Blondie time. When Chris got ill, I was very stressed out. But I never dabble, ever. When you take habit-forming drugs, then you usually have a habit. These people who claim they're dabbling, it's just bullshit."

"I really despised the idea that in order to be in a group and play hard music, you had to be covered in your own vomit."
(Morrissey)

"Everybody vomits now and then."
(Johnny Rotten)

Michael Hutchence, INXS

Billy Idol

"Jane's Addiction was usually most healthy when we first got back into town from a tour, because at some point along the way, everybody usually dropped off their habit. If your problem is heroin, then it's really tough to maintain a habit on the road. The perception is that there's someone standing right next to you going, 'What do you need?' I remember being upset by the fact that that *wasn't* the case. You spend a lot of time being miserable and sick." (Eric Avery, bassist for the group, who were usually so high they were barely able to play)

Anthony Kiedis, Red Hot Chili Peppers

John Lennon

Paul "Kermit" Leveridge, Black Grape

Courtney Love

Frankie Lymon

Phil Lynott, Thin Lizzy

Jim Morrison

"I was told I had to do heroin if I wanted to be great. I spent $500 a day for five years on freebasing heroin. If I hadn't screwed up like that, I'd be on easy street now."
(Dave Mustaine, Megadeth)
(Note: Mustaine cleaned up his act in 1990, and would jump off the Golden Gate Bridge if you told him to.)

Nico, Velvet Underground

Yoko Ono

Jimmy Page, Led Zeppelin

Gram Parsons

"I was very high on heroin when I wrote 'Back in the Saddle.' That riff just floated right through me. Drugs can be a shortcut to creativity. All throughout history, medicine men and priests in all those primitive cultures used drugs to get to that spirit place."
(Joe Perry, Aerosmith)

John Phillips, The Mamas & the Papas

Lou Reed

Keith Richards, Rolling Stones: Had a forty-eight-hour complete blood transfusion (thought it would help him kick his addiction) to prepare for the Stones' 1973 tour

Axl Rose, Guns N' Roses

Johnny Rotten, The Sex Pistols

Andy Rourke, bassist, The Smiths

"People say that my heroin habit split the band up. I had a perfectly healthy habit before the Mondays were even going."
(Shaun Ryder, Black Grape/Happy Mondays)

Nikki Sixx, Mötley Crüe: On December 26, 1987, Sixx was partying down with **Slash** and **Steve Adler** (of **Guns N' Roses**); all of them, with their prodigious capacities for substance abuse, were mixing a cornucopia of booze and drugs when Sixx collapsed. Quick-thinking Slash called 911 and did mouth-to-mouth (if the OD didn't kill him . . .), but Sixx was "dead" when the paramedics arrived. They were able to revive the rocker, who later wrote "Kick Start My Heart" about the experience. "I was strung out bad for over a year," Sixx remembers. "I'd just bought a new house, and it turned into the Hollywood rock 'n' roll headquarters. It was like, 'Here, snort this. Here, shoot this. Here, drink this. Hey, fuck her.' "

Slash, Guns N' Roses

Layne Staley, Alice in Chains

James Taylor

Johnny Thunders, New York Dolls

Pete Townshend, The Who: Once "died" after taking heroin with **Thin Lizzy's Phil Lynott**

Steven Tyler, Aerosmith: Overdosed and was pronounced dead on stage during a show in 1985

"When I tried heroin, it made me feel just right. I thought I wouldn't be able to get through life without it. It was the drug for me."
(Steven Tyler)

Vanilla Ice

Sid Vicious, Sex Pistols, and groupie-girlfriend Nancy Spungen

Charlie Watts, Rolling Stones

Scott Weiland, Stone Temple Pilots

Brian and Dennis Wilson, The Beach Boys

Johnny Winter

Andy Wood, lead singer for Mother Love Bone

Paula Yates

Hooked on a Feeling: The Rock 'n' Roll Pharmacy

Aerosmith's Joe Perry and Steven Tyler: Everything—they were known for good reason as the "Toxic Twins." Now they insist that anyone who works for them abstain from drugs and alcohol—even on their days off! Even when they're nowhere near the band! In fact, they'd better not even be in the same *state* as the band if they're doing that shit!

Gregg Allman: Booze, heroin, cocaine (high on pills and booze, once fell face-forward into a plate of spaghetti during dinner; Cher, who filed for divorce nine days after she married him, said she'd had *no idea he was on drugs* until they were wed)

Syd Barrett, Pink Floyd: Psychedelics (destroyed his mind—and his career in music)

The Beatles: Acid, marijuana

Ozzy Osbourne and Bill Ward, Black Sabbath: Ozzy says there was a two-year period when he and **Bill Ward** took acid every single day. "It was crazy and fun," he reminisced. "It was like the old kid in a candy store. We came from being completely unknown, and suddenly we could get drugs and drinks and sex, and it was all free."

Tommy Bolin, guitarist, Deep Purple: Heroin, cocaine, barbiturates, booze

David Bowie: Cocaine ("There's oodles of pain on that album *[Low]*. That was my first attempt to kick cocaine. And I moved to Berlin to do it. I moved out of the coke capital of the world into the smack capital of the world"). During his addiction, Bowie behaved very bizarrely: he was obsessed with the occult, believed he could walk through walls, dabbled in far-right politics and sadomasochism, had paranoid delusions (such as the idea that his phone was tapped and that he needed to have his swimming pool exorcised), drank his own urine (stored it in the refrigerator to maintain its freshness), and got really *really* into Hitler.

"I've been a really lucky sod. I'm extremely fit. But then, I've never had a brain scan. I remember reading about the effects of vast amounts of [drugs], and the holes they leave in your brain. They specified the amounts you had to take to produce sizable holes, amounts I far exceeded. I thought, 'Oh god, what the hell's going on up there?' "

(David Bowie)

Bobby Brown: Cocaine

James Brown: PCP

Lindsey Buckingham, Fleetwood Mac: Cocaine

Eric Burdon, The Animals: LSD

Belinda Carlisle, The Go-Go's: Cocaine and just about everything else. "I quit, cold-turkey, on my own," she says. "Part of the addiction was physical, but most of it was psychological. It was just a matter of going to meetings, getting a support group, and behavior modification. It took me a while to get out of that mind-set of walking into a restaurant and trying to figure out who was carrying."

Richard Carpenter: Quaaludes

Nick Cave: Heroin (quit in the early nineties), booze: "I used to drink a lot, but in the last three years I really haven't drunk much. Alcohol's the thing that really eats away at you. More than drug-taking by far. I guess crack isn't really something that leads to a long life. But the other stuff's not too bad."

Eric Clapton: Acid, pills, marijuana, cocaine, heroin. Clapton was able to kick heroin, but then turned to booze (a bottle of brandy plus forty or fifty painkillers per day) and used to "streak" quite often when he was high;

roadies used to carry booze on board airplanes so Clapton wouldn't have to wait to be served by the stews; his heavy boozing ultimately landed him in the hospital with a perforated ulcer.

George Clinton: Cocaine (freebaser)

"Magic is, if you're high on psychedelics, having a great big love-beast crawl out of your amplifiers and eat the audience."
(David Crosby)

Kurt Cobain: Just about everything—but mainly heroin. Overdosed and fell into an almost fatal coma in Rome on March 4, 1994 (sixty sedative pills plus champagne). Though the incident was initially classified an accident, the *Los Angeles Times* soon unearthed the fact that it was actually a failed suicide attempt (including a good-bye note).

Joe Cocker: Pot, coke, booze. "[I drink] partly to forget everything—which is what booze is about—and partly because I couldn't find anything decent to smoke in America."

Alice Cooper: He and his band spent $250,000 a year on booze, and he consumed almost two cases of beer per day by himself! "In the end," he admits, "I was throwing up blood." Cleaned up his act in late 1977 by having himself committed to a sanitarium—which probably wasn't too difficult, considering he confessed he hadn't been sober at all in the preceding two and a half years. "I was drinking every day," Cooper confessed. "I was kidding myself. I wore black leather and drank two bottles of whiskey a day. This is the honest-to-God truth. I was in a VO coma—a Seagram's VO coma. . . . I was actually in a coma for days at a time."

Billy Corgan, Smashing Pumpkins: LSD

Hugh Cornwell, The Stranglers: "I got into speedballs, which is mixing a line of heroin with a line of cocaine. You get the up from the cocaine and then the heroin calms you down, so you don't get paranoid." And, "The greatest thing I discovered at university was marijuana."

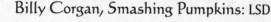

"We were all smoking dope and we were all taking cocaine. This was normal for bands in those days—you started making money and you took what you could lay your hands on. . . . It got to the stage where it was no coke, no gig, and we would see what we could get away with. We'd have the promoter running around trying to find a dealer so we could have some cocaine, and there'd be two thousand people in the hall. We were holding him to ransom and seeing him running around. And you know that he'd find some."
(Hugh Cornwell, The Stranglers)

Elvis Costello: Booze, cocaine

Graham Coxon, guitarist, Blur: Booze

David Crosby: Cocaine, booze, psychedelics

Roger Daltrey, The Who: "Once I got off it, I realized how much the band had deteriorated through playing on speed."

Evan Dando, The Lemonheads: Booze, pot, cocaine, crack. Once nearly broke up the band after a gig where he insisted on playing excerpts from Guns N' Roses "Sweet Child O' Mine" during every single song in the Lemonheads' set.

"Tons of my friends have died recently. It sucks. When my friends die, it makes me want to do more drugs and join them. . . . There's this model I know—I used to go out with her for a little while— and she's been murdered by a bunch of coke dealers because she owed them $50,000. You pay for that stuff in the next life, even if there isn't a next life."
(Evan Dando)
Statements like this are why we should all stay away from drugs.

Roky Erickson, Thirteenth Floor Elevators: Acid, cocaine, heroin, LSD, speed. Busted for possession of two joints, Erickson chose commitment to a psychiatric ward instead of jail time. Unfortunately, he was remanded to an institution for the criminally insane, where he endured three years of heavy medication and shock treatment, causing permanent brain damage and mental illness (example: upon his release, he went to a notary and had the man register a sworn statement that Erickson was an alien from Mars). He remains incapable of caring for himself.

Don Everly: Amphetamines. Attempted suicide twice before he was twenty-five, saying, "I was so high it didn't matter whether I went on living or not."

Perry Farrell: Crack, booze, heroin (arrested October 16, 1991, at a Holiday Inn in Santa Monica, California—reportedly because a horrified maid found freebase "works" in the room)

Bay City Rollers singer Eric Faulkner: ODed on Seconal and Valium on April 14, 1976, and nearly died

Fleetwood Mac: Cocaine (after recording *Rumours*, they actually wanted to give label credit to their dealer since he'd contributed so much to the project, but the man died before the album came out— I'm sure the record execs breathed big sighs of relief)

"As word spread around the Bay Area that the glamorous Fleetwood Mac was recording, the studio's lounges began to fill up with strangers tapping razors on mirrors."
(Mick Fleetwood)

Ace Frehley, Kiss: "I used to sniff glue. It expanded my consciousness better than acid."

Dave Gahan, Depeche Mode: Cocaine, heroin, booze. Depeche Mode wouldn't (couldn't?) tour in support of their album *Ultra*. Why—because they were so messed up on drugs? No—because they were all in recovery: Dave Gahan from heroin, **Martin Gore** from a knockout combo of stress and booze (which eventually caused brain seizures), and Andy Fletcher from a nervous breakdown.

"To get high is to forget yourself. And to forget yourself is to see everything else. And to see everything else is to become an understanding molecule in evolution, a conscious tool of the universe."
(Jerry Garcia)

Oasis's Gallagher brothers: Liam (glue, booze), Noel (marijuana, psychedelics, Ecstasy, booze); both of them: cocaine. Liam was arrested in London in November of 1996 for possession of a small amount of cocaine, then was let off with a caution in January of the following year.

"We can drink more than Liam and Noel Gallagher. These youngsters had to be sent home in a taxi while we were still going for it at seven in the morning under the big Golden Gate Bridge."
(The Edge, U2)

"I think marijuana is the scourge of my generation. I know loads of talented artists and musicians who are still sitting in Manchester in their bedrooms, stoned, because they can't be bothered to get off their asses. If I could turn the clock back, I would never even have started smoking, let alone smoking pot. Or drinking lager, Jack Daniel's, and gin and tonic. If I had my time again, I wouldn't bother. It's starting to affect my memory." (Noel Gallagher)

"I sniffed cans of gas at the age of twelve. Took mushrooms at the age of twelve—proper mushrooms. Not twenty—more like 150. I've done all that." (Noel Gallagher)

Marvin Gaye: Cocaine (made him extremely paranoid: he routinely walked around with a gun, and holed up in his room for days at a time, refusing to eat because he was suspicious the food was poisoned)

Bob Geldof: Cocaine (At a nightclub, Geldof once accepted some cocaine from an attractive woman, who gave him her address; when he showed up later in the evening, her boyfriend was there. Was there a problem? No, the man told Geldof he could "have" the lady as long as Geldof would let him watch—which Geldof did.)

The brothers Gibb (Bee Gees): "I was the piss artist, Barry was the pothead, and Robin was the pillhead." (Maurice Gibb)

Gary Glitter: In his autobiography, Glitter noted that drinking expensive champagne was his "duty to his fans."

Robin Guthrie, Cocteau Twins keyboardist: Cocaine ("I snorted a whole house-worth in two years.")

Jimi Hendrix: Benzedrine, codeine-based cough syrup, methedrine, pot, LSD, cocaine

"Knowing me, I'll probably get busted at my own funeral."
(Jimi Hendrix)

Doug Hopkins, Gin Blossoms: Booze

Billy Idol: Heroin, GHB (ODed on GHB, a horse tranquilizer, in Hollywood in 1994)

Mick Jagger: "[Acid] never gave me brain damage or anything at all like that. I shouldn't really own up to it even now. I took it before it was made illegal."

Alex James, bassist, Blur: Booze

Rick James: Cocaine

Elton John: Cocaine

"I still wake up, seven years since I last had any, having had cocaine dreams where my mother is in the next room about to walk in and I'm there with powder all over my face. I can still taste it, too, running down the back of my throat. You have to fight it because it invades your psyche like you wouldn't believe."
(Elton John)

Brian Jones: Whiskey, pot, pills, acid (former girlfriend Anita Pallenberg says he'd huddle in corners, fearfully ranting about the monsters and armies of black beetles he was seeing while high; when he'd go to rehab, he'd take with him all the drugs that had landed him there in the first place)

"He had an obsession about piercing the [barbiturate] capsules so that they'd get into his bloodstream quicker. He knew all these junkie tricks."
(Keith Richards, on Brian Jones)

Mick Jones, The Clash: "I was so into speed. I mean, I don't even recall making the first album."

Janis Joplin: Heroin, booze ("I think I think too much. That's why I drink.")

"I was just a young chick. I just wanted to get it on. I wanted to smoke dope, take dope, lick dope, suck dope, fuck dope, anything I could lay my hands on—I wanted to do it, man."
(Janis Joplin)

Joy Division: "We were on speed; [Joy Division member] Martin Hannett was into smack." (Bernard Sumner)

"[Martin Gore] used to say to Rob [Gretton], 'Get these two thick, stupid cunts out of my way.' In the studio, we'd sit on the left, he'd sit on the right, and if we said anything like 'I think the guitars are a bit quiet, Martin,' he'd scream, 'Oh my god! Why don't you just fuck off, you stupid retards!' It was all right at first, but gradually he got weirder and weirder."
(Bernard Sumner, on recording Joy Division's *Unknown Pleasures* album)

Arthur "Killer" Kane, New York Dolls: Booze (would get so drunk that he could only pretend to play his bass onstage)

Simon LeBon, Duran Duran: Booze, cocaine

"When I go to a restaurant, I'll have a bottle of wine; in a bar I'll drink cocktails; and at home in front of the TV I'll have beer. Then suddenly I'll realize that I've not gone without a drink for two years. Fuck! I'm an alcoholic! And it's virtually impossible to stop. Every time you try to give up, it's somebody's birthday. It's always somebody's fucking birthday!"
(Simon LeBon)

Lemmy, Motörhead: Booze, pot (busted in 1968), speed (fired from Hawkwind after being busted for possession of the drug). When asked if he had a hangover, Lemmy said, "You have to stop drinking to get a hangover."

"I try to drink a bottle of whiskey a day. Whether I need it or not."
(Lemmy)

Julian Lennon: Booze, cocaine

Marilyn Manson: Cocaine, Special K (animal tranquilizer), and (proudly) just about everything else. (Pooh-poohed accusations by far-righters that he was distributing drugs to the audiences at his concerts: "It is ridiculous. If I had a giant bag of drugs, I would not be passing them out, especially for free. I would be backstage doing them, as I have in the past.")

"When we did *Antichrist Superstar,* we were living in a crack house, and the conditions we were working under made us really unhappy. We did drugs [then] just because we were so freaked out and depressed, and this time [the recording of *Mechanical Animals*] we did them just for fun. This is a very drug-influenced record, but the substances didn't create the sounds . . . sometimes they just made us feel uncomfortable. The thing about drugs is eventually you start feeling normal on them, so sometimes not to do them makes you feel more fucked up than to do them." (Twiggy Ramirez, Marilyn Manson)

Paul McCartney: Marijuana, psychedelics (scandalized the world in 1996 after publicly admitting the Beatles had all "tripped")

Shane McGowan, The Pogues: Booze (would stumble offstage, forget his lyrics, and fall over during his performances—all due to the mossy-toothed singer's love of a wee drop)

"My old man gave me some whiskey when I was real little. It was Hawaiian whiskey, and it had this long Hawaiian name. He said, 'Take a swig and pronounce the name.' After about four swigs, I couldn't pronounce the name because I was too drunk."
(Duff McKagan, Guns N' Roses)

John McVie, Fleetwood Mac: Booze

"John drinks too much. And that's why Chris and John aren't together. Period."
(Stevie Nicks)

John Mellencamp: Booze

"You think I'm an asshole now? You should have seen me when I was drunk."
(John Mellencamp)

The members of Metallica: Booze (their riders require two bottles of Absolut and a case of imported beer backstage)

George Michael: "I'm a grass and occasional Ecstasy man."

Joni Mitchell: "I did some good writing, I think, on cocaine. . . ."

Keith Moon: Anything and everything (routinely drank two bottles of cognac, plus booster shots of champagne and cocaine, daily)

"A day in the life of Keith Moon was however long he was awake. He didn't have a twenty-four-hour clock like the rest of us. If he was awake for five days, that would be his day."
(Roger Daltrey)

"He checked into the psychiatric wing of the Cedars-Sinai hospital because he knew something was wrong. They gave you little tasks to do, and he had carpentry lessons. So he built a drinks tray! Next time I went to see him, they said, 'He's not too good.' They'd caught him drinking aftershave."
(Moon "handler" Dougal Butler)

Stevie Nicks: Cocaine (quit in 1985 after a doctor said she wouldn't have long to live if she continued her habit; Nicks spent twenty-eight days at the Betty Ford Center, which she remembers with a mixture of emotions: "They are hard-nosed. They're harder on you if you're famous—'Oh, if it isn't Miss Special.' It's awful. But it works.")

"We did not realize how scary cocaine was. Everybody said it was okay, recreational, not addictive. Nobody told you that you may end up with a hole through your nose the size of Chicago."
(Stevie Nicks)*

"I want people to know, if they followed my career and wonder what happened between 1988 and 1993, those years are just nearly gone for me. I had just stopped doing cocaine and I was totally fine. But, to soothe everybody's feathers around me, I went to a psychiatrist. Boy, I wish I'd gotten sick that day. He put me on Klonopin, like a Valium thing. By 1989 it wasn't that I didn't write well, I just stopped writing. And because of being on a tranquilizing drug, of course you make very bad decisions. I fired people, I hired people. . . . It nearly destroyed me."
(Stevie Nicks)

"I was with Nikki [Sixx] in a hotel room. We had shot up all the drugs you could possibly shoot up, and then realized, 'Fuck, we're all out.' Then we went and unscrewed the Jack Daniel's bottle and started shooting up alcohol. And I said, 'Dude, what the fuck are we doing?' That was the point when I said, 'Fuck it. I quit.' "
(Tommy Lee, Mötley Crüe)

Chris Novoselic, Nirvana: Took acid and drank heavily after a Florida performance, then divested himself of all his clothing and walked naked around the parking lot yelling, "Cast away your possessions like I have! You're not worth anything!"

Ozzy Osbourne: Booze, drugs (because of his addictions, Ozzy has a marked stutter and a tendency to "zone out" for short periods). In 1978, a soused-to-the-gills Ozzy picked up a shotgun and killed his and his first wife's seventeen cats. (She threw him out of the house and immediately filed for divorce.) Checked into the Betty Ford Clinic in November 1984, but shortly after his release actually *escalated* his old habits—started drinking four bottles of cognac a day, and consuming a thousand bucks'

worth of cocaine each week. During this period, he attempted to kill his wife, **Sharon**, who says, "He had been on an outrageous roll of drug-taking and drinking for a week. He had all these drugs hidden around the house, and he would make concoctions of everything and take it with the booze. He did that for six days, and on the seventh day he seriously tried to strangle me. I hit the alarm button, the cops came within a few minutes, and that was it. I had him arrested and the court put him in a treatment center for three months." Said Ozzy, "That night I mixed some medication I'd been prescribed by a psychiatrist with alcohol and I just blacked out. I woke up the next day [September 3, 1989] in Amersham police station, and I honestly didn't know what was going on. The copper said, 'Do you know why you're here?' And they told me I'd threatened to kill my wife. After that I vowed to lock myself up in rehab until I was right again. But when I came out, I drank again—I couldn't stop. I was a mess." Ozzy has learned his lesson, but admits, "I'm not a saint. I still do the occasional joint, but I don't hit the bar and I don't touch cocaine."

> **"I became what they call a blackout drinker. I didn't know what I was doing, and it was fucking horrendous. I would wake up and think, 'God, what the fuck have I done now?' You wake up covered in blood and you don't know where it's come from. That sort of thing is really scary."**
> *(Ozzy Osbourne)*

"I've come close [to death] so many times I've lost count. I've blacked out, had seizures, had my stomach pumped. They took me to hospital in New Orleans once and I came 'round to find this guy on his hands and knees by the side of my bed going, 'Psst, are you Ozzy Osbourne? Are you dying?' I said, 'I don't know.' He said, 'Before you do, can you give me your autograph?' And shoves this piece of paper into my hand. No respect, these fuckers." (Ozzy Osbourne)

Rick Parfitt, Status Quo: Cocaine

Andy Partridge, XTC: Valium

John Phillips, The Mamas & the Papas: "I volunteered my body as a human test tube for anything I could get my hands on—mescaline, Black Beauties to keep going, reds to come down, hash and grass for any occasion. A friend of ours once brought over a box of free drug samples he had taken from a doctor's office. I went through everything in there, including the female hormone estrogen. . . . [Wife Michelle Phillips] asked me if I was preparing to go through menopause. 'No, but there's probably a little downer buzz in there. . . .'"

Philips once watched his children playing with their "water pistols"—his syringes.

Joe Perry, Aerosmith: Everything, including heroin (says the band changed from "a bunch of musicians dabbling in drugs to a bunch of addicts dabbling in music")

"I only met my son recently, though he's nine now. Before that, I wasn't good enough. He didn't need a junkie, a pill addict, or a slobbering Quaalude idiot hanging around him."

(Iggy Pop)

Iggy Pop: Amphetamines, cocaine, etc. Once, at a party, Iggy ingested a large quantity of speed, then passed out on t'he spot. After twenty minutes, he awoke, said, "Thanks, man—great speed, great party," and took off.

"I took two grams of biker speed, five trips of LSD, and as much grass as could be inhaled before [our gigs]." (Iggy Pop)

Lou Reed: Heroin, speed, booze

"Half of these people turn up at concerts to see if I'm going to drop dead onstage, and they're so disappointed that I'm still around and writing and capable of performing without falling down and stumbling around. But I haven't ODed. . . . These people, they wanted me to OD, but they never offered me the dope to do it with."

(Lou Reed)

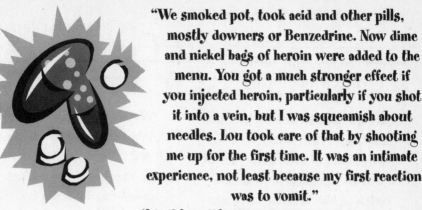

"We smoked pot, took acid and other pills, mostly downers or Benzedrine. Now dime and nickel bags of heroin were added to the menu. You got a much stronger effect if you injected heroin, particularly if you shot it into a vein, but I was squeamish about needles. Lou took care of that by shooting me up for the first time. It was an intimate experience, not least because my first reaction was to vomit."

(John Cale, on Velvet Underground bandmate Lou Reed)

The Rolling Stones: "There was a miscellaneous sum of money at the bottom of the spreadsheet. I would pass over a couple of thousand dollars from that for smack, coke, and grass. I'd divide it out among the band and dock their wages accordingly." And, "I was one of the boys. I'd introduce groupies to them, I'd take drugs with them. On the 1976 Stones tour, there were a hundred of us, and only four or five didn't take drugs." (Sally Arnold, tour manager for the group during the seventies)

Axl Rose, Guns N' Roses: "Right now, drugs get in the way of my dreams and goals. I don't want them around me. Right now, a line of coke puts my voice out of commission for a week. I don't know why. Maybe it's guilt and it's relocated in my throat."

Francis Rossi, Status Quo: Booze, speed, pills, cocaine (once "cut back" to one bottle of scotch and two of wine per day)

"We were the first band on, and we were already high as kites by midday. After we finished, we spent most of the time doing loads of cocaine in the toilets. We didn't spend much time thinking about the starving in Ethiopia."

(Francis Rossi, on Status Quo's performance at the charity concert Live Aid)

Johnny Rotten (a.k.a. John Lydon), The Sex Pistols: Speed (busted in January 1977)

Dave Rowntree, Blur: Booze

Mitch Ryder (. . . and the Detroit Wheels): Acid

Shaun Ryder, Happy Mondays/Black Grape: Heroin, crack, booze

Nikki Sixx, Mötley Crüe: Heroin, booze

"I'm a raving lunatic when I'm wasted." (Nikki Sixx)

"Yeah, I used to be able to drink a lot more than Nikki. We'd be doing shots of Jack Daniel's and I'd drink it all down. And I'd be watching him because he thinks I'm stupid—but I'm not stupid. Out of the corner of my eye, I noticed that as I'd be drinking a shot, he'd be pouring his into my glass."
(Slash)

CAFFEINE MACHINE

"I was a teenage coffee addict. . . . I didn't think it was real bad until I started getting shaky and having stomachaches. Sometimes I couldn't write my name on a check because my hands were shaking so much. Finally, I decided to go cold turkey."
(Debby Boone)

"I've learned drugs can replace religion in men's hearts. Crack and smack, they really suck. My problem was I just had too much free time and too much money. It's a bad combination." (Nikki Sixx)

"I had a bad heroin problem, a bad alcohol problem. I still think about it all the time. I'll be onstage and I'll smell a big puff of pot smoke, and all of a sudden my brain will be cooking up dope."
(Nikki Sixx)

Slash, Guns N' Roses: Booze, heroin. Wasted in Phoenix before a show, Slash once trashed a hotel room, "streaked" through the halls of the hotel, then was hospitalized after cops were called . . . and later, unsurprisingly, he didn't remember a single thing.

"I used to drink every day—a lot. I pass out every night, but it doesn't ever get in the way. I get to rehearsal on time."
(Slash)

"Nobody I know can drink more than Slash."
(Duff McKagan)

Grace Slick: Champagne, brandy

"Anything anybody said I did after nine o'clock at night is probably true."
(Grace Slick)

"People don't want to talk to you, you know, if you're throwing up. Particularly if you're doing it in their room. If I throw up in my room, it's all right." (Grace Slick)

"I can't sing and throw up at the same time." (Grace Slick)

"It did seem impossible for her to go on. . . . She would have needed a portable toilet onstage after every number." (Marty Balin)

"Reporting I'm drunk is like saying there was a Tuesday last week."
(Grace Slick)

Sporty Spice (Melanie Chisholm): Booze

Ringo Starr: Booze (at the height of his addiction, drank sixteen bottles of wine—*per day*)

Dave Stewart, Eurythmics: Hospitalized with a collapsed lung (due to drugs and drink) in 1981

Rod Stewart: Booze, cocaine

"Woody's [Ron Wood] nose was fucked, so we went to the doctor's for advice. He said to use the drug [cocaine] as a suppository. We tried it for a couple of weeks. It had the same effect but was annoying."
(Rod Stewart, on his Faces bandmate)

"I haven't stopped drinking, because she [then-wife Rachel Hunter] likes drinking too. She lets me do a little bit of substance. We did have a falling-out over that when we first met, but she realizes that I never buy it, I never carry it, but if someone's got some I'll have a little line and that will be the end of it." (Rod Stewart)

Sting: Cocaine

Sly Stone: Cocaine (freebaser). "I thought *I* was crazy; then I met Sly. He'd be lying on the piano whacked out of his brain when it was time to do a vocal, and they'd have to lay the microphone next to his head. That's why it came out, 'Waaan chiiiile grows up to beeee!' I had to laugh when I read about this new singing style of Sly's that was so raw. Man, he was just fucked up!" (Bobby Womack)

"There's nothing like throwing up out a bus door going sixty-five miles an hour."
(Izzy Stradlin, Guns N' Roses)

Joe Strummer, The Clash: Had his license taken away in 1986 after a drunk-driving offense

James Taylor: Heroin, booze

Johnny Thunders: Heroin, booze ("I'm addicted to sex, my guitar, and White Russians.")

Peter Tork, The Monkees: Booze ("I was very fortunate, because I found myself to be an alcoholic, and there is a community that is out there to help. . . . Otherwise, I'd be a bubbling pile of protoplasm in the gutter someplace.")

Pete Townshend: Alcohol (used to drink five bottles of brandy a day), amphetamines, heroin

Steven Tyler, Aerosmith: Acid, cocaine, heroin ("My worst experience was shooting cocaine at the Gorham Hotel, having a seizure, and waking up on the floor with people banging on my chest. I was in toxic psychosis. I ran into the bathroom and slammed the door. I was totally out of my mind from the coke in my bloodstream. I took a tube of toothpaste and squeezed it into the cracks of the tiles on the walls because I thought worms and hands were coming to get me.")

"Do you have any idea what it's like seeing your lead singer fall down and not get up? It puts an awful feeling in the pit of your stomach. You fear for his life. You have to stop playing, pick him up, and find out what's wrong with him. And it happened more than once. Those were probably some of the worst moments I've ever had."
(Brad Whitford, Aerosmith)

Adam Clayton and Bono, U2:
Booze

Eddie Van Halen: "There were a couple of years, seriously, where every morning I'd wake up and dry-heave. I'd have to drink a six-pack of beer just to feel normal."

Stevie Ray Vaughan: Booze, cocaine

"By the time we got to recording *Soul to Soul* in '85, it was getting pretty bad. We were paying for the studio time and spending hours upon hours playing Ping-Pong, waiting for our cocaine to arrive before we'd play." (Tommy Shannon, **Double Trouble** bassist)

"We ran into Clapton on a tour of Australia. He was leaving the hotel and I went out to talk to him, hangover and all. He was sober, of course, and really calm, while I sat there downing two or three shots of Crown Royal. And he just sort of looked at me wisely and said, 'Well, sometimes you have to go through that, don't ya?' " (Stevie Ray Vaughan)

"Stevie and I always had adjoining rooms on the road, and we'd leave the door between us open so it was like one big room. We went on a European tour and were at a hotel in Germany. I was lying on my bed, sick as a dog, and I could see Stevie rolling around his bed mumbling shit, and just sticking his head over and vomiting blood all over the floor, too weak to get up and walk to the bathroom. There wasn't much I could do to help him, because I was so sick myself, but I went over. He was gray, so I called an ambulance and they came and got him." (Tommy Shannon)

"I don't have a drink problem—except when I can't get one."
(Tom Waits)

Sid Vicious and Nancy Spungen: Just about anything going. "I take a lot of brandy. Order a large one for me and a small one for Sid. Sid's not supposed to drink, otherwise he'll die." (Nancy Spungen)

"When Sid's out of it, he's a different person. At least if he goes to prison he'll kick his habit." (Fellow **Pistols** member **Steve Jones**)

"I'm glad they didn't have drugs in the sixties when I was in high school, because if they'd had drugs I'd still be in high school."
(Joe Walsh)

Robbie Williams: Pot, speed, Ecstasy, cocaine, heroin. "I used to smoke an incredible amount of weed. Then I took speed—speed was good. . . . I found out that when you come down off your E you can carry on with coke." Took heroin once when "I ran out of coke. . . . The wondrous sense of calm never came."

Brian Wilson: Amphetamines, cocaine, acid, heroin

"I used to write on pills. I used to take uppers and write, and I used to like that effect. In fact, I'd like to take uppers now and write because they give me, you know, a certain lift and a certain outlook. And it's not an unnatural thing. I mean, the pill might be unnatural and the energy, but the song itself doesn't turn out unnatural on the uppers. The creativity flows through. I'm thinking of asking the doctor if I can go back to those, yeah."
(Brian Wilson)

Dennis Wilson: Heroin, coke, booze

Dave Wyndorf, Monster Magnet: Booze and drugs. "I took three years off [between records], but I had no choice. My mind was gone—it was blown from alcohol and drugs. I almost died on our last tour, while we were in Canada."

"I can't understand why anybody should devote their lives to a cause like dope. It's the most boring pastime I can think of. It ranks a close second to TV."
(Frank Zappa)

Like a Rolling Stone: The Keith Richards Drug Primer

"I looked upon myself, in a sort of romantic and silly way, as a laboratory. I wasn't thinking about the ramifications. Then after about ten years, I realized that this experiment had gone on too long. But it was a *smooth* ten years, heh heh, and I never got a cold. And the minute I quit, I got a cold."

"Somewhere early on in this [1998] tour, somebody came through with a little taste, you know. 'Cause in a way, you like to test yourself. Never say no. You can quit it, it's no big deal. . . . I loved it when I was doing it and developed a very strong relationship with the residue of the poppy in all its forms."

"I find it a bit of a drag that certain people need to project their death wishes on me. I've no preoccupation with death whatsoever."

"I only get ill when I give up drugs."

"I think drugs are purely a matter for the person concerned. It's like a blow job—in some states that's still illegal. It's just a matter of how much people are prepared to put up with so-called authorities prying into their lives."

"I'm extremely careful. I've never turned blue in someone else's bathroom. I consider that the height of bad manners. I've had so many people do it to me, and it's not really on, as far as drug etiquette goes, to turn blue in someone else's john."

"I've been drunk for twenty-seven years."

Needle Drops

Scott Weiland's love affair with heroin

"You don't age. You don't age until you stop doing it. Keith Richards looked great until 1981."

Scott Weiland, talented singer for Stone Temple Pilots, began his long relationship with "horse" in 1993. "When I tried heroin for the first time," he remembered, "it seemed to make all those insecurities, all those feelings of inadequacy, just go away. . . . I thought, 'Wow, this is how everybody feels, this is how normal people feel on a day-to-day basis.' I mean, that's besides the rush, which lasts for a very short time. But the important thing for me was that I felt normal. Once you become strung out, physically, which takes maybe a month or two of doing it every day, you have no choice. It becomes as necessary as food or water."

"There's no way you can place the blame on anyone but yourself—although, because I'm a drug addict, I don't believe I have control over what I do when I start using it, because I feel totally powerless."

Weiland, who has been to rehab more than a dozen times to date, lost his job as lead singer of the band he'd founded—due to his addiction. The straw that broke the camel's back? "The day the limos came to pick us up to go to Anchorage, Alaska, and do a show, I called Dean [DeLeo] to tell him I had slipped two times: 'I've got a little bit of a habit. I'm going to bring meds so I can detox on the road—just Vicodin and Valium.' Then Dean called back and said, 'We canceled the shows. We can't rely on you.' I was like, 'What do you mean? It was only a three-day slip!' He said, 'We're tired of this; we don't want anything to do with you.' I just said, 'Fine! Have a good life.'"

"You don't ever want to fix in the bathroom, 'cause the security guards are always looking in there trying to find shoplifters. I used to go down to the parking structure, sit between two cars, wrap a shirtsleeve around my arm, and shoot up right there. I was much more inclined to shop once I got loaded, but by the end of the run all I wanted to do was watch *Beavis and Butt-head*."

Stoned
Temple
Pilot

Sick Again

Let's Go Crazy

"I'm warming up to the idea of an asylum."
(John Lennon)

The undeniably high stress level of the rock life can lead to substance abuse, criminal behavior, and health problems—including mental illness. Craig Adams of The Mission had a nervous breakdown during the band's 1988 U.S. tour, and had to quit the group temporarily; Kurt Cobain had what one bystander described as a breakdown during a performance in Rome (stormed offstage, climbed into the rafters of the building, and screamed at the audience), and nervous breakdowns have plagued the Smashing Pumpkins' Billy Corgan, John Lennon, Brian Wilson of the Beach Boys, Kylie Minogue, and (!) Donny Osmond.

> BREAKDOWN DEAD AHEAD
>
> Rockers on Prozac
>
> **Damon Albarn, Blur**
>
> **Cher**
>
> **Shaun Ryder**
>
> **Bernard Sumner, New Order**

"I don't think I'm easy to talk about. I've got a very irregular head. And I'm not anything that you think I am anyway."
(Syd Barrett)

Syd, one of the most talented and innovative musicians of the sixties, was undone by heavy psychedelic drug usage and had to leave Pink Floyd because he was too fried to carry on. Barrett's mental meltdown made him behave strangely—and sometimes criminally: A woman once showed up at the door of Barrett's manager, claiming she'd been beaten and locked in a room in Barrett's house for a week, having been given nothing to eat but a few crackers.

FEAR AND TREMBLING

"The ocean scares me."
(Brian Wilson)

Fear of flying: Joan Baez, David Bowie, Whitney Houston, Lenny Kravitz, Mike Oldfield

The Cure's Robert Smith is so afraid of flying that he insists on journeying by sea, racking up huge travel expenses.

Liam Gallagher and Alison Moyet are agoraphobic.

Madonna is afraid of thunder.

Prince is afraid of heights and dirt.

"I got treated for depression last year. So I look at life a little different after shock treatment."
(Greg Dulli, Afghan Whigs)

Jonathan Davis, lead singer for the idiotically named Korn, suffers regular panic attacks. "My psychiatrist says he should be helping me," says Davis, "but he's just looking for ways to get me high. But maybe I *should* start taking antidepressants, or go to AA. Because when the band's joking around, the only time I feel comfortable—like I can join in—is when I'm drunk." Davis also claims he suffers nightmares and post-traumatic stress disorder from his previous job as a coroner's assistant.

"The band weren't getting on, and the touring meant I hadn't had any fresh real-life experiences to inspire my writing, especially the lyrics.
Then I started taking too many drugs—anything to be creative. I'd walk round the pond and talk to the ducks, out of my mind on Ecstasy. That gave me an idea for a track. I had the engineers rig up a microphone on a rowing boat, and I went out on the lake and recorded the ducks. *The Duck Symphony*, it was called. There's still a tape of it out there somewhere."
(Andy Cairns, Therapy?)

> "If I was eating a curry, I couldn't
> wait to throw it up so that I could
> have the next one."
> *(Elton John, on his bulimia)*

Andy Fletcher, keyboardist for Depeche Mode, spent a month in the hospital to combat depression and "obsessive-compulsive disorder" in 1993. Soul Asylum's Dave Pirner became an outpatient at a psychiatric institution after suffering career-related depression, Iggy Pop spent time in a Detroit mental hospital in the seventies, and Lou Reed had shock treatment as a young man. Fleetwood Mac had a couple of mentally suspect guitarists (even prior to the arrival of Lindsey Buckingham): Jeremy Spencer toured with a miniature Bible tacked into the lining of his coat, and would hang milk-filled condoms from his guitar's tuning pegs; and in 1977, original Mac axman Peter Green was committed to a mental institution in England after firing a pistol in the general direction of a courier attempting to deliver a royalty check.

DISAPPEARING ACTS

Michael Schenker, lead guitarist, UFO

Vanished after a June 17, 1977, concert in Leeds. Six months later, he resurfaced, explaining that he had wanted to quit the band but didn't know how to say so in English, so he'd just packed up and left. (Gotta love that.) Schenker rejoined the band and stayed with them until 1980.

DISAPPEARING ACTS

Joe Strummer, The Clash

On April 26, 1982, Strummer, on his way to rehearsal, hopped aboard a train and headed for parts unknown. No one in the band knew what he'd done or where he'd gone, and their U.K. tour had to be canceled. Three weeks later, Strummer turned up in London, saying he'd been exhausted and doubtful about the band's career, so had gone to Paris to live "like a bum." Strummer's disappearance was later found to be a strange publicity stunt cooked up by their manager, Bernie Rhodes.

> "I ran out of ideas and I just got zapped. I had personal problems that totally zapped me, that took three or four years to recover from. That's where I got the stomach. I laid around and got fat. . . . I stayed in my room and wouldn't see anyone. I reclused it, definitely. I don't know how, but I somehow got into weird stuff in my head. All mind and no activity."
> *(Brian Wilson)*

DISAPPEARING ACTS

Richey James Edwards, Manic
Street Preachers

**Alcoholic and anorexic, Edwards had
long suffered from depression
resulting in severe self-mutilation
and substance abuse. On February 1,
1995, Edwards, on the eve of a U.S.
tour with the band, checked out of
his London hotel and hasn't been
seen since (his abandoned car was
found two weeks later at the Severn
Bridge, near the English-Welsh
border). Various sightings (including
one in a Canary Islands bar in
December of 1998) have proven to
be hoaxes or mistakes.**

When Beach Boy Brian Wilson
suffered a mental breakdown
(paranoid, he believed "wall of
sound" producer Phil Spector was
out to get him, and that Bob
Dylan was part of a plot to
"destroy the whole of music"—an
opinion with which I'd agree), he
went in search of help—and
found his savior in the form of
quack psychiatrist Eugene Landy.
Landy got Wilson off the hard
stuff, although he substituted
some mood-altering concoctions
of his own—and ultimately lost
his medical license in 1989
because of this and other serious
charges, such as having sex with
one of his female patients. During
his Landy period, Wilson, who
called Landy "master," published a book about his life, of which *Rolling
Stone* wrote, "The autobiography reads like some slick parody of the end of
Psycho, with the psychiatrist telling the police, 'Brian was never all Brian,
but he was often only Landy. Now the Landy half has taken over. Probably
for all time.'" Wilson has since taken out a restraining order preventing
Landy from contacting him at all.

**"He's my boss, and I like him as my
boss. I just toe the line. But I just
don't think I could walk away. First of
all, I'd be afraid. I wouldn't know where
to live. I wouldn't know how to live."**
(Brian Wilson)

**"We've exchanged names. I'm 'Eugene
Wilson Landy' and he's 'Brian Landy
Wilson.' We've kind of merged."**
(Eugene Landy)

Need You Tonight

The tragic saga of Hutchence and Yates

The sad, sad story of the doomed romance of **Michael Hutchence** and **Paula Yates** ranks right up there with the tearjerker of a tale about prototypical punk pair **Sid Vicious** and **Nancy Spungen**. Why don't these rock 'n' roll love affairs ever have happy endings? Well, the female half is usually no wide-eyed Cinderella (in fact, her main goal at the beginning of the relationship may not be lifelong romance, but simply a quick one-nighter to notch another famous moniker into her bedpost), and I don't think you could classify too many self-obsessed rock stars as Prince Charmings. Add the two needy, narcissistic personalities together and you get a recipe for disaster.

Paula Yates was raised by what she called a "lurid flirt" of a mother, and described herself as a "whining, clinging child" who was anorexic from a very young age. Yates was precocious in every way—she lost her virginity at age twelve, was dabbling in drugs at fourteen, and at nineteen had already been featured in *Penthouse*. Paula's first major rock-star score was the **Boomtown Rats'** resident do-gooder, **Bob Geldof**, whom she pursued with no holds barred, earning herself a well-deserved nickname, "the Limpet." In her ongoing quest to nab her man, Yates once followed the band to Paris, where she loitered outside their hotel in freezing weather, clad in a mere wisp of a dress, until he broke down and invited her in. They were together full-time after that, finally marrying three years after

having their first strangely named child (Yates's menagerie currently includes Fifi Trixibelle, Peaches, Pixie, and of course Heavenly Hiraani Tigerlily). It wasn't exactly a match made in heaven, though—both were constantly unfaithful, and Geldof, a very private man, couldn't abide Paula's bottomless craving for and tireless pursuit of publicity.

Yates got herself a gig hosting a British music TV show, *The Tube*, on which she interviewed Michael Hutchence, lead singer for INXS. Hutchence had dated some of the world's most beautiful women (including supermodel Helena Christensen, with whom he had a five-year relationship), but was oddly attracted to the oddly attractive Yates— and the feeling was most certainly mutual. (The pair actually met at a hotel later that evening, but nothing came of it.) Yates began obsessing about Hutchence, and taped a photo of him to her refrigerator; when Geldof noticed it and asked when she was planning to remove it, Paula replied, "When I get him." She "got him," all right, a few years later—but Geldof had to hear the news from their young daughter ("Mummy and Michael were kissing in your bed," she told her daddy). Being a liberal sort, Geldof let Paula go with grace, and at the beginning it seemed as though the three were going to have a fairly amicable relationship. But that changed when Yates began making oblique digs at her ex-husband—by publicly talking up her new lover, whom she called a "sexy love god" who had "the Taj Mahal of crotches," and who, she said, was "just so kind, so good—and so bad." The friendship went completely down the drain, and accusations began to fly—Paula even publicly accused Geldof of having sex with her tart of a mother. Yikes!

Meanwhile, Yates and her new man were living the rock life to the hilt, dabbling in drugs and strange sex. A police raid on their London apartment (the cops were tipped off by a maid) turned up weird sex toys, plus a stash of opium wrapped in candy paper; drug charges were brought but subsequently dropped. Unfortunately, this meant that Hutchence didn't get help for his by-now full-blown heroin addiction—a habit that probably contributed to his ever-present thoughts of suicide, and eventual strange death in November of 1997. Found in an Australian hotel room, Hutchence was hanging by a belt from the door; he'd also suffered a broken hand (from punching a wall earlier in the day), a split lip, bruised face, and assorted lacerations. Rumors of autoerotic asphyxiation quickly surfaced, and were as quickly pooh-poohed—until Paula spilled a few beans. A few months after her lover's death, Yates was interviewed by the Australian version of *60 Minutes*, during which she seemed to confirm the lurid rumors: "Michael was the kind of man who would try everything," she said. "There was nothing he hadn't tried. . . . He didn't mean to die."

In April of 1998, Yates suffered a nervous breakdown, and was treated at a London clinic (she was also kicked out of rehab for having an affair with a fellow patient). Then, the following month, in a Sydney hotel room, she was found hanging sans clothing in a grotesque mimicry of Hutchence's death pose, with a noose around her neck, hovering near death's door. It remains to be seen what will become of this troubled woman (who by this point is a little long in the tooth to be chasing rock stars).

Another One Bites the Dust

"Idiots that believe their own hype, guys who start believing their own stuff, wind up in the most romantic place of all—six feet underground."
(Gene Simmons)

Drug Overdoses, Drug-Related Deaths

"Goddamn it! He beat me to it!"
(Janis Joplin, upon learning of Jimi Hendrix's death)

Punker G. G. Allin (36), heroin, 1993

Florence Ballard, The Supremes, alcohol, 1976

Lester Bangs (33), rock critic and singer, Darvon, April 3,1982

Mike Bloomfield (37), blues guitarist, Valium, February 15, 1981: Bloomfield, a heroin addict, was found dead in his car in San Francisco.

Tommy Bolin, guitarist, Deep Purple/James Gang, heroin, cocaine, barbiturates, alcohol, Newport Hotel (Miami), December 4, 1976: Bolin was talking on the phone when he suddenly passed out. His bodyguard threw him in the shower and revived him, then put him to bed, but Bolin died in his sleep of drug-induced suffocation.

John Bonham, Led Zeppelin, choked on his own vomit after drinking about forty shots of vodka at Jimmy Page's Windsor estate, September 25, 1980

Tim Buckley (28), folk-rocker, heroin and morphine, June 29, 1975: At a party thrown by a UCLA grad student, Buckley took what he thought was cocaine—and died because it was heroin. The student was convicted of involuntary manslaughter for supplying the illicit substance, but because Buckley had used the drug without his knowledge, his sentence was light: four months, plus four years probation.

Paul Butterfield (45), May 4, 1987

David Byron (38), Uriah Heep, drug-related heart attack, February 19, 1980

Miss Christine, GTOs (Frank Zappa's manufactured groupie-girl band, of which Pamela Des Barres was also a member), heroin, November 5, 1972

Gene Clark, The Byrds, alcohol, 1991

Steve Clark, Def Leppard, alcohol and prescription drugs, January 8, 1991: Used to booze-and-drug it up with fellow Lep guitarist and party partner Phil Collen, until Collen quit. Clark didn't, and delved deeper into substance abuse as his isolation from the rest of the band increased—exacerbated by his unreliability. Clark spent time in six different rehabilitation facilities, but was still on the hard stuff (prescription anti-depression medication, plus painkillers) at the time of his death. The coroner cited the cause of death as respiratory failure due to a compression of the brain stem resulting from a mix of booze and prescription medications.

Brian Cole, vocalist and bassist with The Association, heroin, August 2, 1972

Darby Crash, The Germs, heroin, December 7, 1980

Brian Epstein (32), **Beatles** manager, sleeping pills (Carbitrol), August 27, 1967: Epstein's death was ruled accidental because of his regular "incautious self-overdoses."

Pete Farndon, The Pretenders, heroin and cocaine "speedball" (died while taking a bath), April 14, 1983

Alan Freed, pioneering DJ, alcohol, 1965

Jerry Garcia, health complications during heroin withdrawal, 1995

"Jerry died broke. We only have a few hundred thousand dollars in the bank."
(Grieving spouse Deborah Koons Garcia)

Lowell George (34), vastly overweight member of Little Feat, drug-induced heart failure/overdose, at a motel in Arlington, Virginia, June 29, 1979

Andy Gibb (30), inflammatory heart virus (related to drug abuse), March 9, 1988

Dwayne Goettel, Skinny Puppy, heroin, August 1995

Rick Grech (44), **Blind Faith**, March 17, 1990

Bill Haley, alcohol, 1981

Tim Hardin (39; "If I Were a Carpenter"), heroin, Los Angeles, December 29, 1980

Eddie Hazel, **P-Funk**, alcohol, 1992

Jimi Hendrix, sleeping pills and wine, September 18, 1970: Attended a dinner party in London on September 17 and took nine sleeping pills the same night—not a good combination with the red wine he'd already consumed: cause of death was cited as "inhalation of vomit due to barbiturate intoxication."

Greg Herbert (30), saxophonist for **Blood, Sweat and Tears**, Amsterdam, January 31, 1978

Bob Hite (36), **Canned Heat**, drug-related heart attack, April 1981

James Honeyman-Scott (25), **The Pretenders**, booze and cocaine (died in his sleep), June 16, 1982

Shannon Hoon (23), **Blind Melon** lead singer, heroin, October 21, 1995: died on the Melon's tour bus in a New Orleans parking lot.

Brian Jones (27), **Rolling Stones** (fired from the band a month previously), alcohol and barbiturates, July 3, 1969: A knockout combo of wine, vodka, brandy, and barbiturates weren't the ticket for a midnight swim— Jones drowned; at the time of death, his heart and liver were almost completely destroyed due to substance abuse.

"I would say manslaughter. I think he was pretty out of it. He'd let these builders in and they were sort of running his house, you know, and having fun playing with this stoned-out rock star. I think that maybe somebody held him under the water for a joke and he didn't come up. Murder? No. I think stupidity."
(Keith Richards, on Brian Jones's death)

Janis Joplin (27), heroin, October 4, 1970

Paul Kossoff (26), guitarist for **Free**, health complications due to drug use, March 19, 1976: died of heart and kidney failure during a transatlantic flight. Kossoff had previously been hospitalized for heroin-related health problems, including a near overdose.

Frankie Lymon (25), heroin (ODed at his mother's apartment in New York), February 28, 1968

Phil Lynott (34), **Thin Lizzy**, heroin (was in a drug-induced coma for eight days prior to his death), January 4, 1986

Jimmy McCulloch (26), **Wings**, September 27, 1979

Robbie McIntosh, drummer, **Average White Band**, September 23, 1974: At a North Hollywood party, McIntosh and bandmate **Alan Gorrie** took something they thought was cocaine, but which was really strychnine-cut heroin. Both got violently ill, and worried fellow party-goer **Cher** called her doctor to describe the symptoms. The physician recommended immediate hospitalization for McIntosh, and Cher left with Gorrie after being assured McIntosh would be taken to the hospital. Unfortunately, he wasn't: his wife was persuaded to let him recover in their hotel room, where he died a few hours later. (Gorrie was nursed back to health by Cher.)

"Pigpen" (Ronald) McKernan (27), **Grateful Dead**, stomach hemorrhage caused by cirrhosis of the liver (booze), March 8, 1973

"He was a juicer, man. It did him in."
(Jerry Garcia)

"The services were a bummer, man. Strictly for the straights."
(Jerry Garcia)

Clyde McPhatter, complications from drug and alcohol abuse, 1972

Jonathan Melvoin (34), keyboardist for **Smashing Pumpkins**, heroin, July 12, 1996: After a long night of partying with Pumpkins drummer **Jimmy Chamberlin**, Melvoin died in a New York City hotel room. Previously during the same tour, there had been two overdose incidents involving Chamberlin and Melvoin: once in Thailand and once in Portugal, where both were revived with Adrenalin shots to the heart.

ESPRIT DE CORPSE

"It might be nice [when I die] to have myself propped up in a chair where people get in line and come up and have a picture taken with me, put glasses on me, and it looks like we're just hanging out. I want a full hour [of] prime time on MTV. But they didn't even give that to Michael Hutchence, so I know I'm shooting a little high. . . . I have a coffin in my house, and I've been in it for long periods of time, and I don't think I want to be in it for that long."
(Dave Navarro)

"This Smashing Pumpkins guy is just another worthless bum. It was the same with Kurt Cobain—why couldn't the press tap into what a coward this guy was for leaving his wife without a husband and his kid fatherless?"
(Gene Simmons, Kiss)

Keith Moon (31), The Who, Hemenephrin (drug used in the treatment of alcoholism), September 7, 1978

"I think someone looked down and said, 'Okay, that's your ninth life.' "
(John Entwistle, on the death of Keith Moon)

Jim Morrison, drug-induced heart attack, July 3, 1971

"I wouldn't recommend [Jim Morrison's] lifestyle to anyone. It killed him."
(Ray Manzarek)

Billy Murcia (21), New York Dolls, November 6, 1972: Died indirectly as a result of heroin abuse—had gone home with a woman after a show in London and was using; when he nodded out, she panicked and poured coffee down his throat, causing suffocation.

Brent Mydland (38), Grateful Dead, July 26, 1990

Brad Nowell (28), guitarist and lead singer for Sublime, heroin (overdosed in a San Francisco motel room), May 25, 1996

Malcolm Owen, singer for The Ruts, heroin (ODed in his mother's bathtub), July 14, 1980

Gram Parsons, cocaine/speed/morphine/booze, September 1973

"Yeah, Gram Parsons, he had it all sussed. He didn't stick around. He made his best work and then he died. That's the way I want to do it. I'm never going to stick around long enough to churn out a load of mediocre crap like all those guys from the sixties ended up doing. I'd rather kill myself. I mean, Parsons's exit was perfect."
(Elvis Costello)

Jon Jon Paulus (32), The Buckinghams, drug-related heart failure, March 26, 1980

Kristin Pfaff (27), bassist for Hole, heroin, 1994

Rob Pilatus, Milli Vanilli, alcohol and prescription drugs (found in a German hotel room), April 1998

Elvis Presley, a cornucopia of drugs (exhaustively detailed in the five thousand Elvis books that have come out since his death), 1977

"Makes you feel sad, doesn't it? . . . Yeah, it's just too bad it couldn't have been Mick Jagger."
(Malcolm McLaren, on Elvis Presley's death)

"Fuckin' good riddance to bad rubbish."
(Johnny Rotten, ditto)

Carl Radle (34), Derek and the Dominoes, Delaney and Bonnie, liver failure (probably caused by heavy drug abuse), May 30, 1980

David Ruffin (50), The Temptations, June 1, 1991

Stefanie Sargent (20s), Seven Year Bitch guitarist, heroin, 1993

Bon Scott, AC/DC, February 19, 1980 (died in his car with a half-bottle of whiskey still in his stomach; just thirty-three at the time of his death, Scott already had significant heart and liver damage from years of heavy boozing)

Will Shatter (31), vocalist/bassist for Flipper, heroin, 1987

Hillel Slovak (25), Red Hot Chili Peppers guitarist, heroin, June 1988

Bob Stinson (35), **The Replacements**, complications from drug and alcohol abuse, February 18, 1995

Vinnie Taylor (25), **Sha Na Na**, heroin, hotel room in Charlottesville, Virginia, April 19, 1974

Gary Thain (27), **Uriah Heep**, heroin (found by his girlfriend in his bathtub), February 1976

Johnny Thunders (38), **New York Dolls**, cocaine/methadone, hotel room in New Orleans, April 23, 1991

Sid Vicious (21), **Sex Pistols**, heroin overdose, February 2, 1979: After killing groupie-girlfriend **Nancy Spungen**, Vicious was jailed and released on bail, then tried to commit suicide by slashing every vein in his body with a razor and broken lightbulb. Jailed again for a fracas with **Patti Smith**'s brother (see page 240), he was released into his mother's custody, and immediately picked up his heroin habit again, continuing to use until he died from an overdose. A year after her son's death, his mother, **Anne Beverly**, admitted she'd purchased the drugs that killed him, but said she'd done it out of the kindness of her heart, simply to save him from another arrest. "I suppose it was fate, really," the noble woman said. "He died because I tried to help him."

Gene Vincent (28), early rock 'n' roller ("Be-Bop-a-Lula"), seizure resulting from drug and alcohol abuse, October 12, 1971

Danny Whitten (29), guitarist for **Buffalo Springfield** and **Crazy Horse**, heroin, Los Angeles, October 18, 1972

Alan Wilson (27), **Canned Heat**, sleeping pills, September 3, 1970: Wilson, who was almost blind, was prone to bouts of serious depression. He was found with an empty barbiturate bottle in his hand in fellow Heat member **Bob Hite**'s Topanga Canyon garden.

Andrew Wood (24), vocalist for **Mother Love Bone**, heroin, 1990: Smoked a lot of pot in addition to taking heroin, and went to rehab in Seattle in March of 1990; four months afterward, his girlfriend, Xana, found him lying unconscious on his bed, with a used hypo nearby. Wood was taken to the hospital, where he was placed on life support—but it wasn't enough to save him, and he died when they pulled the plug three days later.

Chris Wood, Traffic, alcohol, 1983

Vehicle Accidents

Duane Allman (24), motorcycle crash (Macon, Georgia), October 29, 1971: Allman swerved to avoid an oncoming truck, which hit him anyway. He was dragged along, still on his motorcycle, for fifty feet, and died three hours later during surgery.

Stiv Bators, Dead Boys, hit by a car (thought he was unhurt, but died in his sleep that night), Paris, June 4, 1990

Marc Bolan, killed in a car crash on Barnes Common in England (the driver, Bolan's girlfriend, Gloria Jones, survived), September 16, 1977

Johnny Burnette (30), rockabilly innovator ("Train Kept A-Rollin' "), boating accident on Clear Lake in California, August 1964

Chris Burton, Metallica, tour bus crash (the band was traveling between Stockholm and Copenhagen), September 27, 1986: Burton was asleep in his bunk when the bus driver lost control. Burton was thrown through a window and the bus landed on top of him, killing him instantly.

Tommy Caldwell, bassist for the **Marshall Tucker Band,** car crash in Spartanburg, South Carolina, April 28, 1980

Harry Chapin, car crash on the Long Island Expressway, July 16, 1981: A tractor hit Chapin's car and caused the gas tank to explode (Chapin also suffered a heart attack, the coroner found, but whether it was a cause or a result of the accident no one knows).

Eddie Cochran ("Summertime Blues"), car crash on the way to Heathrow Airport, April 17, 1960: The taxi in which Cochran was riding was hurled into a lamppost after losing a tire. Cochran was thrown through the windshield, and died without regaining consciousness. The car's two other passengers were unhurt.

Allen Collins, Lynyrd Skynyrd, car crash, 1990

Jim Croce (30), plane crash near Natchitoches, Louisiana (crashed into a tree just after takeoff), September 20, 1973

Razzle Dingley, Hanoi Rocks, car crash (Mötley Crüe's Vince Neil was driving, and was convicted of vehicular manslaughter; see page 257), 1984

Falco (40), singer/songwriter ("Rock Me Amadeus"), car crash (his vehicle collided with a bus), Puerto Plata, Dominican Republic, February 1998. Falco was rushed to the hospital after the crash, in which he suffered severe head injuries, but died shortly afterward.

Richard Fariña, motorcycle crash, 1966

Keith Godchaux (32), Grateful Dead keyboardist, car crash, 1980

Rock impresario Bill Graham, helicopter crash (on his way home from a concert, Graham's private chopper hit electrical wires and exploded), 1991

Buddy Holly, The Big Bopper (J. P. Richardson), and Ritchie Valens, plane crash, February 3, 1959: A bad storm in the area (they were flying through the Midwest) meant pilots had to be able to fly by instruments alone, which the pilot of Holly's plane, who'd flunked an instruments test, hadn't been told by air traffic controllers.

Tim Kelly (35), Slaughter guitarist, head injuries from a crash (his car ran into a jackknifed trailer in Arizona), February 6, 1998

Lynyrd Skynyrd members Ronnie Van Zant and Steve and Cassie Gaines, plus Skynyrd manager Dean Kilpatrick and a roadie, the pilot and copilot, plane crash (Mississippi swampland), October 20, 1977: The chartered aircraft, which had been showing signs of wear and tear, was due to be traded in by the group at their next stop.

Ricky Nelson, plane crash (rumors persist that Nelson and his companions were freebasing in the DC-3, causing it to combust), December 31, 1985

Berry Oakley (24), Allman Brothers, November 11, 1972: One year and thirteen days after Duane Allman's fatal crash (and just three blocks from the site), Oakley, who had been deeply depressed by Allman's death, ran his motorcycle into a city bus and was thrown twenty yards. He appeared to be unhurt but died of a cerebral hemorrhage shortly after his arrival at a nearby hospital.

Cozy Powell (50), car crash (into the center divider of an English highway in his Saab), April 5, 1998: Cozy was traveling waaaay over the legal speed limit, and in bad weather to boot.

Otis Redding and four members of his band, the Bar-Kays (Ronnie Caldwell, Carl Cunningham, Phalon Jones, Jimmy King), plane crash (small craft went down in Wisconsin's Lake Monona), 1967, just three days after recording his biggest hit, "(Sitting on) The Dock of the Bay"

Lynn Strait, Snot, car crash, December 11, 1998: Strait was en route from Santa Barbara to L.A. when he got involved in a three-car pileup on an exit ramp.

Stevie Ray Vaughan, helicopter crash, August 27, 1990: Vaughan's helicopter crashed into a manmade ski slope in dense fog in Wisconsin; unbeknownst to the passengers, the plane's pilot had been involved in two prior aircraft accidents.

Clarence White, Byrds, hit by car (driver was drunk) while loading equipment into a tour van outside a nightclub, July 14, 1973

I'm Outta Here: Suicides

"I tried to commit suicide one day. It was a very Woody Allen-type suicide. I turned on the gas and left all the windows open."
(Elton John)

"Elton was destined to tie the knot. And I don't think he was very sure about it—he was getting more and more depressed. He talked about going to end it all. . . . I was coming out of my room and walking down the hall when I smelled gas. Someone had left the oven on in the kitchen. I walk into the kitchen and there's Elton, lying on the floor with the gas oven open. And my immediate thing should have been, 'My god, he's tried to kill himself!' The thing was, I started laughing—because he'd taken a pillow . . . and he'd opened all the windows!"
(Bernie Taupin)

"The public hungers to see talented young people kill themselves."
(Paul Simon)

Kurt Cobain, shooting, 1994 (no, there was no conspiracy, and Courtney didn't do it)

Ian Curtis (23), epileptic, angst-ridden singer of Joy Division, hanging (found in his Manchester home), May 18,1980: Said bandmate Pete Hook: "The great tragedy of Ian's death was that all he really wanted to be was successful. And he missed it—by a week." (The band had a hit single just after Curtis died.) Curtis's suicide note included these lines: "At this very moment I just wish I were dead. I just can't cope anymore."

Tommy Evans, Badfinger, hanging (three years after the suicide of Pete Ham, Evans reformed the band, but success wasn't forthcoming and Evans became severely depressed), 1983

Pete Ham (27), Badfinger, hanging (found in the garage of his home in London; he'd been suffering from financial problems and depression), April 23, 1975

STAYIN' ALIVE

Unsuccessful suicide attempts

Angie Bowie

Marianne Faithfull

Gary Glitter

Billy Joel

Elton John

Sinéad O'Connor

Vanilla Ice

"One night, nobody was paying any attention to me, so I thought I'd commit suicide. So I went in the bathroom, broke a glass, and slashed my chest with it. It's a really good way to get attention. I'm going to do it again, particularly as it doesn't work."

(Sid Vicious)

Doug Hopkins, **Gin Blossoms**, fired by the band on December 3, 1993, and checked into rehab at St. Luke's Hospital in Phoenix, where he stole a pistol and used it to commit suicide

Richard Manuel, **The Band**, hanging (Florida motel room), 1986

Phil Ochs (35), hanging (found at his sister's house in Queens), April 9, 1976: Years of heavy alcohol abuse led to mental illness—Ochs was in the habit of wandering the streets in a delusional fog, ranting and raving.

Del Shannon, shooting, 1990: Shannon was depressed and schizophrenic, and was also bummed out that he was losing his hair, and about the constant fighting going on between his kids and his new wife, who were their age.

Rozz Williams (34), **Christian Death**, hanging, April 1, 1998

Wendy O. Williams (48), **The Plasmatics**, shooting (in a forest near her home in Connecticut), April 2, 1998: Said Williams's former boyfriend, Rod Swenson, who found the body: "She felt she was past her peak and found it difficult to lead a normal life. This was something she had planned; it was no spur-of-the-moment thing." Part of her suicide note read: "For me, much of the world makes no sense, but my feelings about what I am doing ring loud and clear to an inner ear and a place where there is no self, only calm." Williams had previously attempted a gruesome suicide by trying to bang a knife deep into her chest with a hammer; the blade got stuck in her sternum and she was afraid to remove it, so she went to the hospital. If at first you don't succeed . . .

Murder, Death by Violence

Shirley Brickley (32), founding member of the **Orlons**, shot (murdered), October 13, 1977

Sam Cooke, shot, December 1964: At the Hacienda Motel in L.A., Cooke brought a woman back to his room, then made advances, which scared her to death—she thought he was planning to rape her, so she took off with his clothing. Cooke hotfooted it after her, arriving at the motel manager's door wearing only his jacket and shoes. Cooke banged on the manager's door, and she mistook him for a robber and shot him three times with a .22. The verdict was justifiable homicide.

King Curtis (37), saxophonist, knifing (Curtis was fighting with people on his stoop, one of whom stabbed him), August 1971

Mal Evans (40), roadie and bodyguard to the **Beatles** (and assistant general manager of their company, Apple), shot to death by cops, January 4, 1976: Evans's girlfriend walked into their apartment and found him crying, cradling a rifle in his hands. She in turn called some friends; unable to wrest the gun away from him, they called police. When the cops arrived, they asked Evans to put the gun down; instead, he pointed it at them, and they fired four times, killing him instantly.

Rhett Forrester (37), singer for early eighties hard-rockers **Riot**, murdered in his car by unknown gunmen at an intersection in Atlanta, January 22, 1994

Marvin Gaye, shot, April 1, 1984: Shot to death by his booze-addled father, with whom he'd been having a violent argument. Dad was sentenced to five years' probation.

Al Jackson (39), drummer for **Booker T. and the MGs**, shot in his Memphis home (his wife was questioned—she'd been arrested but not charged earlier in the year for shooting him in the chest), October 1, 1975

John Lennon, shot, December 8, 1980: Killed by obsessed stalker/fan John Chapman.

Felix Pappalardi, bassist for **Mountain**, shot dead by his wife, Gail Collins, April 17, 1983

Nancy Spungen, stabbed, October 12, 1978: Called in by a drug-addled, nearly incoherent **Sid Vicious**, cops found Nancy in the couple's hotel-room bathroom, dead of a stab wound. (When the police asked why he'd done it, he replied it was because he was a "dog, a dirty dog.") Ten days later, Vicious was released into the custody of his mother, and that very night attempted suicide, slicing open every vein in his arms and legs. What did Mom do—call the paramedics? Rush him to the hospital? No—sat with her son as he started bleeding to death. When Pistols manager **Malcolm McLaren** and Joe Stevens, Vicious's "keeper," arrived unexpectedly, she ordered them to stay out of it. They wouldn't, of course—and while they were waiting for help to arrive, Stevens taped Vicious's confession. Sid said he and Nancy, who were living at New York's Chelsea Hotel, had tried to score some heroin, but their dealer didn't have any, so he gave them downers instead. The pills didn't help—in fact, they only aggravated Sid's withdrawal agonies, so he visited each room in the Chelsea, banging on the doors and demanding drugs. This went on until he was accosted by a janitor, who ordered him to desist. The argument flared into violence, and the janitor broke Sid's nose. Upon returning to his room, seriously jonesing Sid argued with Nancy, who slapped his face, irritating his sore nose, which so enraged him that he grabbed a hunting knife and stabbed her in the stomach. Minutes later, they kissed and made up, and Sid ran off to a methadone clinic. Upon his return, he found Nancy dead—evidently, she hadn't felt the wound was serious, so hadn't bothered to put pressure on it or cover it.

Peter Tosh (42), shot by burglars at his home in Jamaica, September 1987

Accidents Will Happen

Johnny Ace, blues balladeer ("Pledging My Love"), died on Christmas Eve 1954 at the Houston City Auditorium while playing Russian roulette.

Jeff Buckley (son of **Tim**) took a swim in the Mississippi on May 29, 1997, got caught in strong currents created by the wake of a boat, and drowned (body found June 4, 1997).

Sandy Denny, Fairport Convention, injuries sustained in a fall down a flight of stairs, April 21, 1978: Although she didn't seem seriously injured at the time, she died four days later as a result of an undetected cerebral hemorrhage.

Mama Cass Elliot (32), **The Mamas & the Papas,** heart attack (after choking on a sandwich and inhaling her own vomit), London, July 29, 1974. Despite bandmate **John Phillips**'s assertion that she'd died of a heroin overdose, the coroner who performed the autopsy noted that her "heart muscle had turned to fat due to obesity."

Kevin Gilbert (29), ex-boyfriend of **Sheryl Crow** and the originator of the "Tuesday Music Club" (a loose jam session of area musicians, of which Crow was a member), autoerotic asphyxiation (wearing a black hood, Gilbert died of "asphyxia due to partial suspension hanging"), May 18, 1996. Gilbert was reportedly responsible (although uncredited) for much of the music on Sheryl's hit *Tuesday Night Music Club* album. Says Sheryl of her ex, "As long as I knew him, he struggled with life, as if every single event in life was out to bring him down or trip him up. His perception of the world, from a narcissistic standpoint, was one of darkness, unhappiness. Yeah, he had an accident, but I know the music he was working on at the time was pretty dark, really gothic." Thanks for being so sympathetic, babe.

Les Harvey (25), **Stone the Crows,** electrocution, May 1972. Harvey had wet feet during a gig in Wales, and made the fatal mistake of touching a live microphone.

Terry Kath (31), guitarist for Chicago, died while playing Russian roulette at a buddy's California home in 1978. Kath had been prone to bouts of depression, and the death was ruled accidental.

Steve Marriott, Small Faces, fell asleep with a cigarette burning, causing a fatal fire at his Essex home in April of 1990.

Nico, Velvet Underground, brain hemorrhage after a bike fall in Ibiza (found lying by the side of the road), 1988

LOCATION, LOCATION, LOCATION

Fast Fact: Both Keith Moon and Mama Cass died at Harry Nilsson's London apartment.

Jeff Porcaro, Toto, heart attack caused by a reaction to pesticides with which he'd been spraying his garden

Keith Relf (33), Yardbirds, electrocution, May 14, 1976: found holding a live electric guitar by his young son in their basement

John Rostill, bassist with the Shadows, electrocution (playing guitar in his home studio), November 1973

Dennis Wilson (39), Beach Boys, December 28, 1983: Wilson, a booze-and-cocaine binger, was drinking heavily (vodka and wine) on a boat in Marina Del Rey (Los Angeles) and diving into the water to find "treasure"; he drowned during one of his dives.

Now Will You Leave Me Alone

(Madonna's desired tombstone inscription)

Index

Boy George . . . 27, 39, 44, 119, 131,
    135, 136, 137, 138, 139, 174, 178, 180,
    181, 192, 196, 197, 213, 246, 271
Boyd, Patti . . . 54, 199, 200, 251
Bramlett, Bonnie . . . 225
Brando, Marlon . . . 60, 147
Brandon, Kirk . . . 196
Brandy . . . 99, 101, 102
Branson, Richard . . . 115
Braxton, Toni . . . 169
Breen, Bobby . . . 60
Brice, Fanny . . . 127
Brickell, Edie . . . 220
Brickley, Shirley . . . 317
Brinkley, Christie . . . 56, 200
Brinsley Schwarz . . . 93
Britton, Chris . . . 271
Brix . . . 213
Bronski Beat . . . 197
Brown, Adrienne . . . 246
Brown, Arthur . . . 77
Brown, Bobby . . . 276
Brown, Ian . . . 160, 246
Brown, James . . . 127, 225, 246, 276
Browne, Jackson . . . 13
Bruce, Jack . . . 17
Bruce, Lenny . . . 60
Bruni, Carla . . . 199
Buckingham, Lindsey . . . 52, 79, 133,
    145, 172, 213, 226, 276, 300
Buckinghams, The . . . 310
Buckley, Jeff . . . 319
Buckley, Tim . . . 271, 305, 319
Budgie . . . 213
Buell, Bebe . . . 71, 117, 127, 136, 190,
    200, 201
Buffalo Springfield . . . 18, 53, 182, 311
Burdon, Eric . . . 145, 154, 171, 175,
    276
Burke, Clem . . . 134
Burnel, J. J. . . . 6, 123, 186, 193, 198,
    239
Burnette, Johnny . . . 312
Burr, Raymond . . . 95
Burroughs, William . . . 21, 60

Burrows, Brian . . . 186
Burton, Chris . . . 312
Bush . . . 24, 27, 190, 212, 220
Bush, Kate . . . 99
Butler, Dougal . . . 232, 284
Butler, Geezer . . . 87, 108
Butter Queen, The . . . 202
Butterfield, Paul . . . 126, 305
Butthole Surfers, The . . . 27
Buzzcocks, The . . . 25
Byrds, The . . . 54, 66, 93, 205, 306, 314
Byrne, David . . . 39, 55, 127, 131, 145
Byron, David . . . 305

C

Cabaret Voltaire . . . 24
Cairns, Andy . . . 77, 79, 299
Cakes, Patti . . . 202
Caldwell, Ronnie . . . 314
Caldwell, Tommy . . . 312
Cale, John . . . 10, 44, 197, 289
Campbell, Luther . . . 98
Campbell, Naomi . . . 100, 199
Canned Heat . . . 307, 311
Cantrell, Jerry . . . 85
Capote, Truman . . . 136
Captain & Tennille, The . . . 130
Captain Beefheart . . . 7, 83, 108, 118,
    170
Captain Sensible . . . 79
Caravan . . . 238
Cardigans, The . . . 39
Carey, Mariah . . . 36, 98, 140, 182, 262
Carlisle, Belinda . . . 13, 50, 174, 227,
    276
Carpenter, Karen . . . 34, 145
Carpenter, Richard . . . 34, 276
Carr, Lucas . . . 90
Carrere, Tia . . . 101
Carroll, Lewis . . . 60
Cars, The . . . 27
Carter, Jimmy . . . 133
Carter, Kelly . . . 201
Cass, Mama . . . 106

D

Howlett, Liam . . . 127
Hucknall, Mick . . . 44, 133, 140, 155, 188, 195
Hunter, Ian . . . 15, 139, 160
Hunter, Meredith . . . 82, 265
Hunter, Nancy . . . 200
Hunter, Rachel . . . 201, 216
Hutchence, Kelland . . . 263
Hutchence, Michael . . . 36, 76, 79, 84, 123, 124, 154, 200, 215, 234, 263, 272, 302, 303, 304
Huxley, Aldous . . . 60
Hynde, Chrissie . . . 14, 50, 117, 174, 193, 213, 214

I

Ian, Janis . . . 196
Ice Cube . . . 174
Ice-T . . . 14
Icicle Works . . . 25
Idol, Billy . . . 75, 93, 134, 135, 149, 174, 176, 228, 251, 272, 281
Iha, James . . . 213
Iman . . . 199
Imbruglia, Natalie . . . 33, 216
Indigo Girls, The . . . 197
Interior, Lux . . . 171
INXS . . . 76, 84, 200, 218, 234, 272, 303
Iommi, Tony . . . 3
Iron Maiden . . . 65
Irwin, Elaine . . . 200
Isaak, Chris . . . 14, 102, 191, 200

J

J. Geils Band, The . . . 28, 220
Jackson, Al . . . 317
Jackson, Janet . . . 36, 155, 174, 179, 187, 191, 215
Jackson, Joe . . . 52, 174
Jackson, LaToya . . . 134, 174
Jackson, Michael . . . 9, 113, 134, 135, 168, 174, 225

Jagger, Bianca . . . 61, 215, 233
Jagger, Mick . . . 8, 14, 26, 33, 34, 37, 44, 49, 61, 82, 100, 106, 114, 124, 128, 136, 139, 142, 143, 160, 163, 169, 179, 183, 196, 197, 200, 205, 214, 215, 218, 219, 233, 258, 272, 281, 310
Jam, The . . . 123, 240, 261
James, Alex . . . 281
James, Ella . . . 37
James Gang, The . . . 305
James, Rick . . . 56, 144, 252, 281
James, Wendy . . . 174
Jamiroqui . . . 25, 165
Jane's Addiction . . . 11, 65, 272
Jean, Wyclef . . . 16
Jefferson Airplane/Starship . . . 98, 115, 171, 246
Jenkins, Stephen . . . 216
Jesus and Mary Chain, The . . . 141
Jethro Tull . . . 18, 163, 168
Jewel . . . 36, 52, 102
Joel, Billy . . . 56, 200, 316
Johansen, David . . . 33, 36, 102, 119, 128
John, Elton . . . 32, 36, 38, 56, 57, 83, 84, 86, 98, 100, 103, 119, 129, 130, 134, 136, 140, 146, 156, 158, 163, 165, 169, 183, 184, 194, 196, 238, 241, 281, 300, 315, 316
Johnny Hates Jazz . . . 25
Johnson, Brian . . . 36
Johnson, Don . . . 101
Johnson, Holly . . . 196
Johnston, Tom . . . 252
Jones, Brian . . . 175, 187, 200, 209, 210, 281, 307
Jones, Davy . . . 209
Jones, Gloria . . . 312
Jones, Howard . . . 175
Jones, John Paul . . . 230, 242
Jones, Mick . . . 31, 93, 146, 282
Jones, Phalon . . . 314
Jones, Quincy . . . 205
Jones, Rickie Lee . . . 14, 216
Jones, Robert . . . 168

N

O

P

S

Line art courtesy of:
ArtParts
Hemera Technologies Inc.
Nova Development
NVTech
T/Maker Company

Courtesy of Star File Photo Agency, Inc.:
Elton John (page 32): Bob Gruen
Steven Tyler (page 35): Steve Joester
Courtney Love (page 41): Todd Kaplan
Marilyn Manson and Rose McGowan (page 43): Jeffrey Mayer
David Bowie (page 47): Mick Rock
George Michael (page 59): Todd Kaplan
Madonna (page 69): Todd Kaplan
David Lee Roth (page 97): Vinnie Zuffante
Kurt Cobain (page 109): Jeffrey Mayer
Courtney Love (page 121): Vinnie Zuffante
Billy Idol (page 135): John Lee
Jimmy Page and Robert Plant (page 148): Ken Kaminsky
Bono (page 152): Todd Kaplan
Sting (page 167): Jeffrey Mayer
Boy George (page 181): Bob Gruen
Rod Stewart (page 217): Larry Kaplan
Ozzy Osbourne (page 222): Jeffrey Mayer
Axl Rose (page 229): Bob Leafe
Led Zeppelin (page 230–31): Bob Gruen
Ozzy Osbourne (page 266): Laurie Paladino
Stevie Nicks (page 285): Todd Kaplan
Scott Weiland (page 297): Chuck Pulin